ving
itch

Chihiro Ishizuka

1

Contents

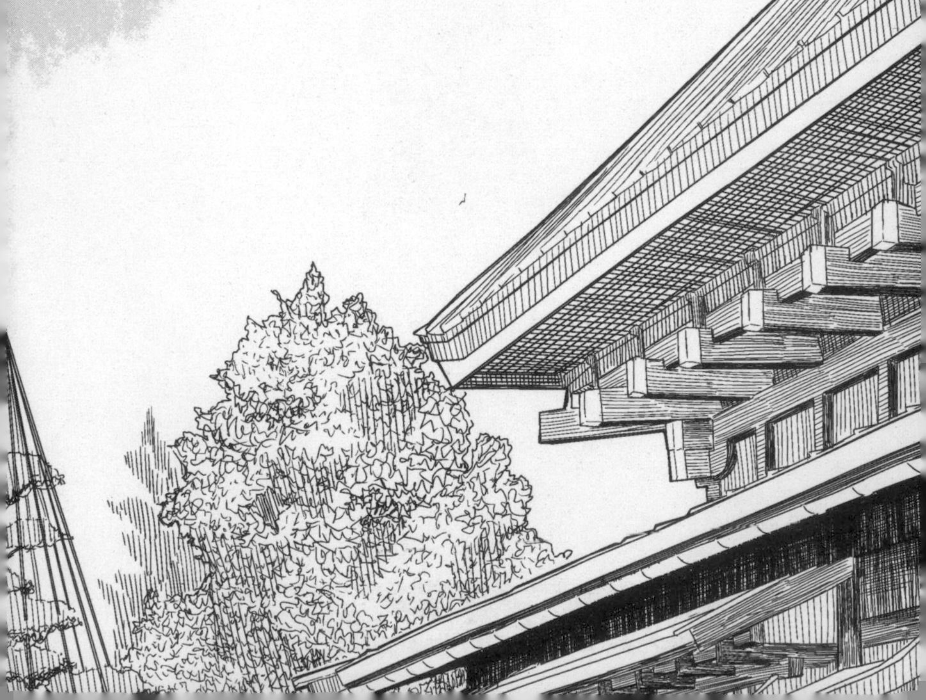

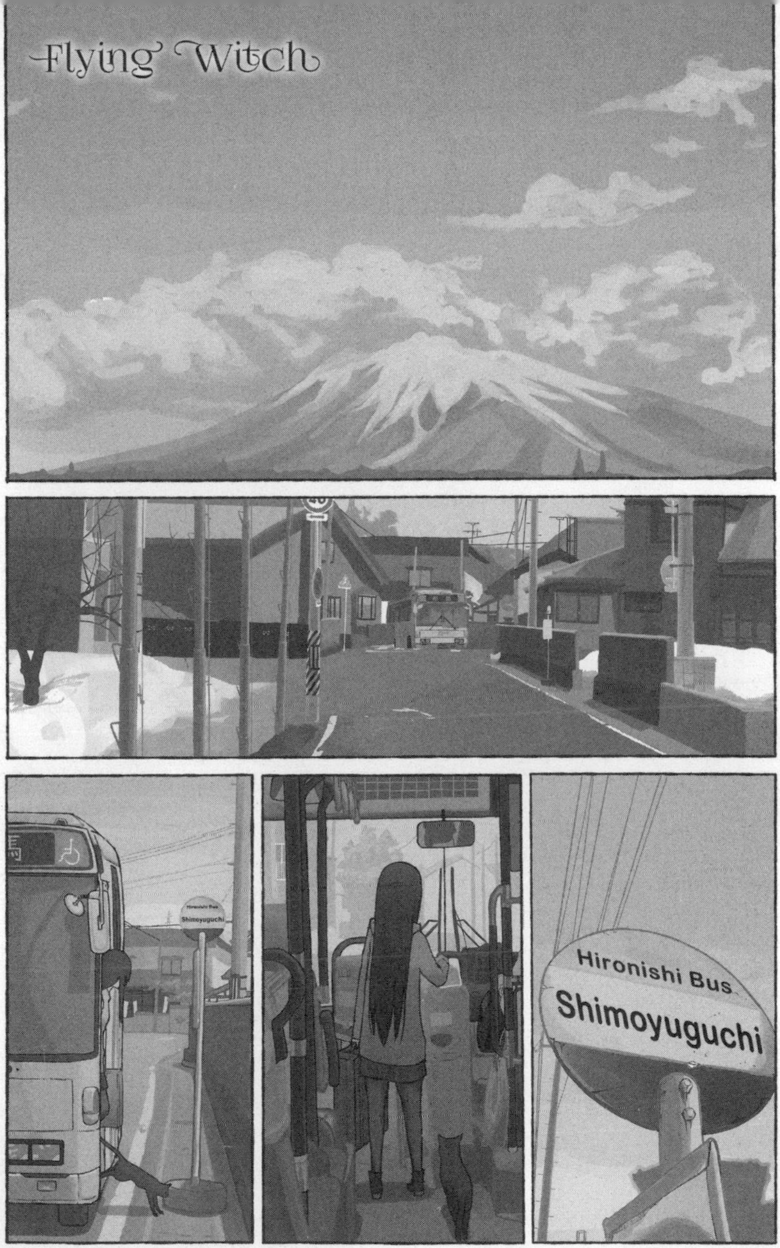
Flying Witch
Hironishi Bus
Shimoyuguchi
Hironishi Bus
Shimoyuguchi

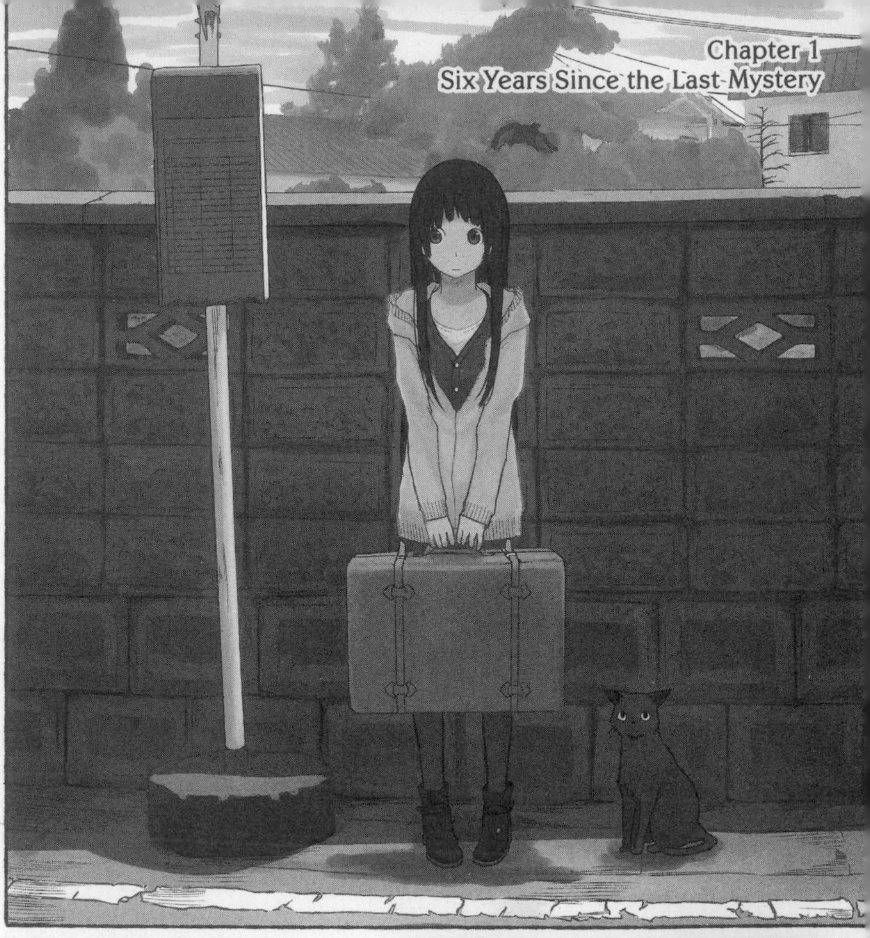
Chapter 1
Six Years Since the Last Mystery

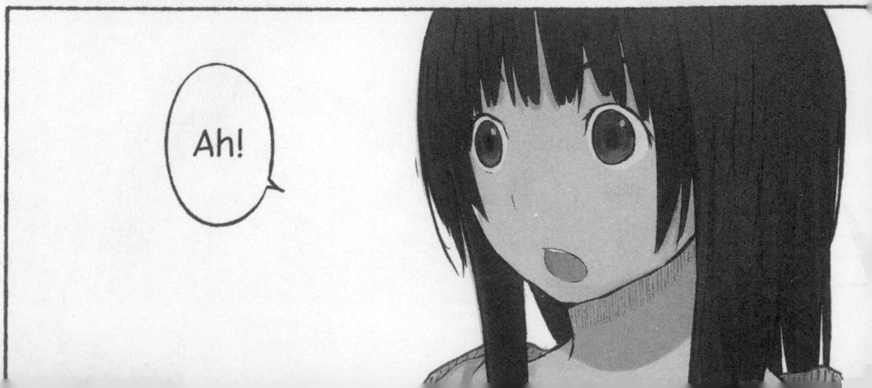
Ah!

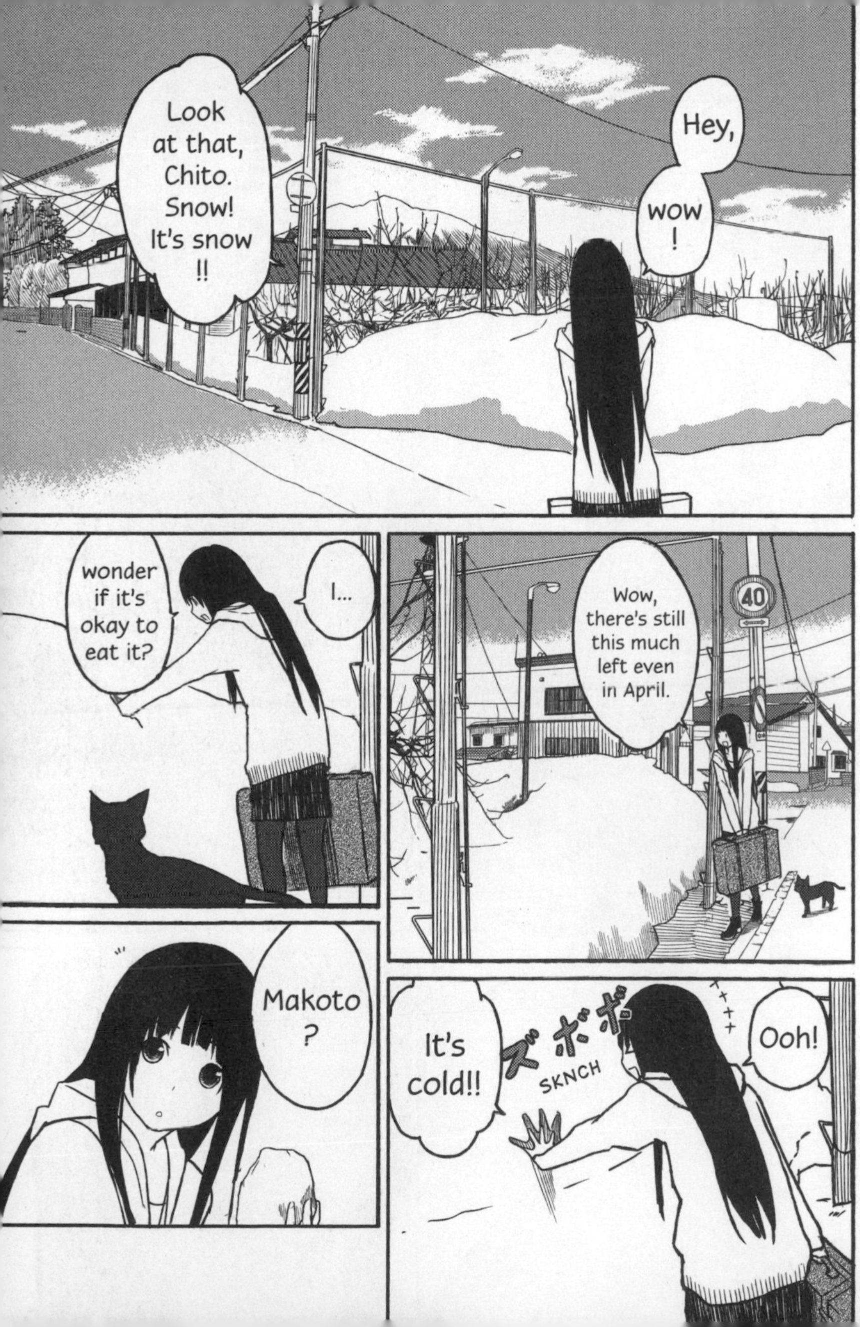
Hey,
wow!
Look at that, Chito. Snow! It's snow!!
Wow, there's still this much left even in April.
I...
wonder if it's okay to eat it?
Ooh!
SKNCH
It's cold!!
Makoto?

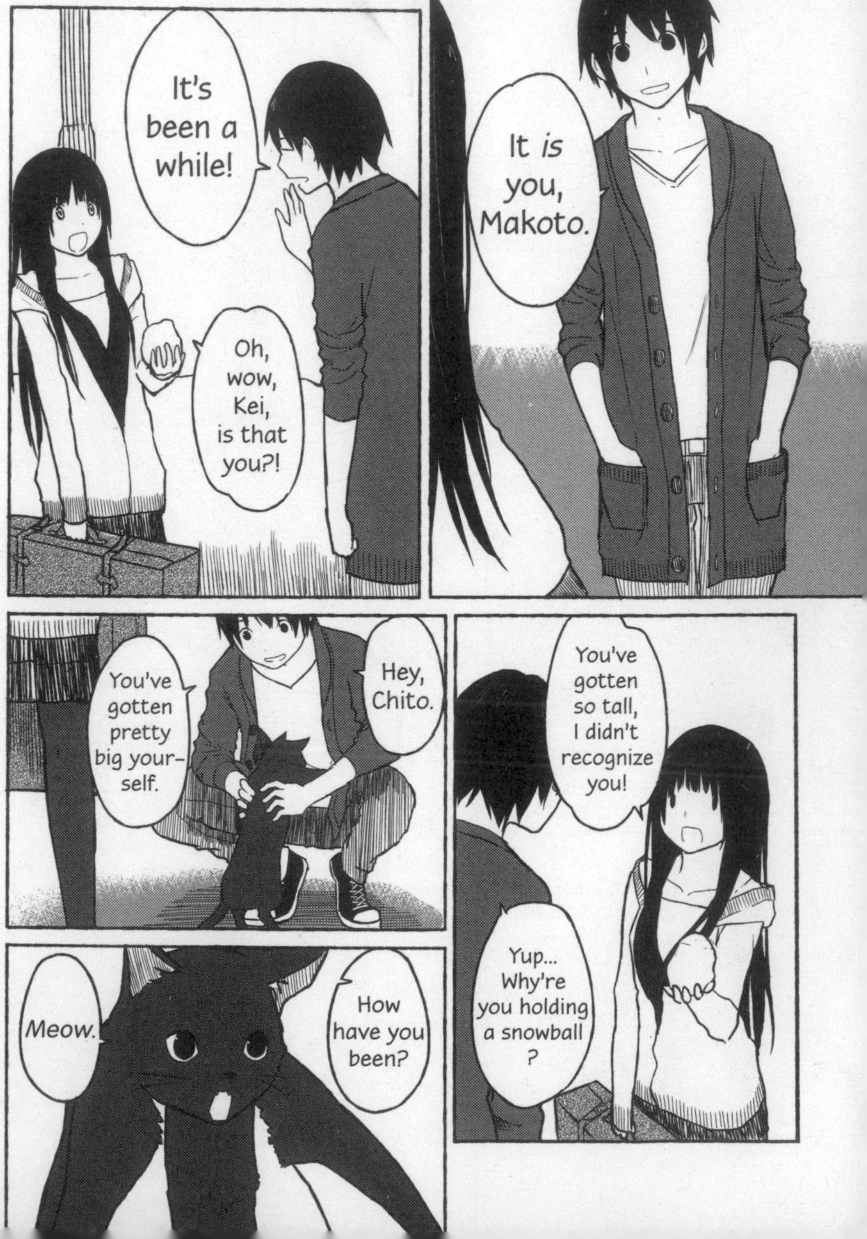
It *is* you, Makoto.
It's been a while!
Oh, wow, Kei, is that you?!
You've gotten so tall, I didn't recognize you!
Yup... Why're you holding a snowball?
Hey, Chito.
You've gotten pretty big your-self.
How have you been?
Meow.

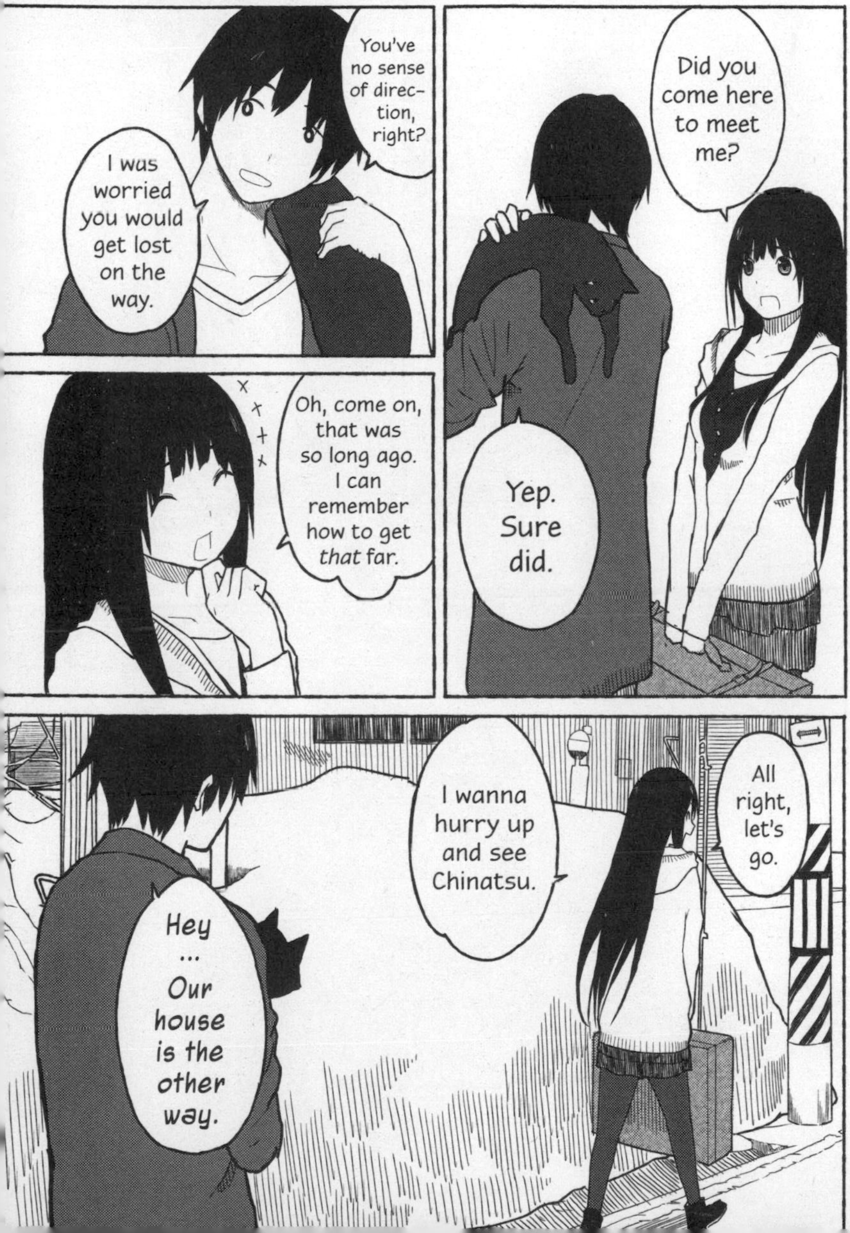
Did you come here to meet me?
Yep. Sure did.
You've no sense of direc-tion, right?
I was worried you would get lost on the way.
Oh, come on, that was so long ago. I can remember how to get *that* far.
All right, let's go.
I wanna hurry up and see Chinatsu.
Hey ... Our house is the other way.

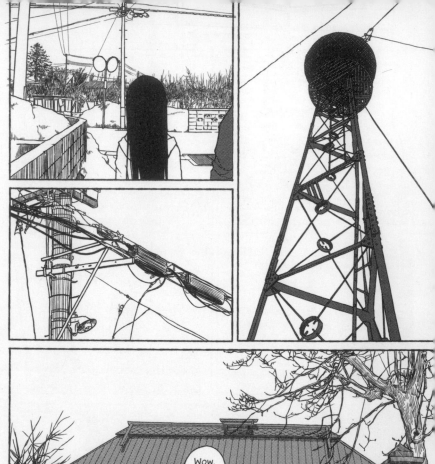

Wow, this takes me back...

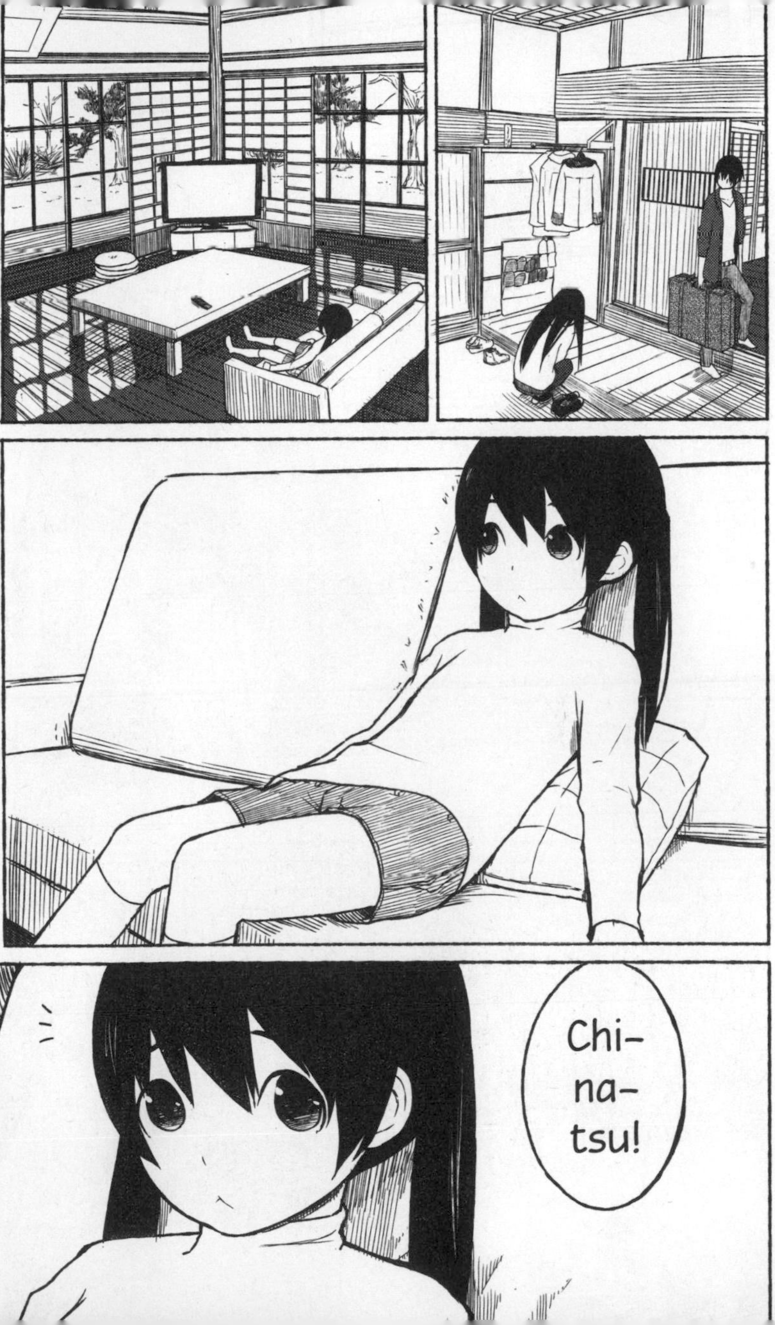
Chi-na-tsu!

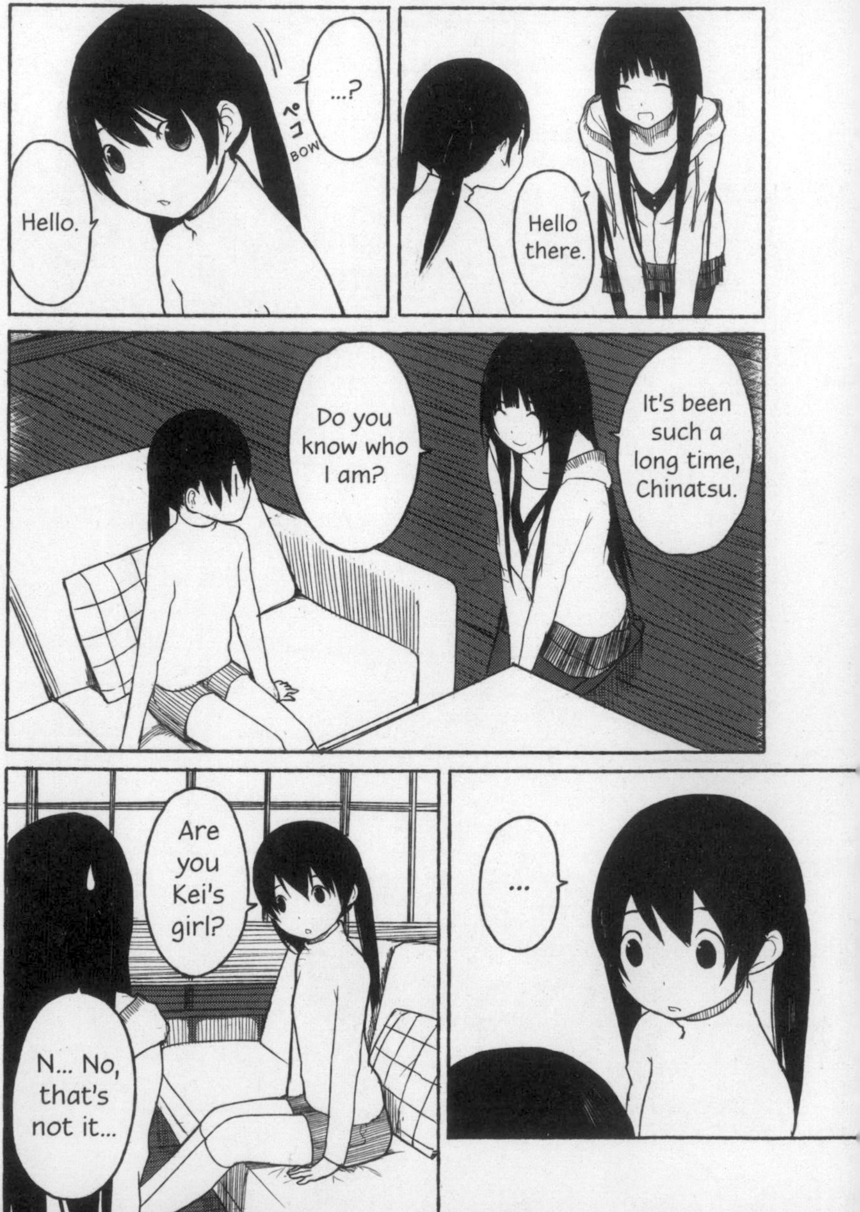
Hello there.
...?
ペコ
BOW
Hello.
It's been such a long time, Chinatsu.
Do you know who I am?
...
Are you Kei's girl?
N... No, that's not it...

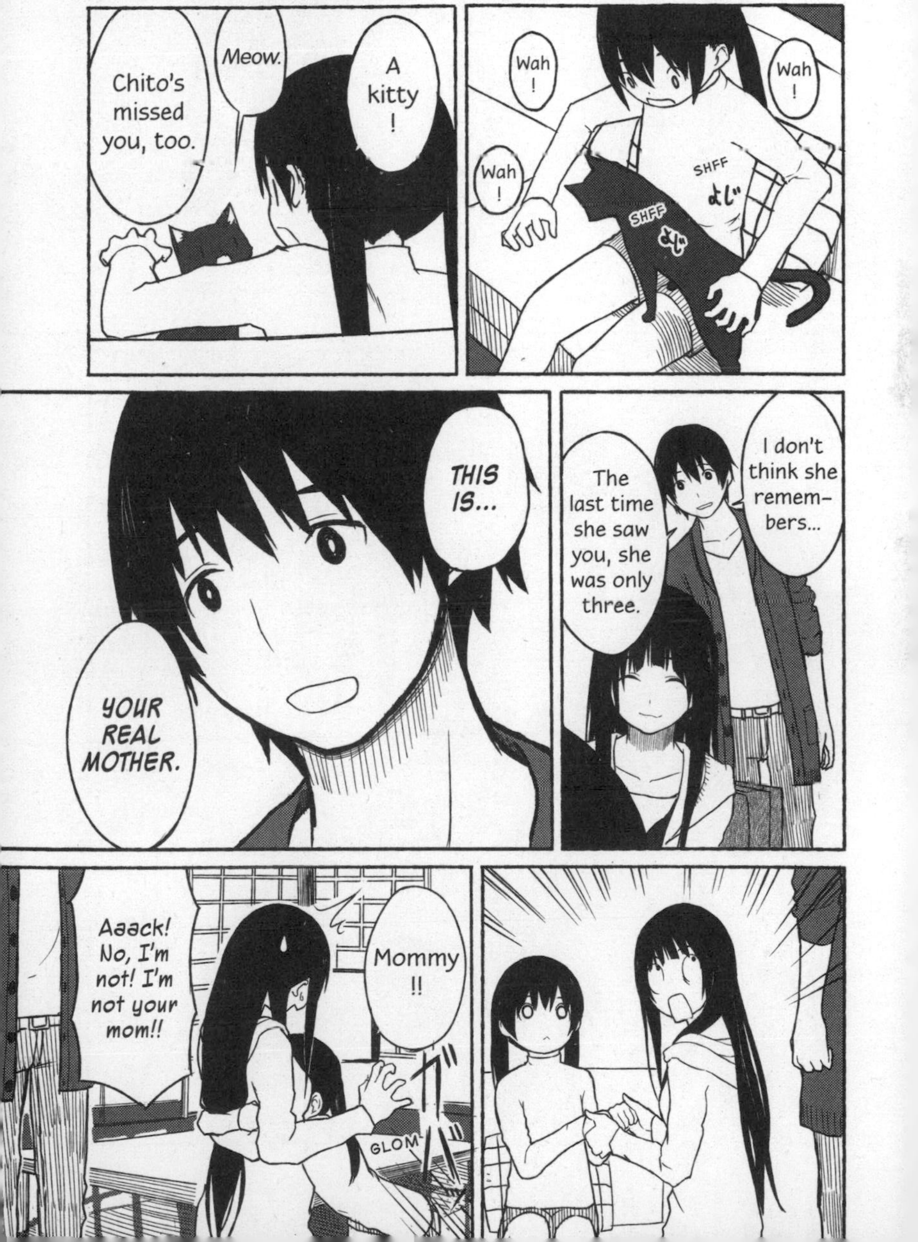
Wah!
Wah!
Wah!
SHFF
よじ
SHFF
よじ
A kitty!
Meow.
Chito's missed you, too.
I don't think she remem-bers...
The last time she saw you, she was only three.
THIS IS...
YOUR REAL MOTHER.
Mommy!!
Aaack! No, I'm not! I'm not your mom!!
GLOM

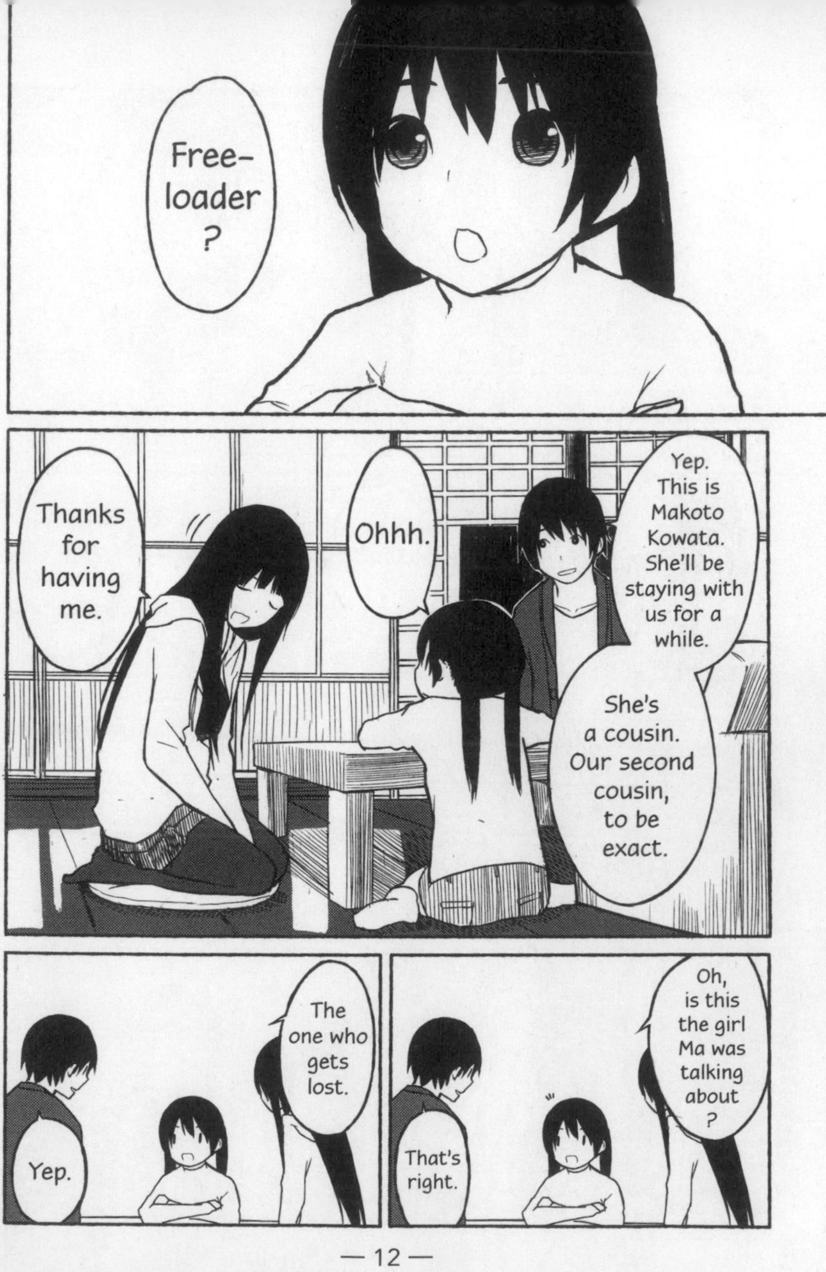
Free-loader?
Yep. This is Makoto Kowata. She'll be staying with us for a while.
She's a cousin. Our second cousin, to be exact.
Ohhh.
Thanks for having me.
Oh, is this the girl Ma was talking about?
That's right.
The one who gets lost.
Yep.

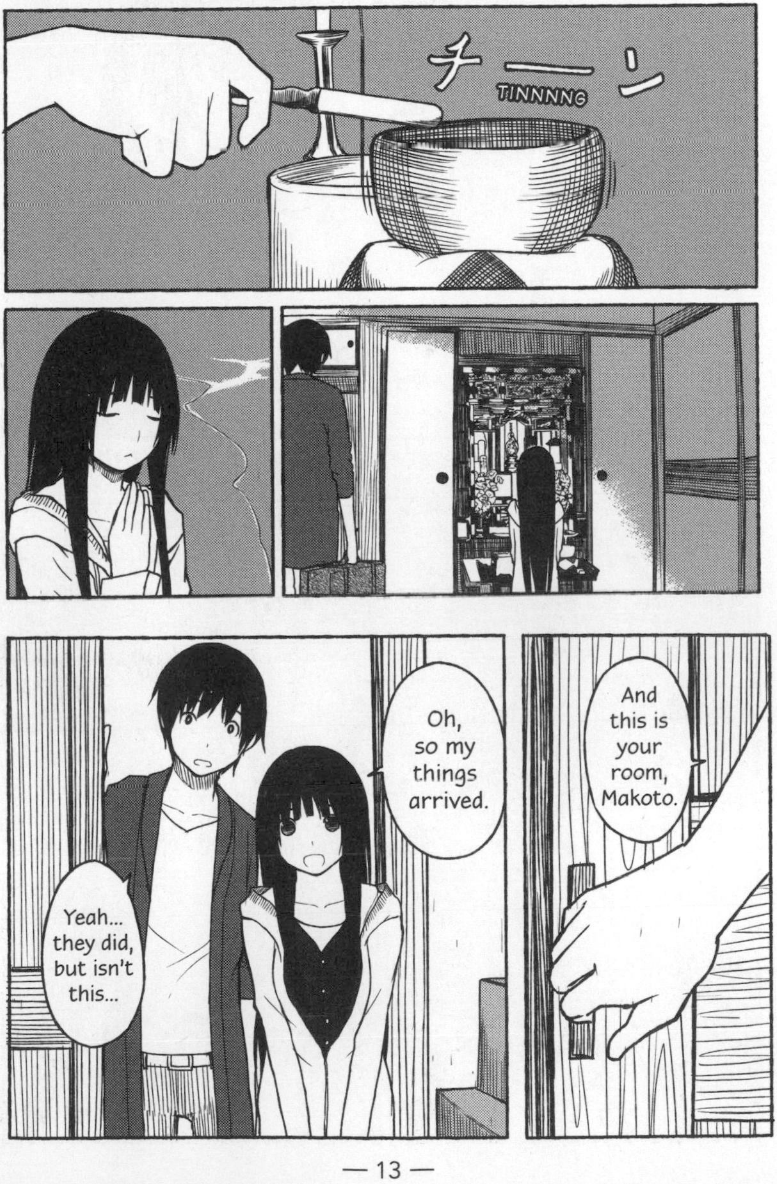
チーン
TINNNNG
And this is your room, Makoto.
Oh, so my things arrived.
Yeah... they did, but isn't this...

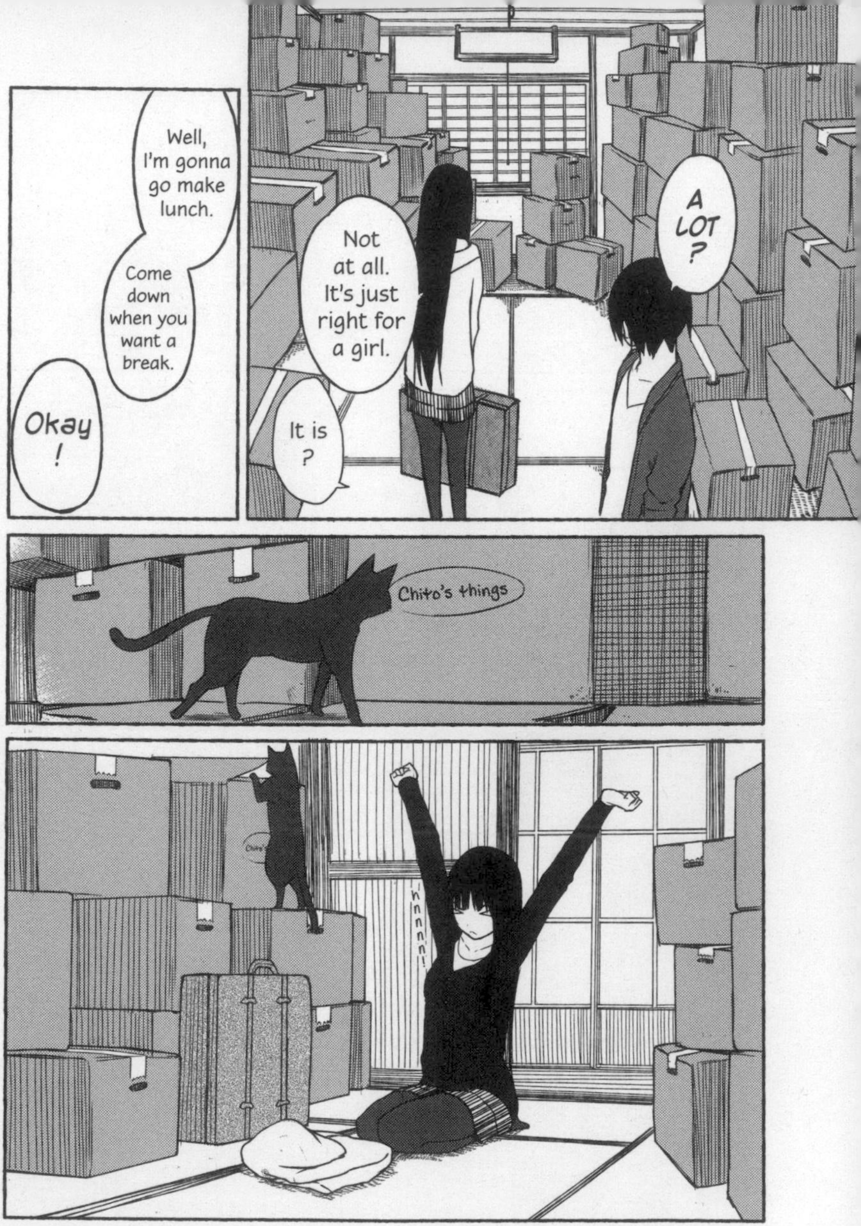
A LOT?
Not at all. It's just right for a girl.
It is?
Well, I'm gonna go make lunch.
Come down when you want a break.
Okay!
Chito's things

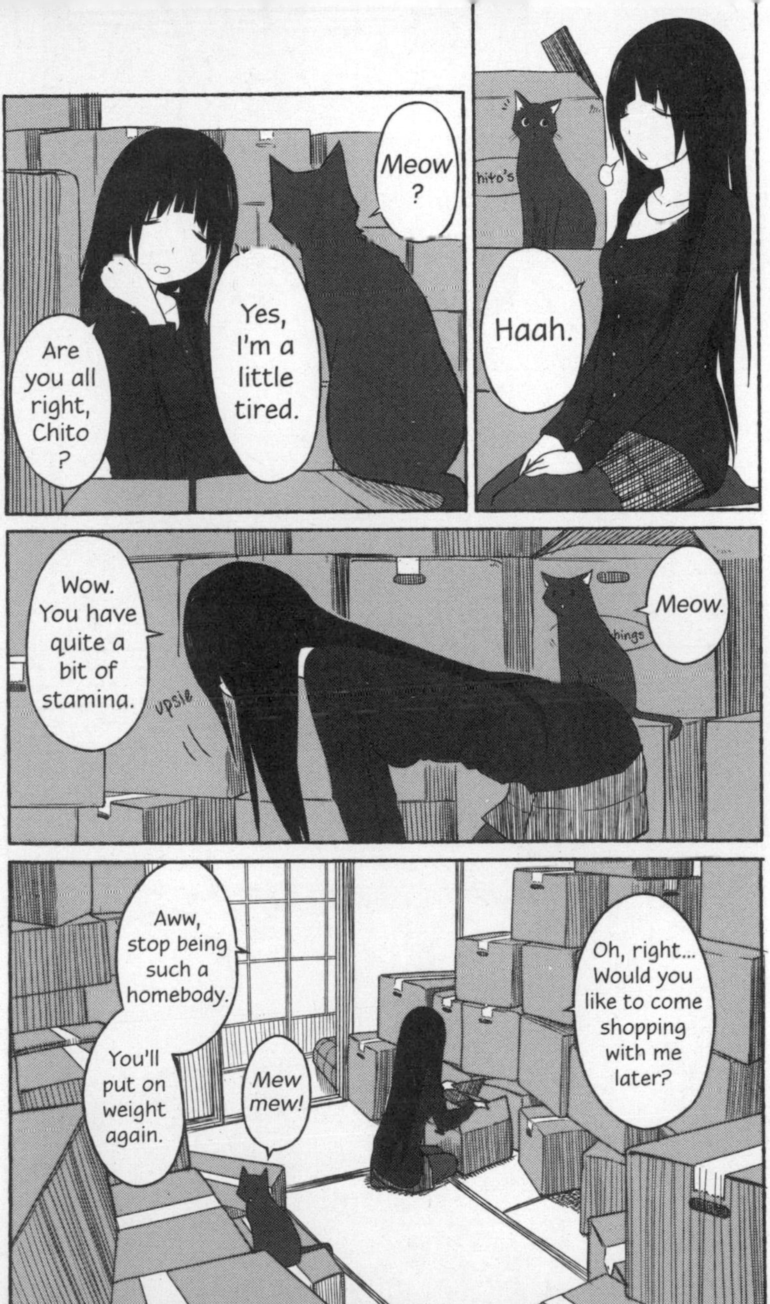
Haah.
Meow?
Yes, I'm a little tired.
Are you all right, Chito?
Meow.
Wow. You have quite a bit of stamina.
Oh, right... Would you like to come shopping with me later?
Mew mew!
Aww, stop being such a homebody.
You'll put on weight again.

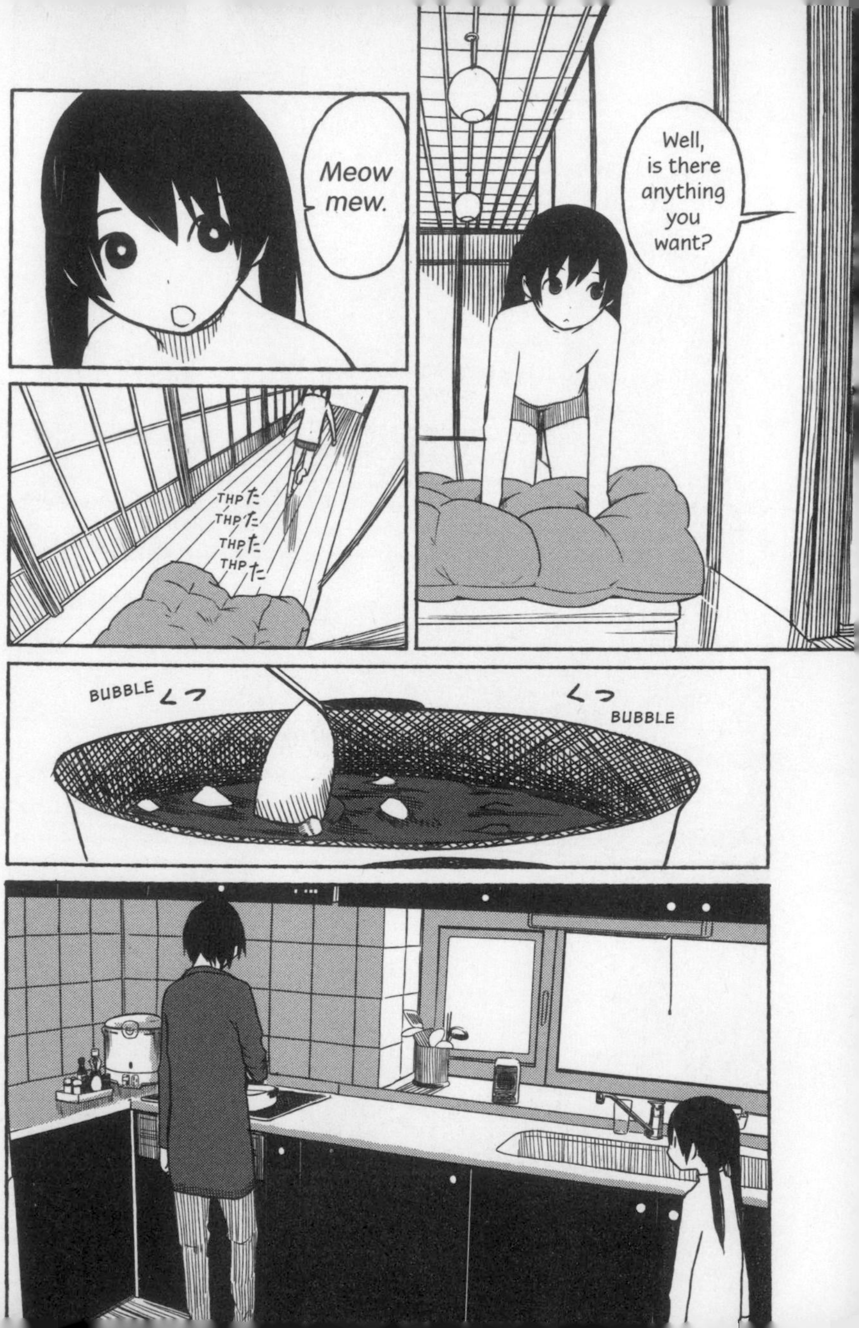
Well, is there anything you want?
Meow mew.
THP た THP た THP た THP た
くっ BUBBLE
BUBBLE くっ

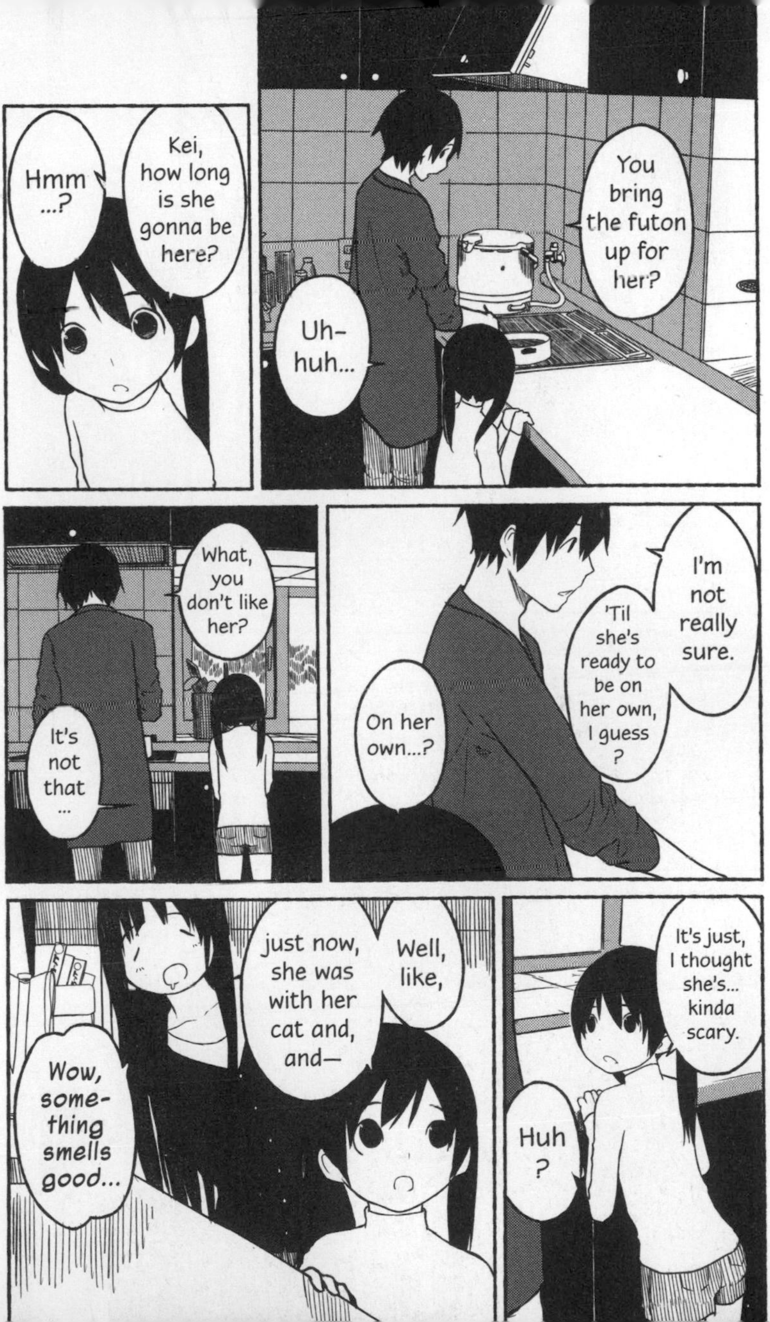
You bring the futon up for her?
Uh-huh...
Kei, how long is she gonna be here?
Hmm ...?
I'm not really sure.
'Til she's ready to be on her own, I guess ?
On her own...?
What, you don't like her?
It's not that ...
It's just, I thought she's... kinda scary.
Huh ?
Well, like,
just now, she was with her cat and, and—
Wow, something smells good...

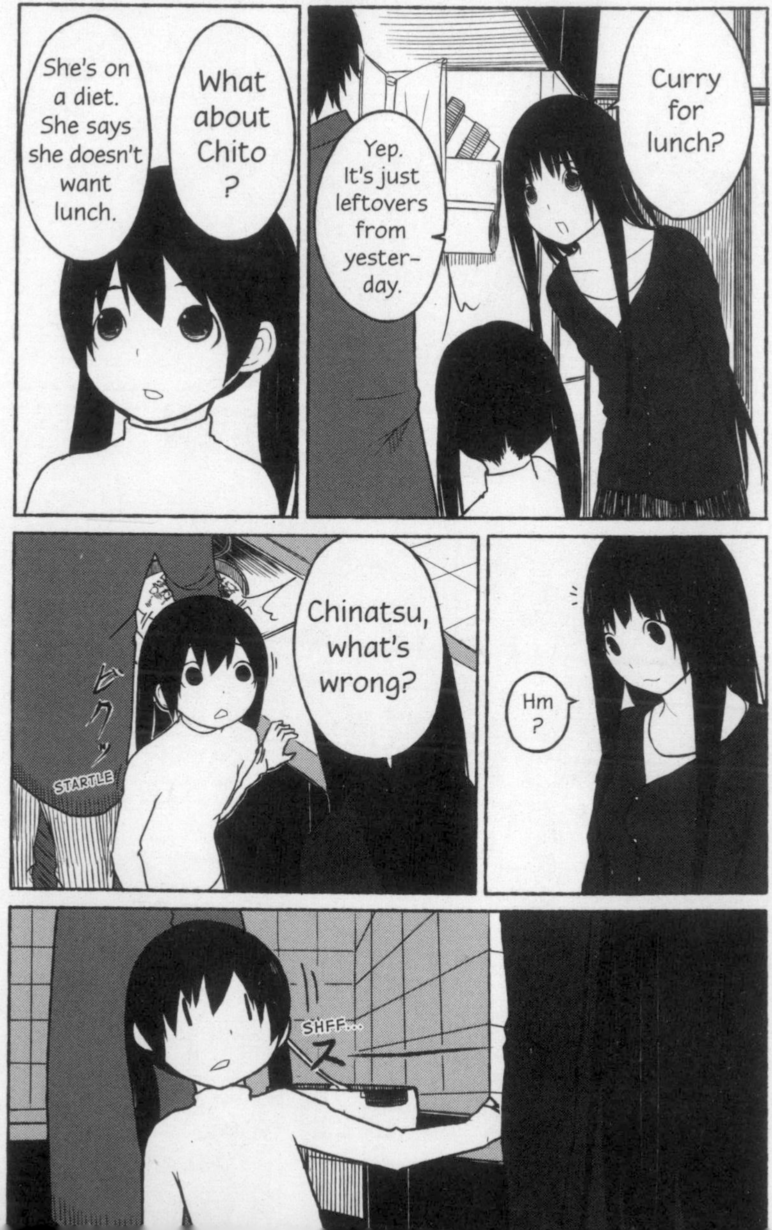
Curry for lunch?
Yep. It's just leftovers from yester-day.
What about Chito ?
She's on a diet. She says she doesn't want lunch.
Hm ?
Chinatsu, what's wrong?
ビクッ
STARTLE
SHFF...
ス

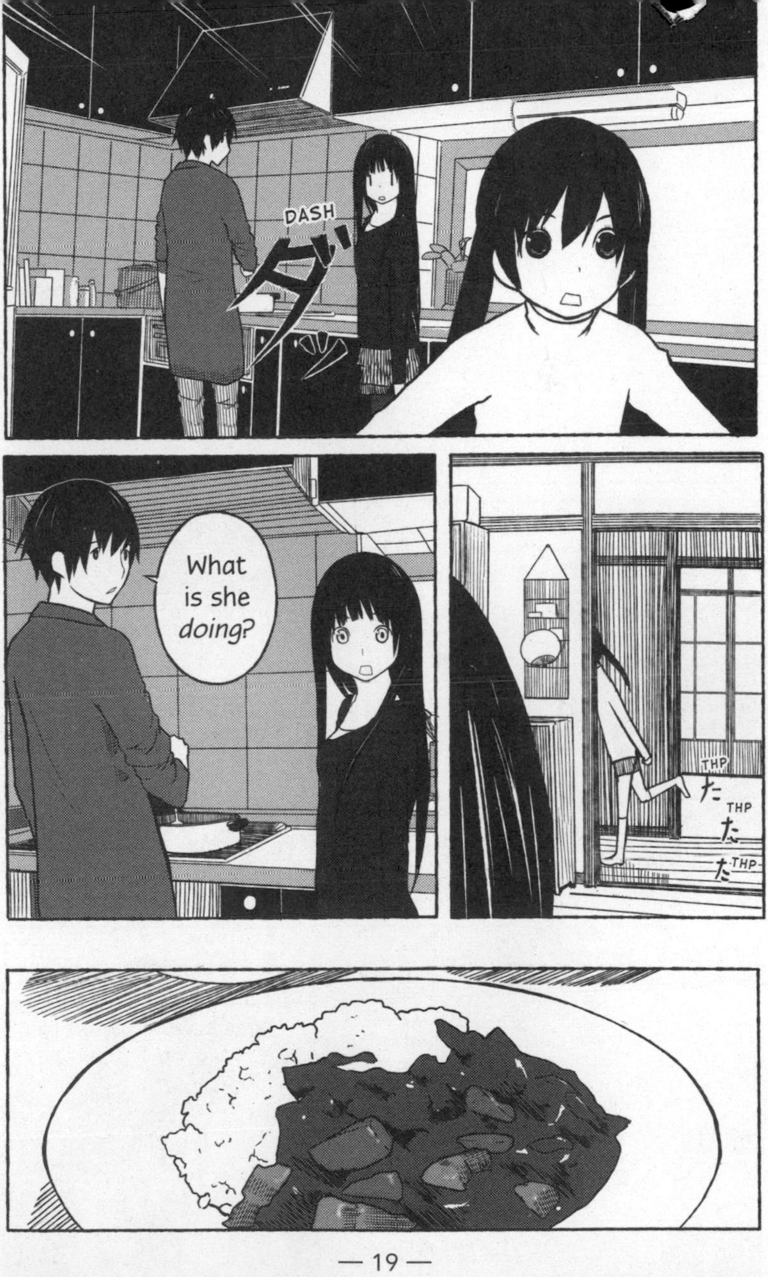
DASH
THP
た
THP
た
THP
た
What is she doing?

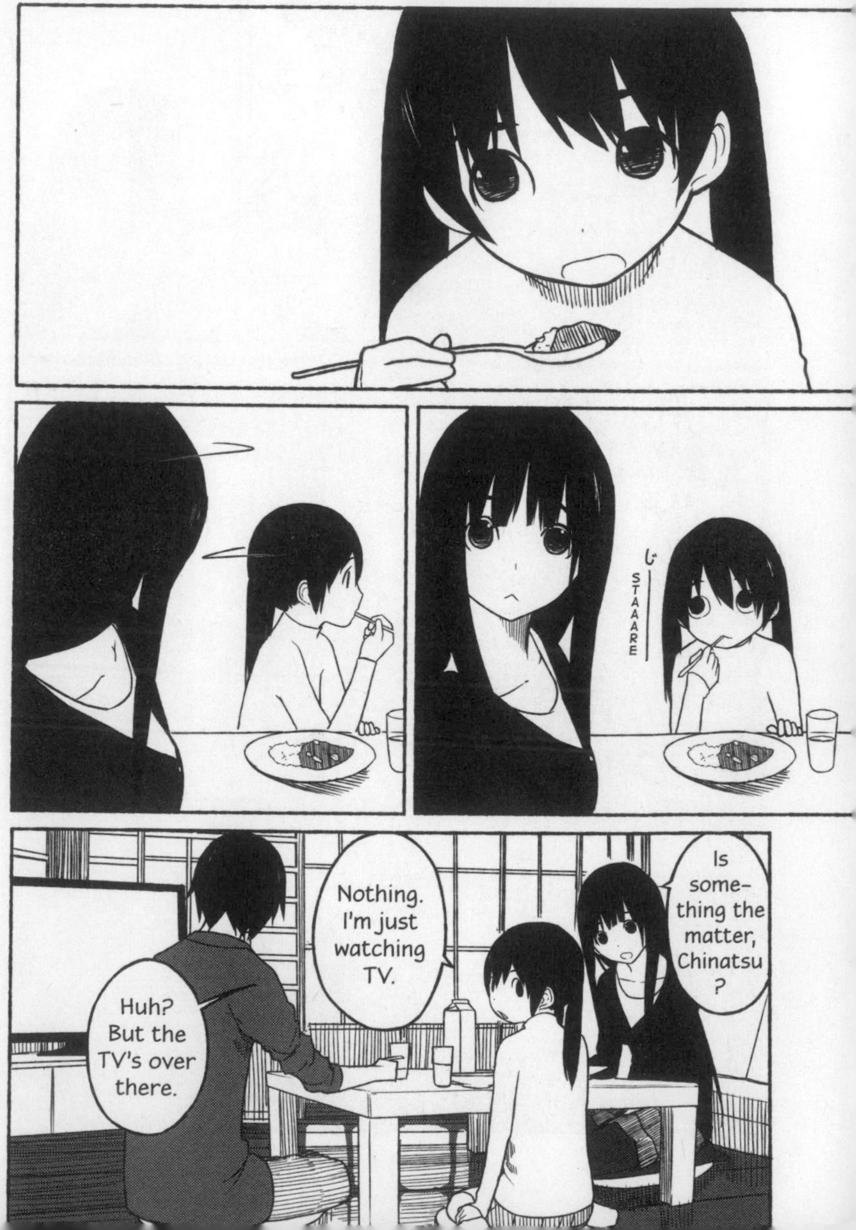
じ
STAAARE
Is some-thing the matter, Chinatsu?
Nothing. I'm just watching TV.
Huh? But the TV's over there.

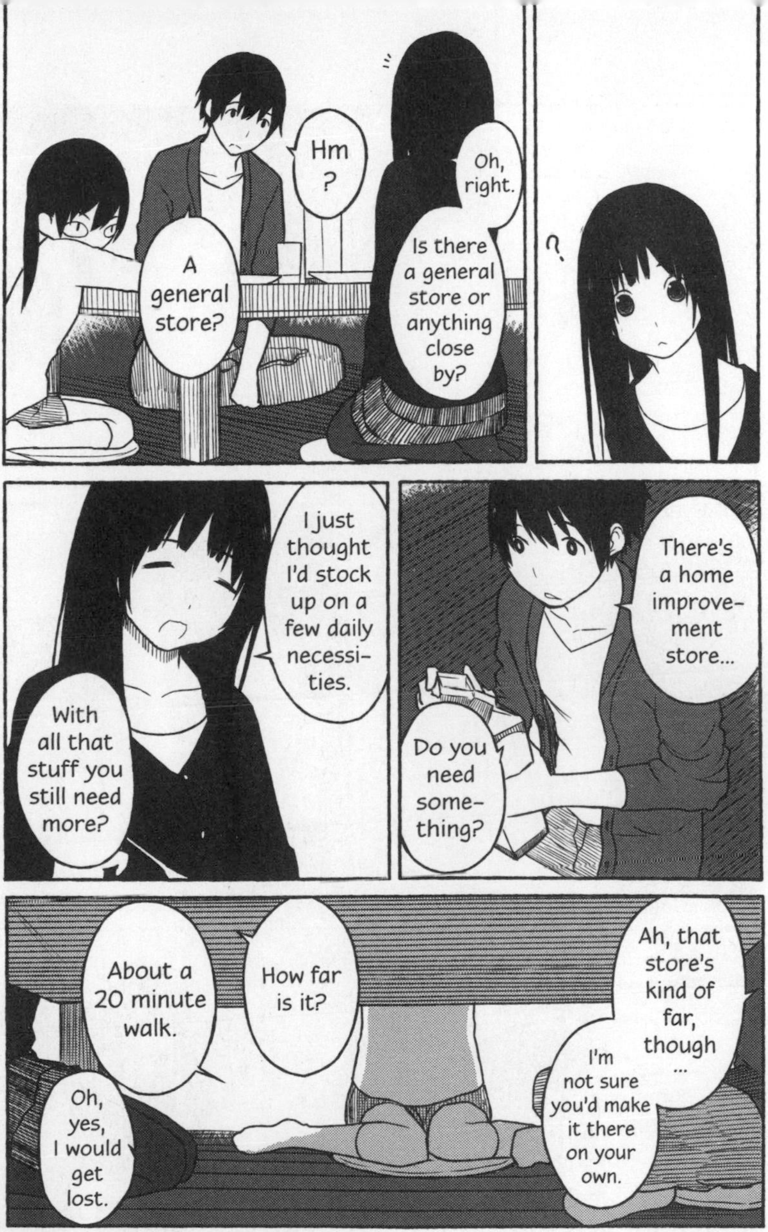
?
Oh, right.
Is there a general store or anything close by?
Hm?
A general store?
There's a home improvement store...
Do you need something?
I just thought I'd stock up on a few daily necessities.
With all that stuff you still need more?
Ah, that store's kind of far, though ...
I'm not sure you'd make it there on your own.
How far is it?
About a 20 minute walk.
Oh, yes, I would get lost.

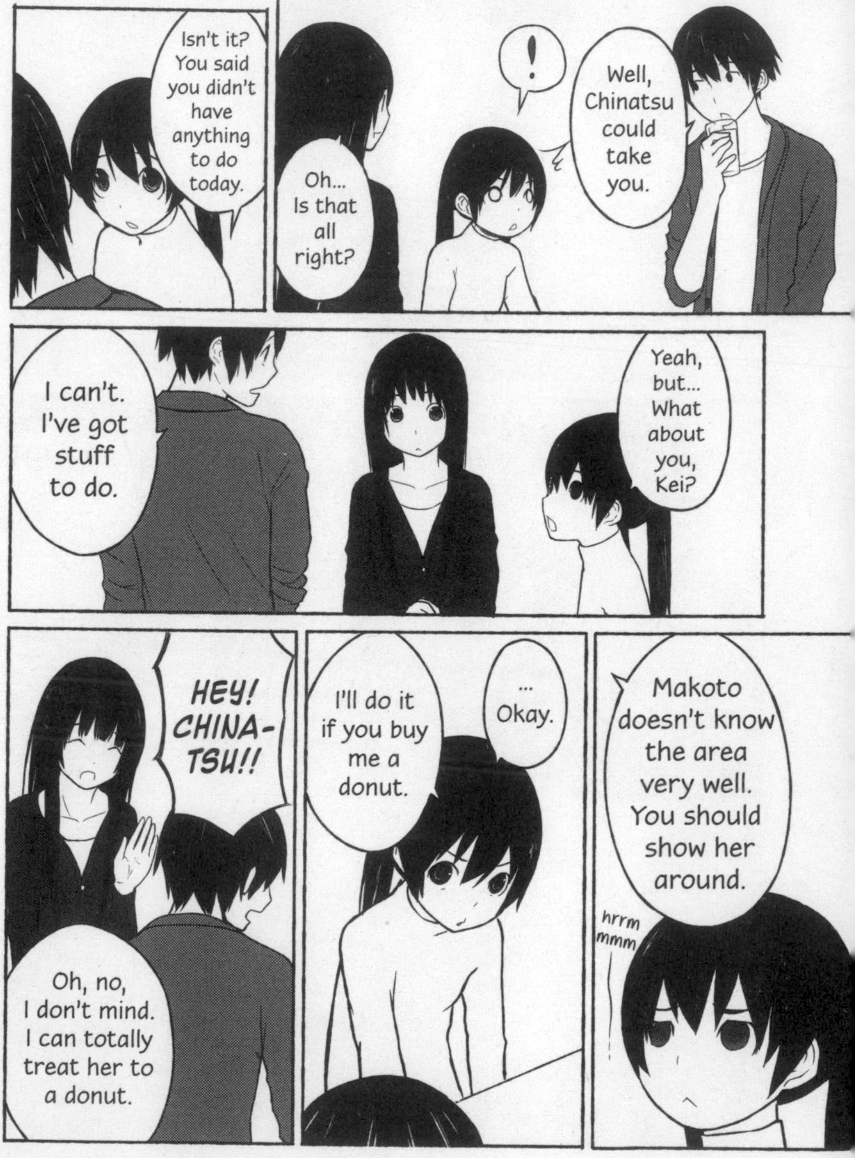
Well, Chinatsu could take you.
!
Oh... Is that all right?
Isn't it? You said you didn't have anything to do today.
Yeah, but... What about you, Kei?
I can't. I've got stuff to do.
Makoto doesn't know the area very well. You should show her around.
hrrm mmm
... Okay.
I'll do it if you buy me a donut.
HEY! CHINA-TSU!!
Oh, no, I don't mind. I can totally treat her to a donut.

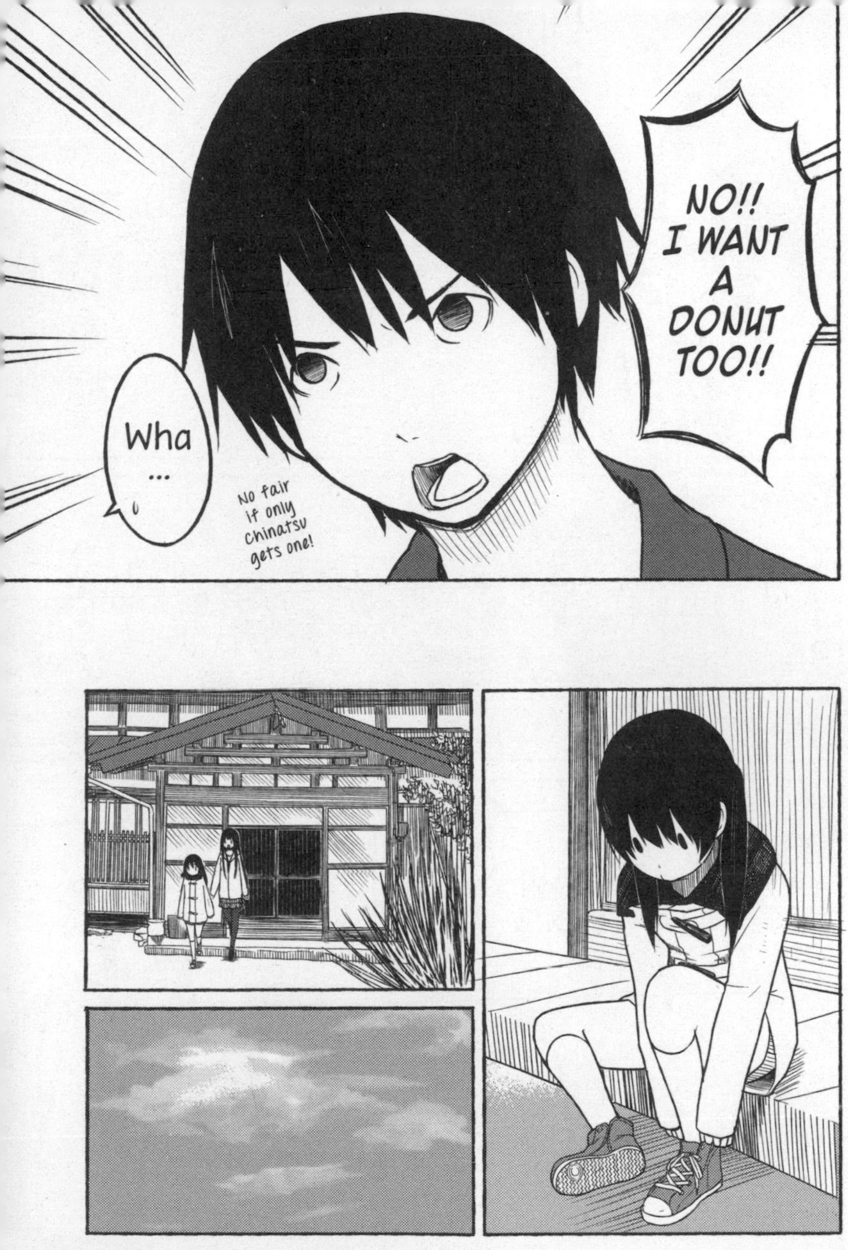
NO!! I WANT A DONUT TOO!!
No fair if only Chinatsu gets one!
Wha...

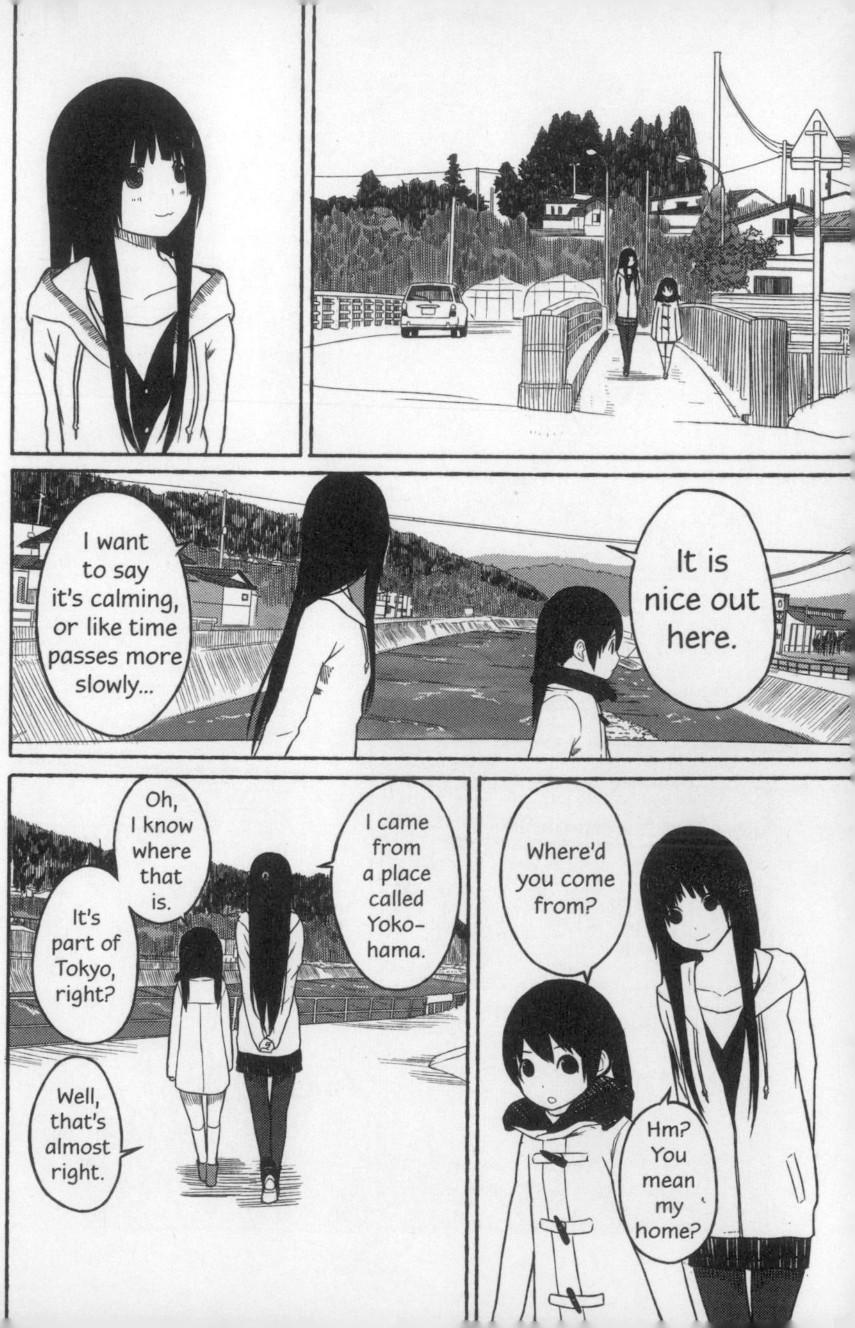
It is nice out here.
I want to say it's calming, or like time passes more slowly...
Where'd you come from?
Hm? You mean my home?
I came from a place called Yoko-hama.
Oh, I know where that is.
It's part of Tokyo, right?
Well, that's almost right.

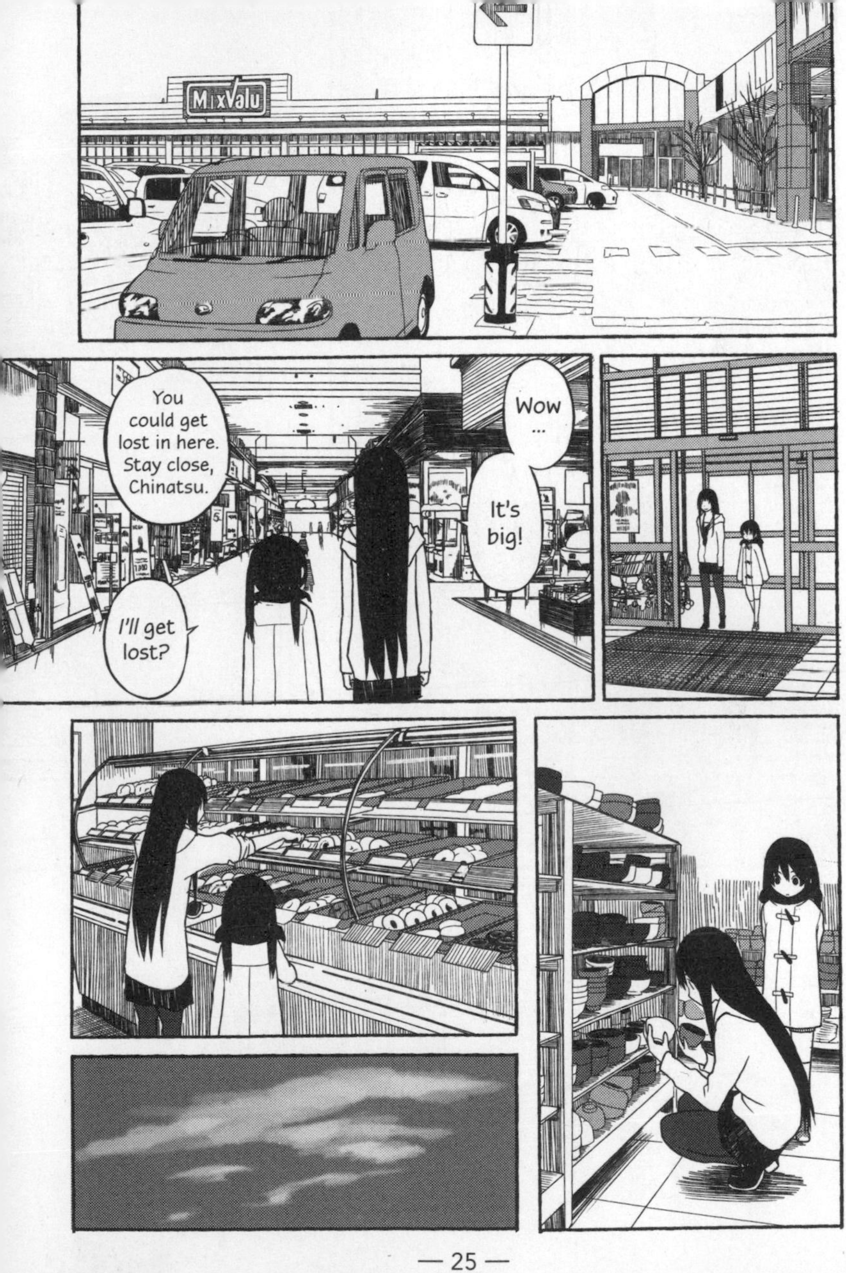
MixValu
Wow ...
It's big!
You could get lost in here. Stay close, Chinatsu.
I'll get lost?

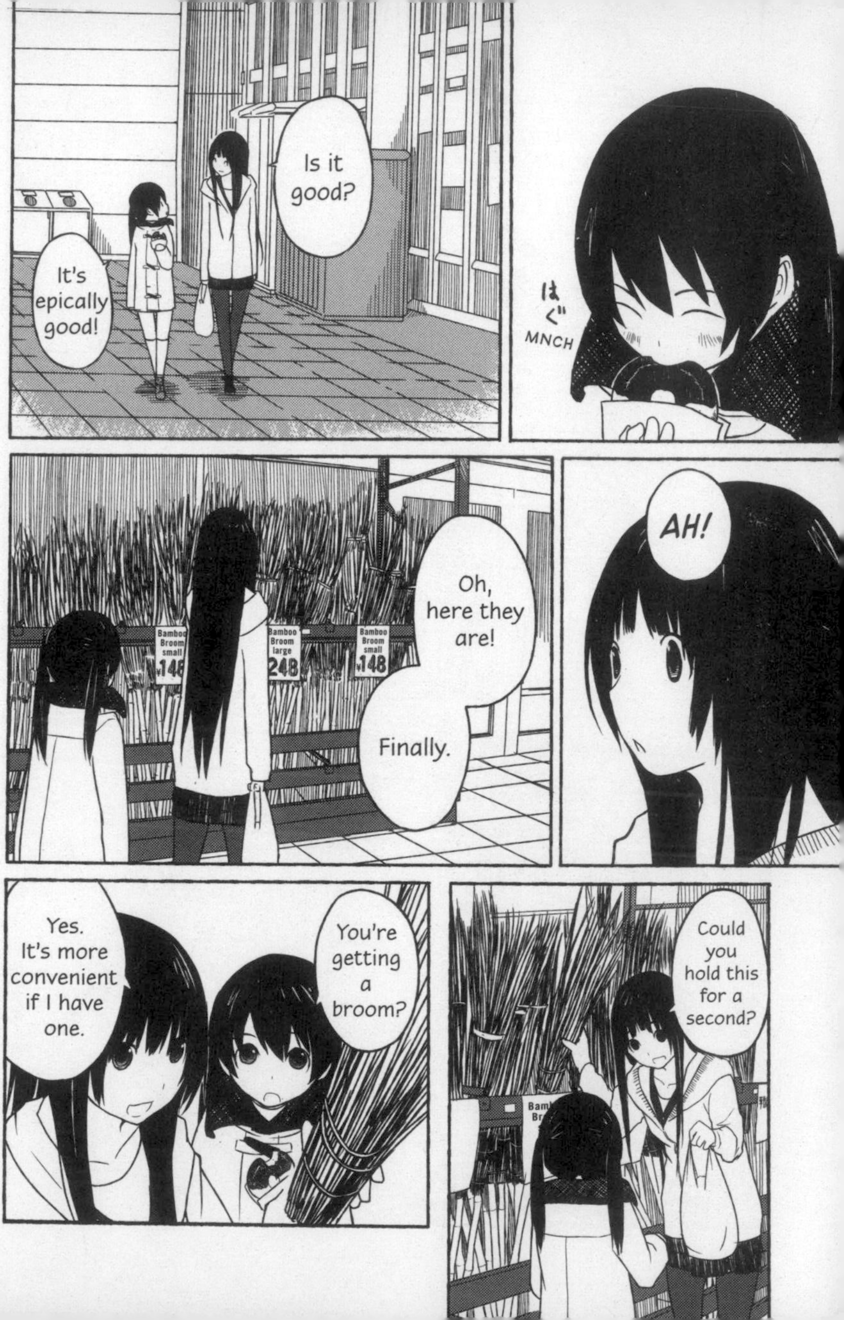
はぐ
MNCH
Is it good?
It's epically good!
AH!
Oh, here they are!
Finally.
Bamboo Broom small ¥148
Bamboo Broom large 248
Bamboo Broom small ¥148
Could you hold this for a second?
You're getting a broom?
Yes. It's more convenient if I have one.

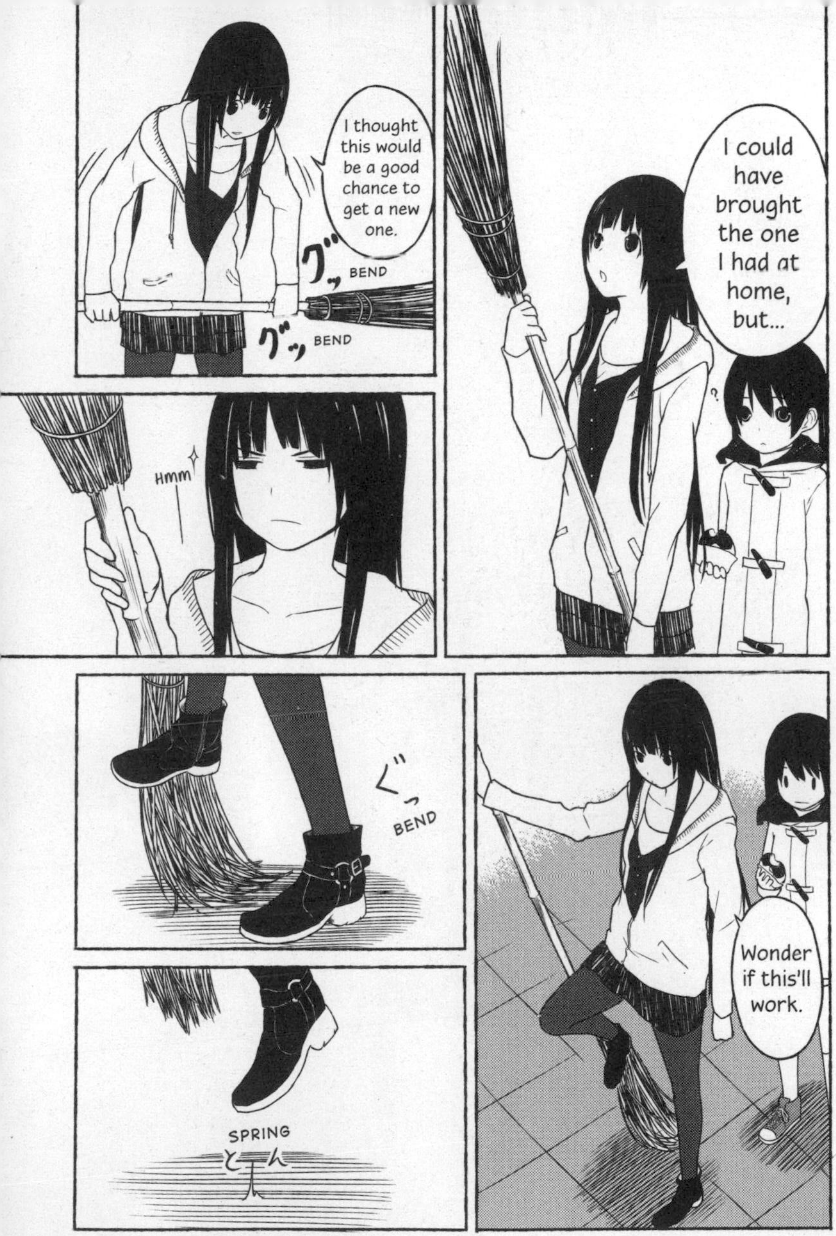
I could have brought the one I had at home, but...
I thought this would be a good chance to get a new one.
グッ BEND
グッ BEND
Hmm
Wonder if this'll work.
ぐっ BEND
SPRING
とん

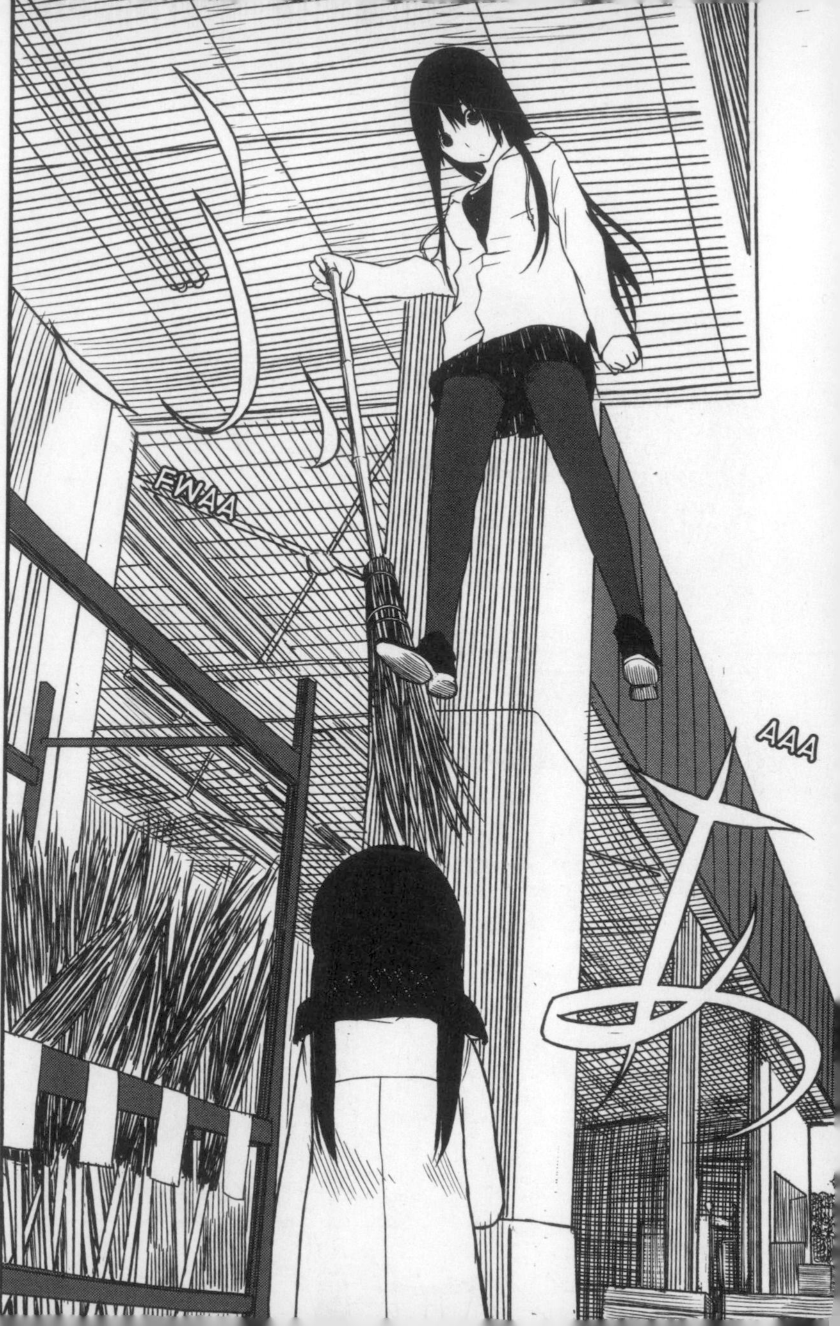
AAA
FWAA

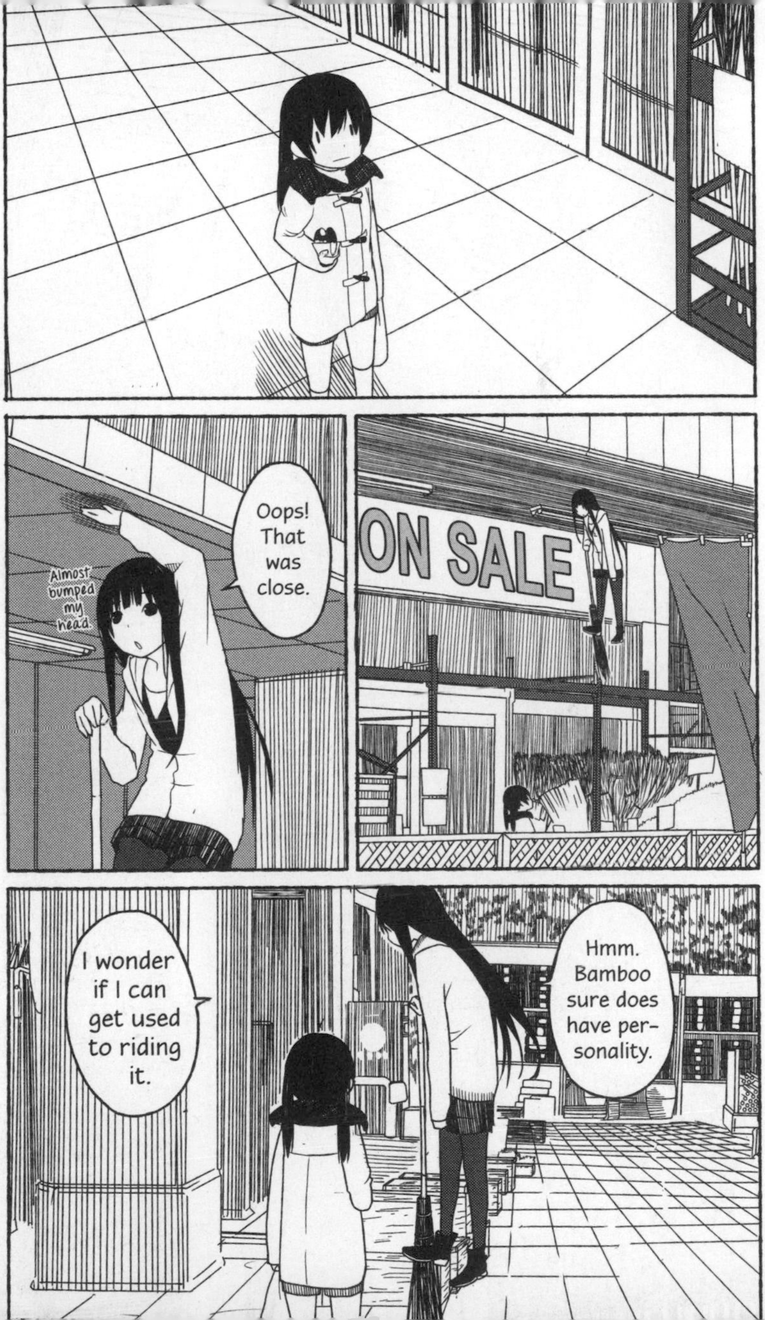
ON SALE
Oops! That was close.
Almost bumped my head.
Hmm. Bamboo sure does have personality.
I wonder if I can get used to riding it.

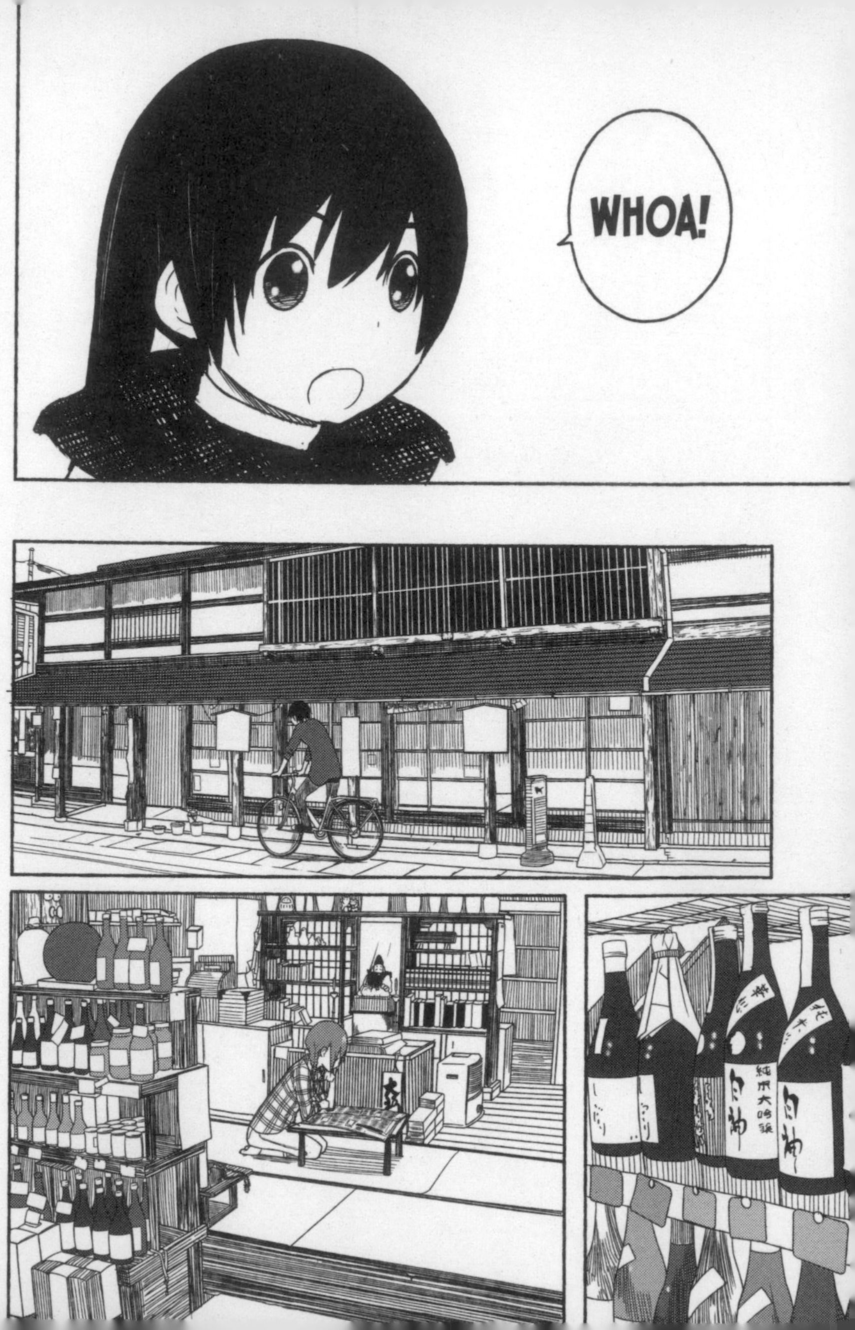
WHOA!

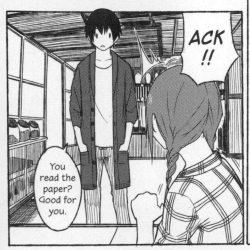

ACK !!
You read the paper? Good for you.
Huh, so you got a cousin staying over?
A boy?
How lewd.
Nah, a girl. My age.
'Scuse me?

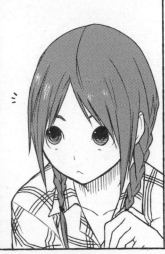

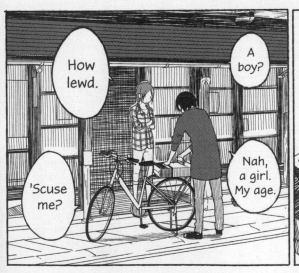

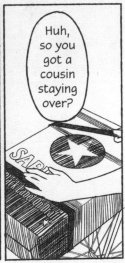

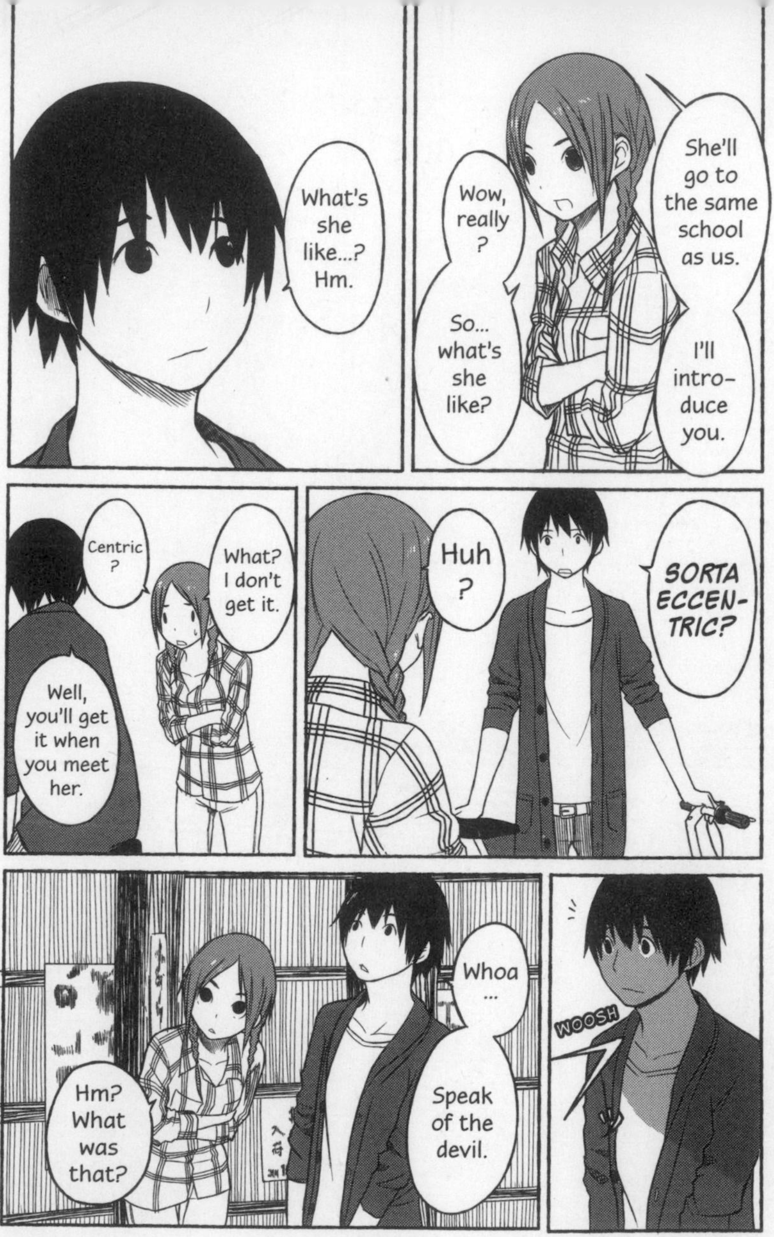
She'll go to the same school as us.
I'll introduce you.
Wow, really?
So... what's she like?
What's she like...? Hm.
SORTA ECCENTRIC?
Huh?
What? I don't get it.
Centric?
Well, you'll get it when you meet her.
WOOSH
Whoa...
Speak of the devil.
Hm? What was that?

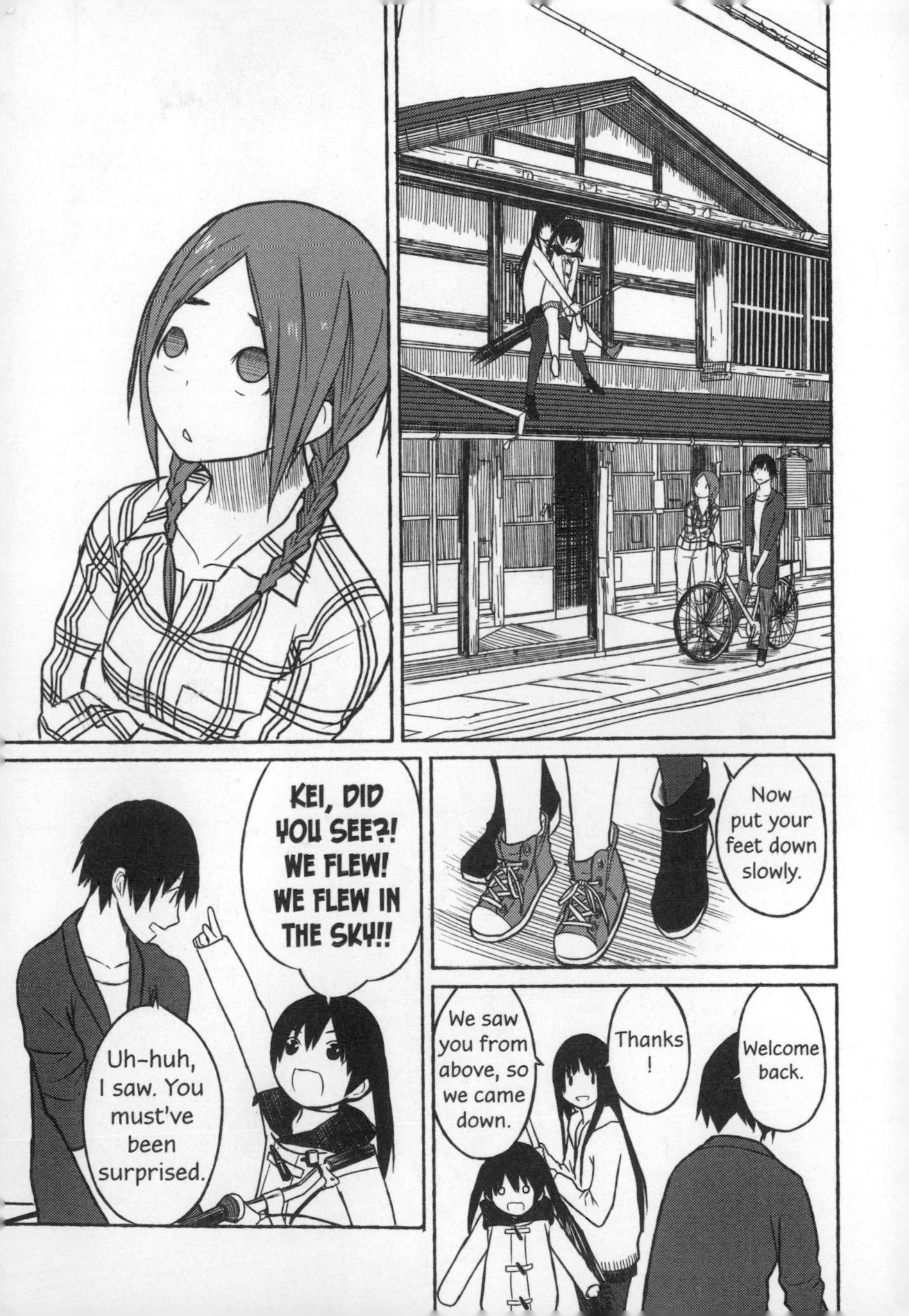
Now put your feet down slowly.
Welcome back.
Thanks!
We saw you from above, so we came down.
KEI, DID YOU SEE?! WE FLEW! WE FLEW IN THE SKY!!
Uh-huh, I saw. You must've been surprised.

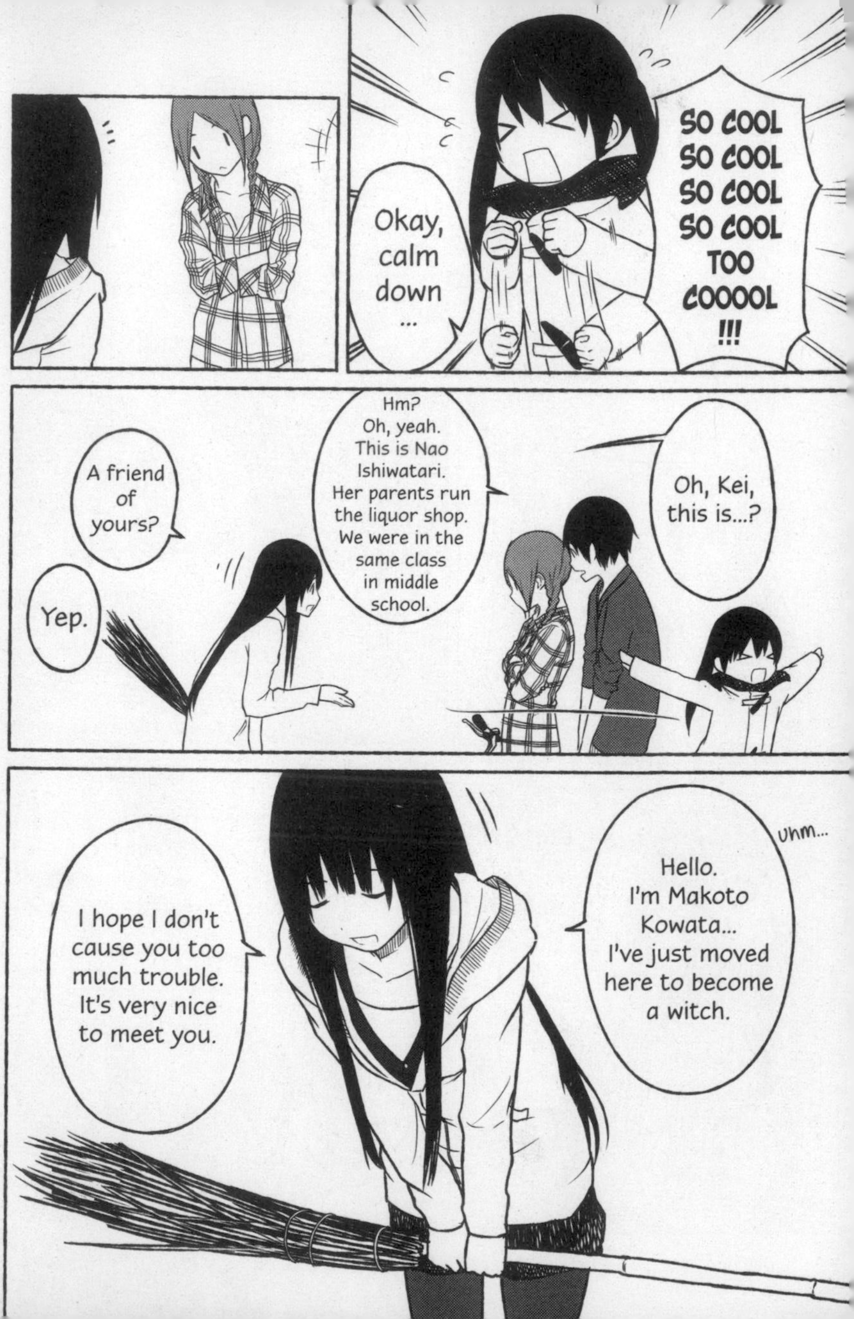
SO COOL SO COOL SO COOL SO COOL TOO COOOOL !!!
Okay, calm down ...
Oh, Kei, this is...?
Hm? Oh, yeah. This is Nao Ishiwatari. Her parents run the liquor shop. We were in the same class in middle school.
A friend of yours?
Yep.
uhm...
Hello. I'm Makoto Kowata... I've just moved here to become a witch.
I hope I don't cause you too much trouble. It's very nice to meet you.

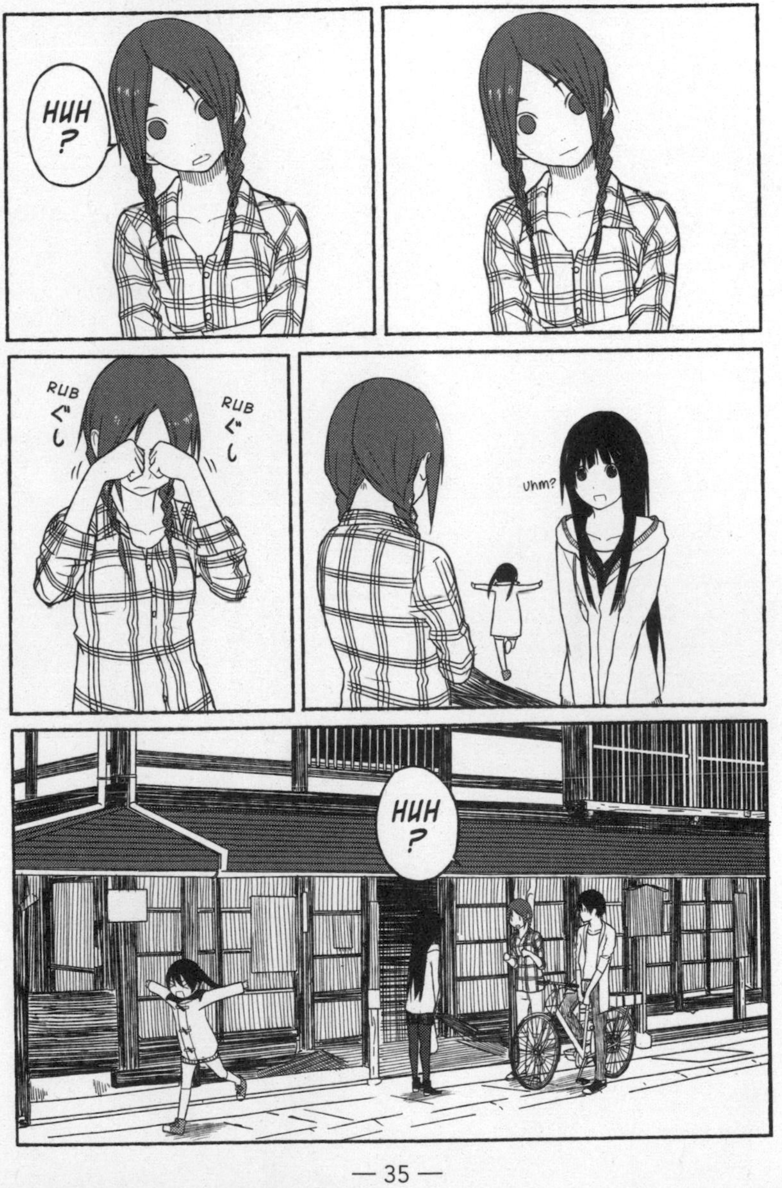
HUH ?
Uhm?
RUB ぐし
RUB ぐし
HUH ?

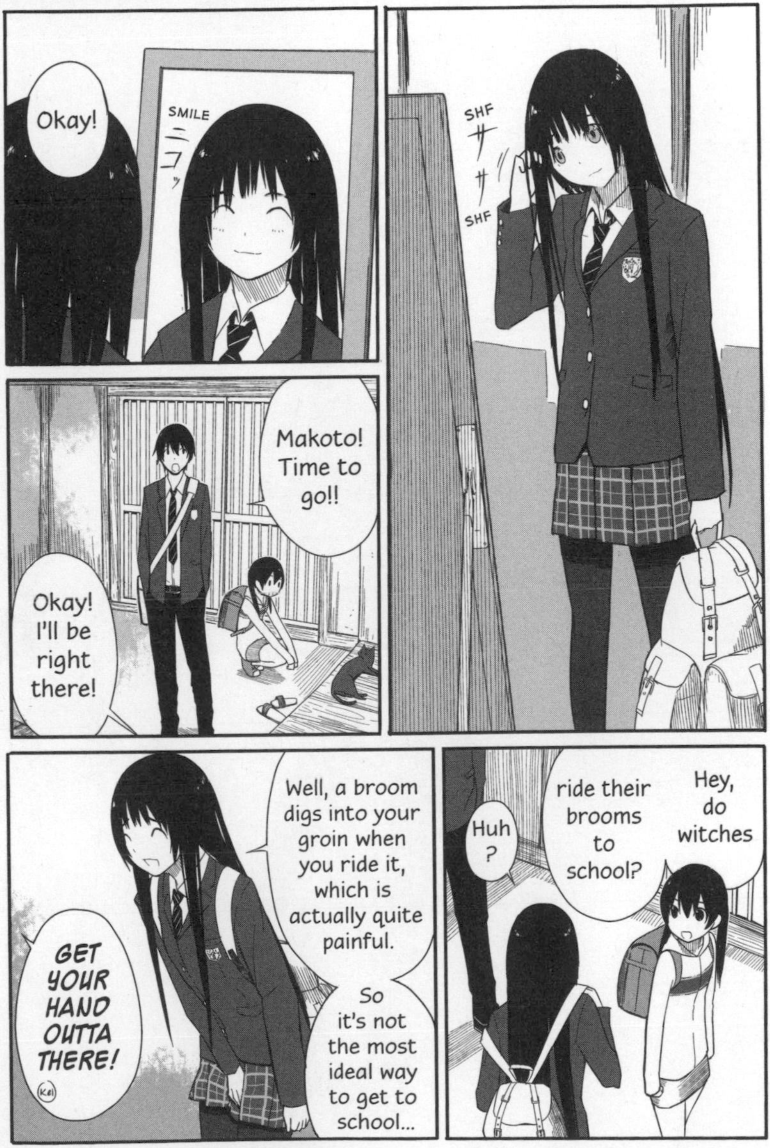
SHF
SHF
Okay!
SMILE
ニコッ
Makoto! Time to go!!
Okay! I'll be right there!
Hey, do witches ride their brooms to school?
Huh?
Well, a broom digs into your groin when you ride it, which is actually quite painful.
So it's not the most ideal way to get to school...
GET YOUR HAND OUTTA THERE!
Kei

Chapter 2
Roadside Panacea

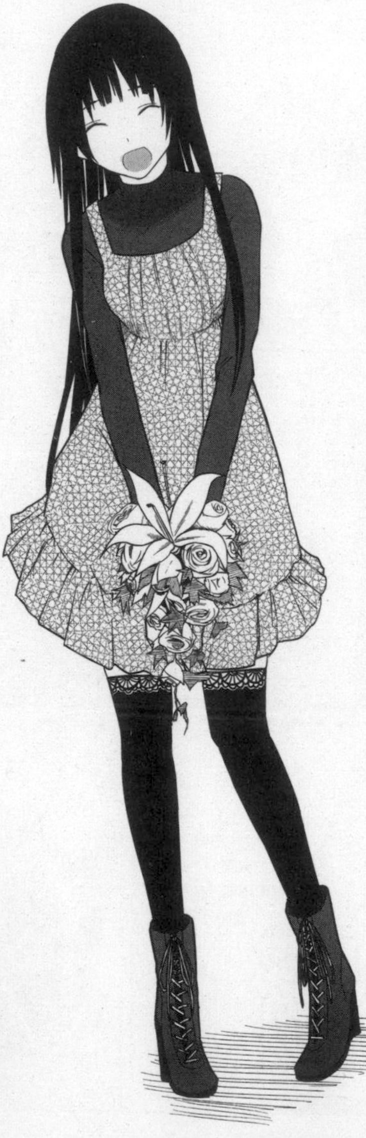

Ah!

Hey, here's your class.

WAAH!!!

BAM

It's Nano!!

THUP ᴀᴀᴀ
THUP THUP
THUP THUP

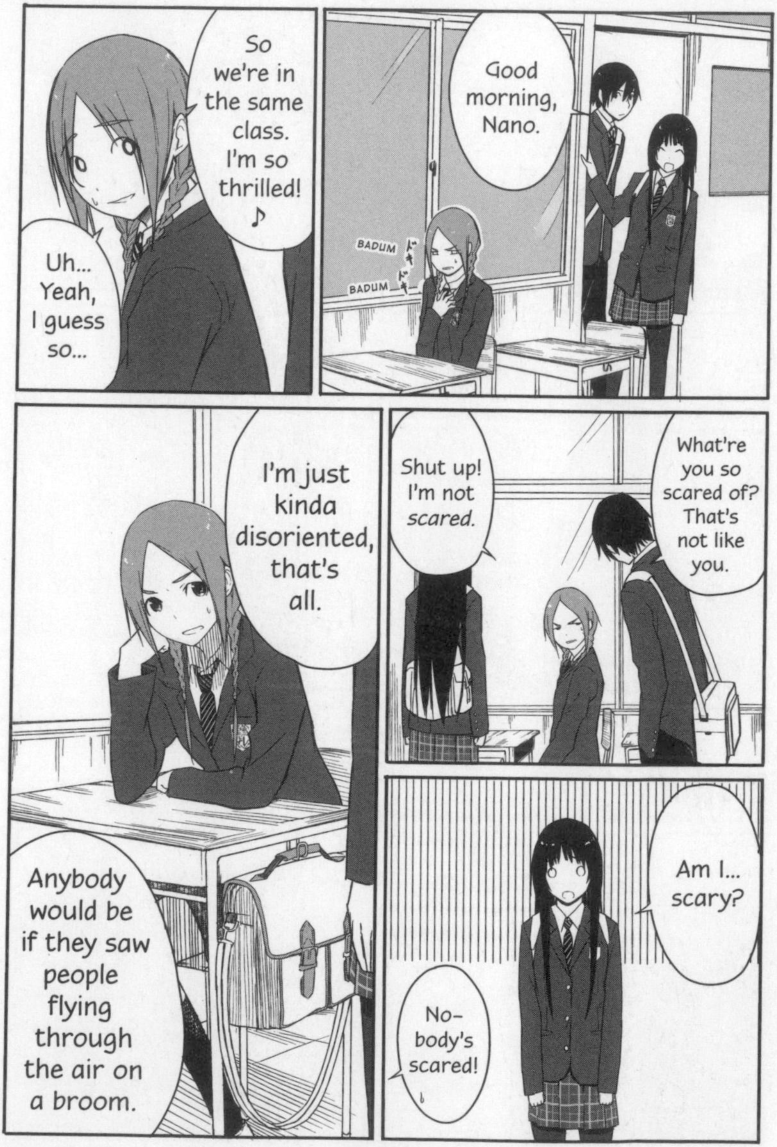
Good morning, Nano.
BADUM
ドキ
BADUM
ドキ
So we're in the same class. I'm so thrilled! ♪
Uh... Yeah, I guess so...
What're you so scared of? That's not like you.
Shut up! I'm not *scared.*
Am I... scary?
No-body's scared!
I'm just kinda disoriented, that's all.
Anybody would be if they saw people flying through the air on a broom.

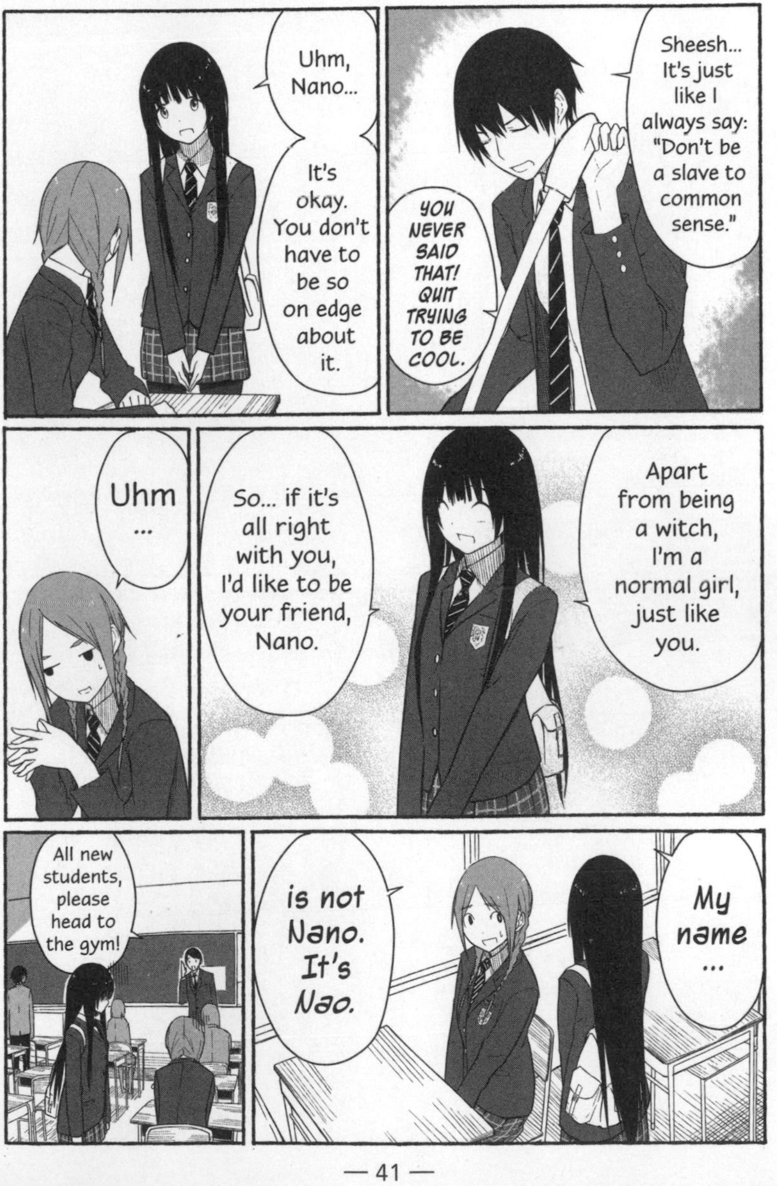
Sheesh... It's just like I always say: "Don't be a slave to common sense."
YOU NEVER SAID THAT! QUIT TRYING TO BE COOL.
Uhm, Nano...
It's okay. You don't have to be so on edge about it.
Apart from being a witch, I'm a normal girl, just like you.
So... if it's all right with you, I'd like to be your friend, Nano.
Uhm ...
My name ...
is not Nano. It's Nao.
All new students, please head to the gym!

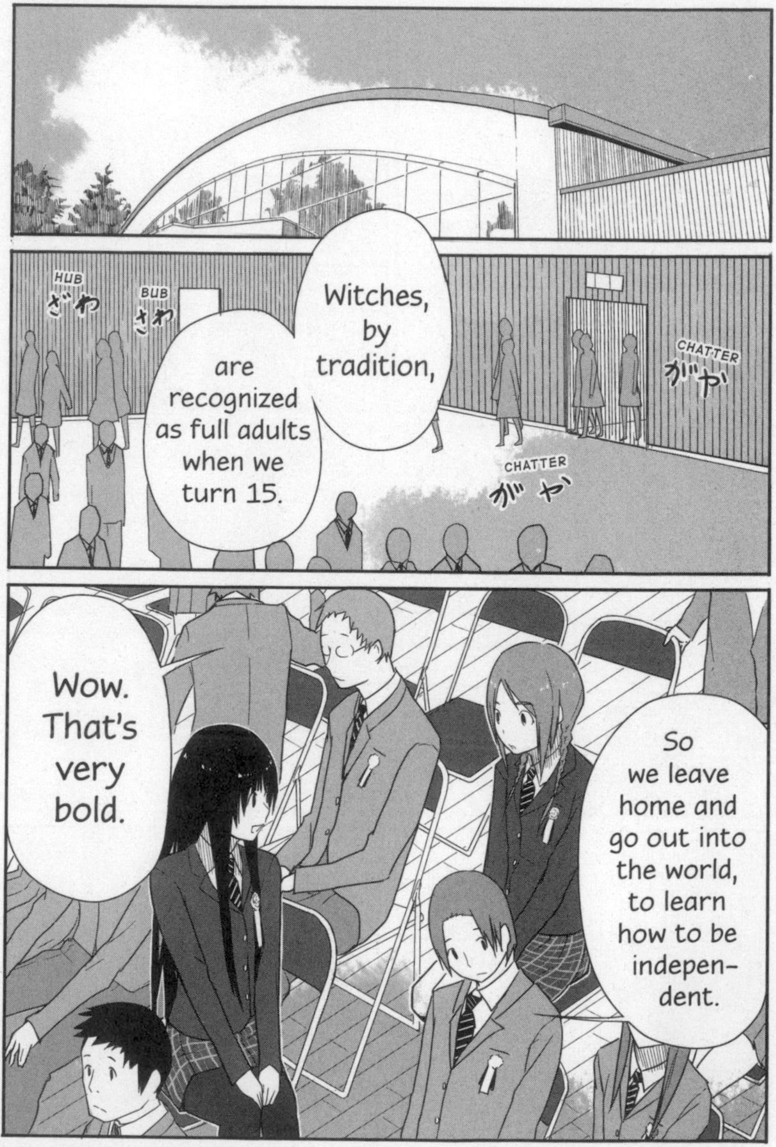
CHATTER
がや
Witches, by tradition,
are recognized as full adults when we turn 15.
CHATTER
がや
BUB
さわ
HUB
ざわ
So we leave home and go out into the world, to learn how to be indepen-dent.
Wow. That's very bold.

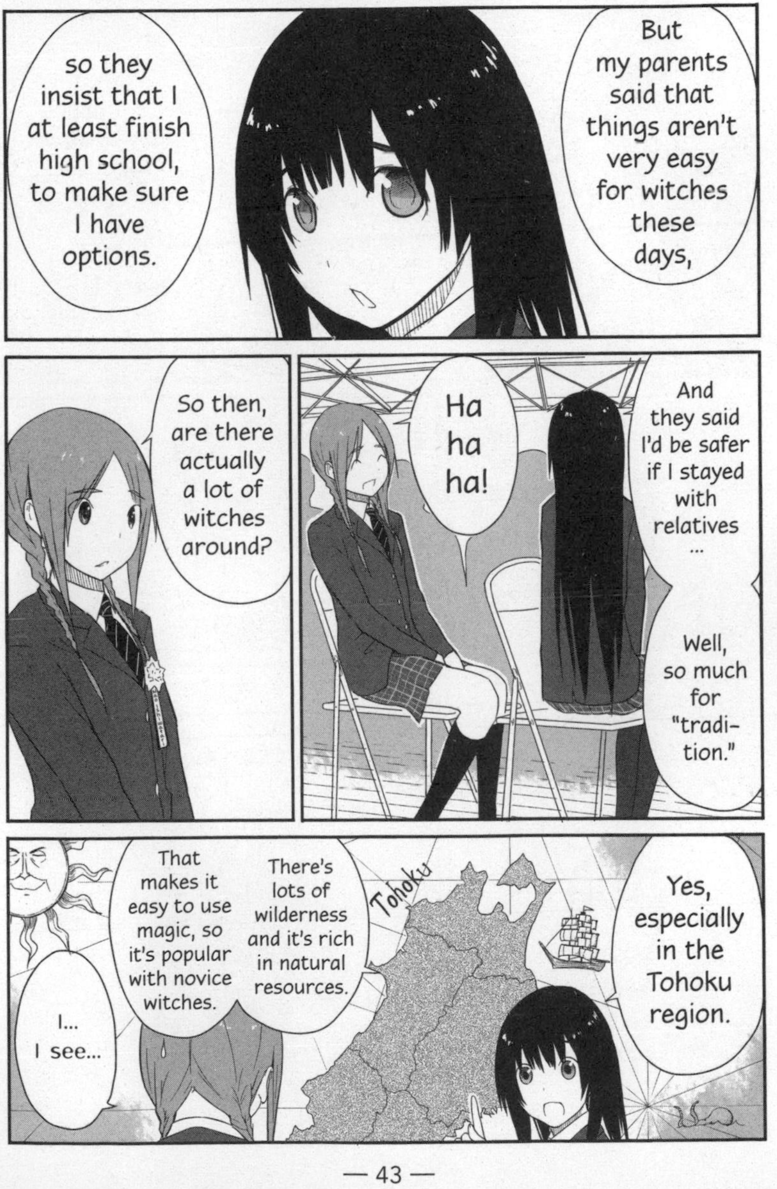
But my parents said that things aren't very easy for witches these days,
so they insist that I at least finish high school, to make sure I have options.
And they said I'd be safer if I stayed with relatives ...
Ha ha ha!
Well, so much for "tradi- tion."
So then, are there actually a lot of witches around?
Yes, especially in the Tohoku region.
Tohoku
There's lots of wilderness and it's rich in natural resources.
That makes it easy to use magic, so it's popular with novice witches.
I... I see...

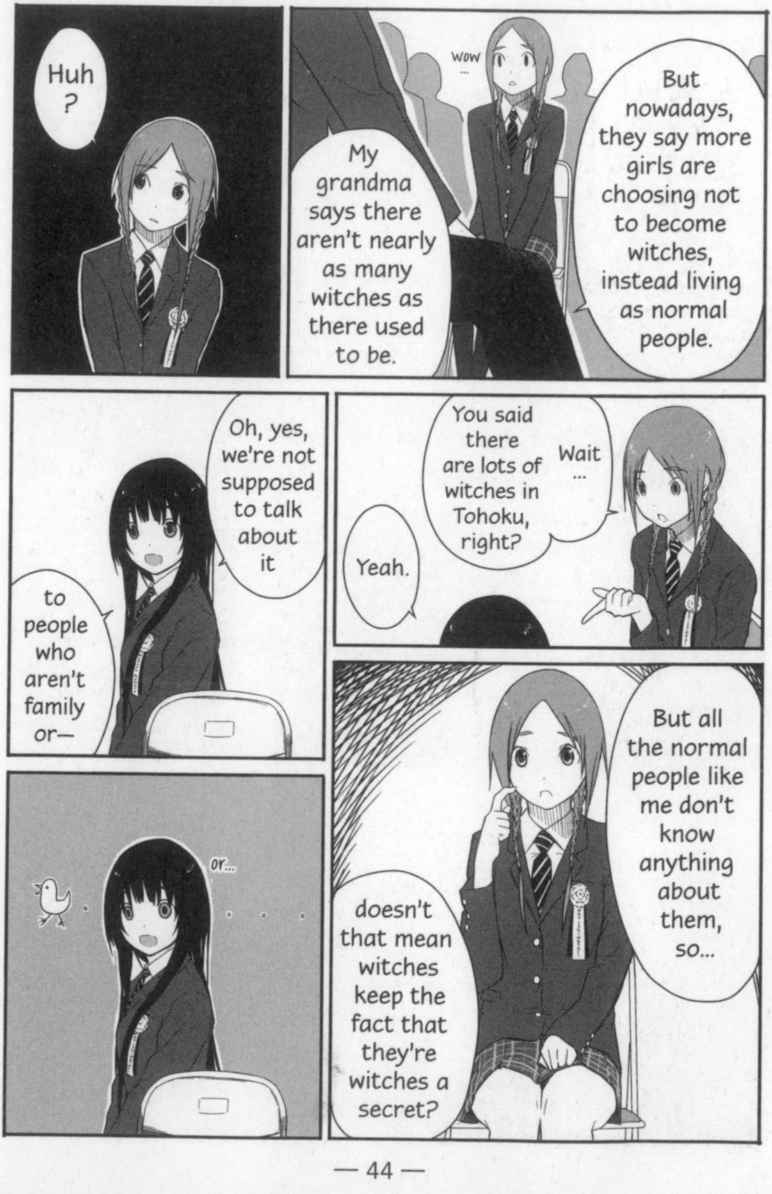
But nowadays, they say more girls are choosing not to become witches, instead living as normal people.
Wow...
My grandma says there aren't nearly as many witches as there used to be.
Huh?
Wait...
You said there are lots of witches in Tohoku, right?
Yeah.
Oh, yes, we're not supposed to talk about it
to people who aren't family or—
But all the normal people like me don't know anything about them, so...
doesn't that mean witches keep the fact that they're witches a secret?
or...

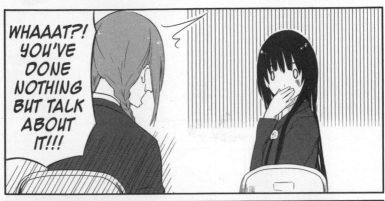

WHAAAT?! YOU'VE DONE NOTHING BUT TALK ABOUT IT!!!
Nooo, don't drag me into any weird witchy stuff...
N-No, no, it's all right! There's no punishment or anything...
oh no oh no
It's more like, we should try to keep it a secret if we can. I think.
But that's super vague?!
Okay, then...
your classes will start tomorrow.
Study hard, and have a good year.

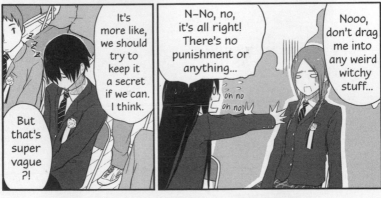

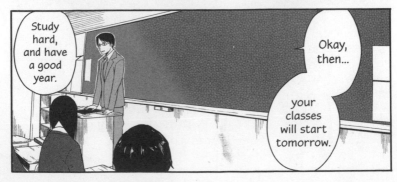

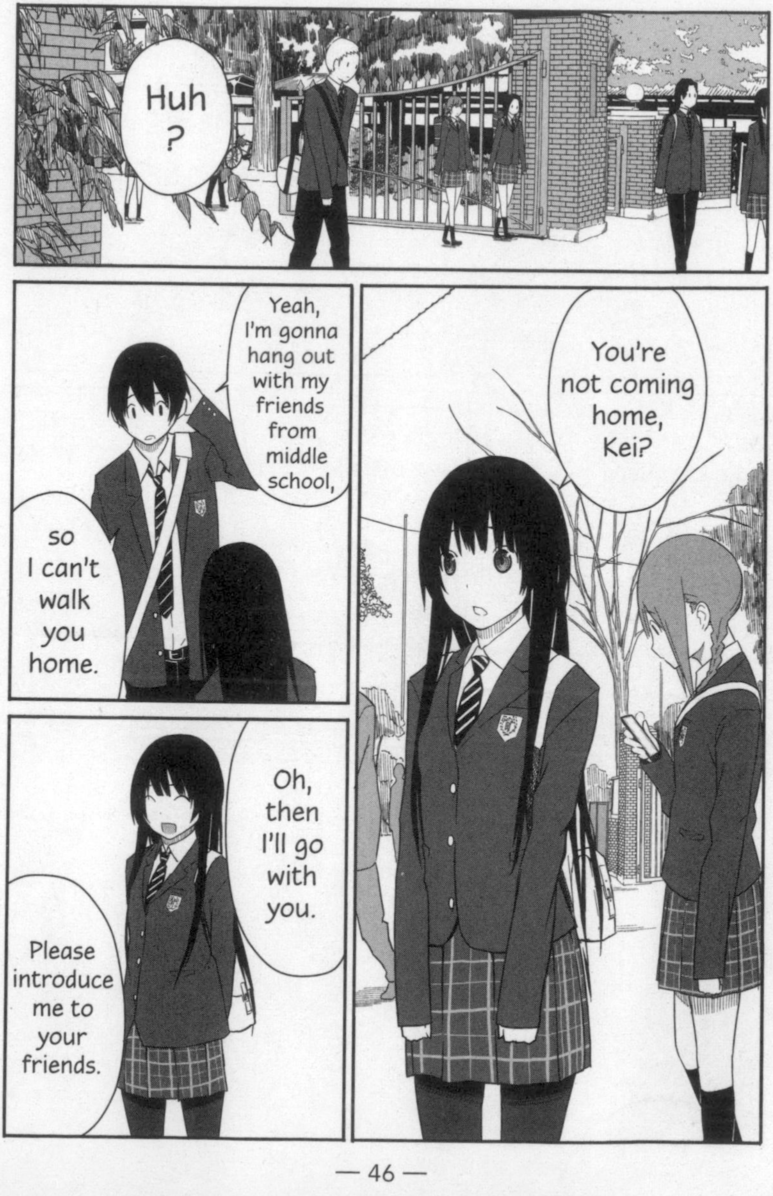
Huh?
You're not coming home, Kei?
Yeah, I'm gonna hang out with my friends from middle school,
so I can't walk you home.
Oh, then I'll go with you.
Please introduce me to your friends.

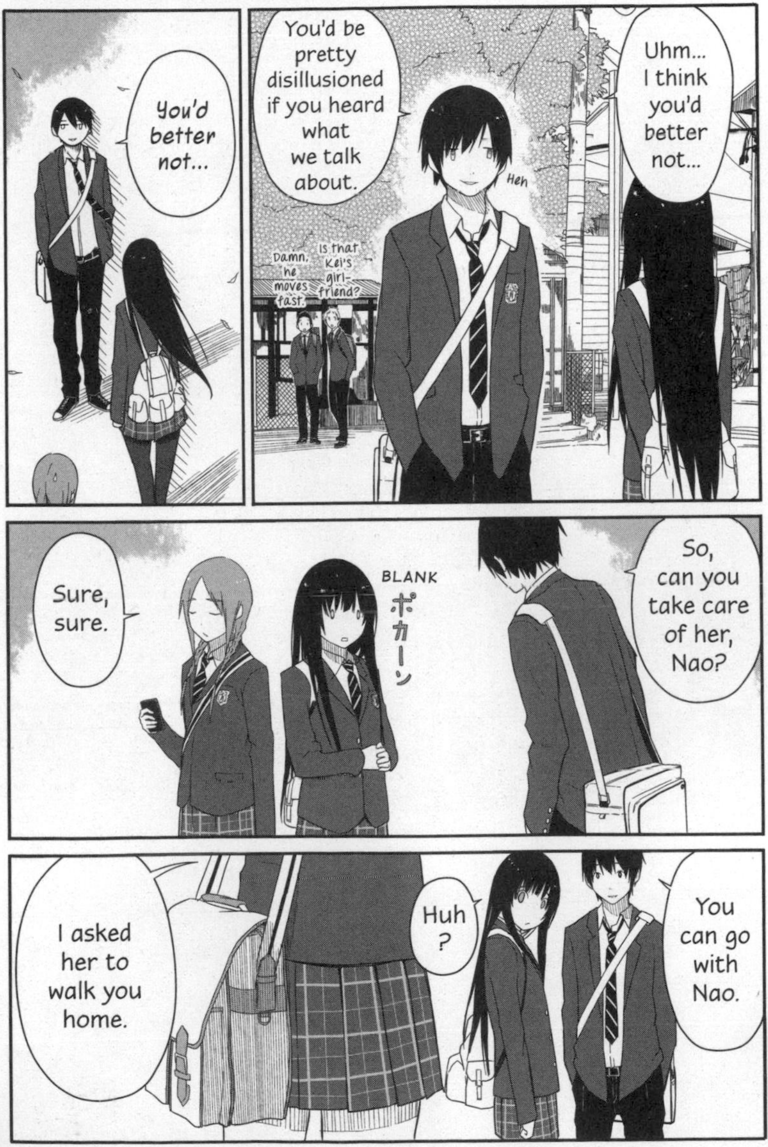
Uhm... I think you'd better not...
You'd be pretty disillusioned if you heard what we talk about.
Heh
Is that Kei's girl-friend?
Damn, he moves fast.
You'd better not...
So, can you take care of her, Nao?
BLANK
ポカーン
Sure, sure.
You can go with Nao.
Huh?
I asked her to walk you home.

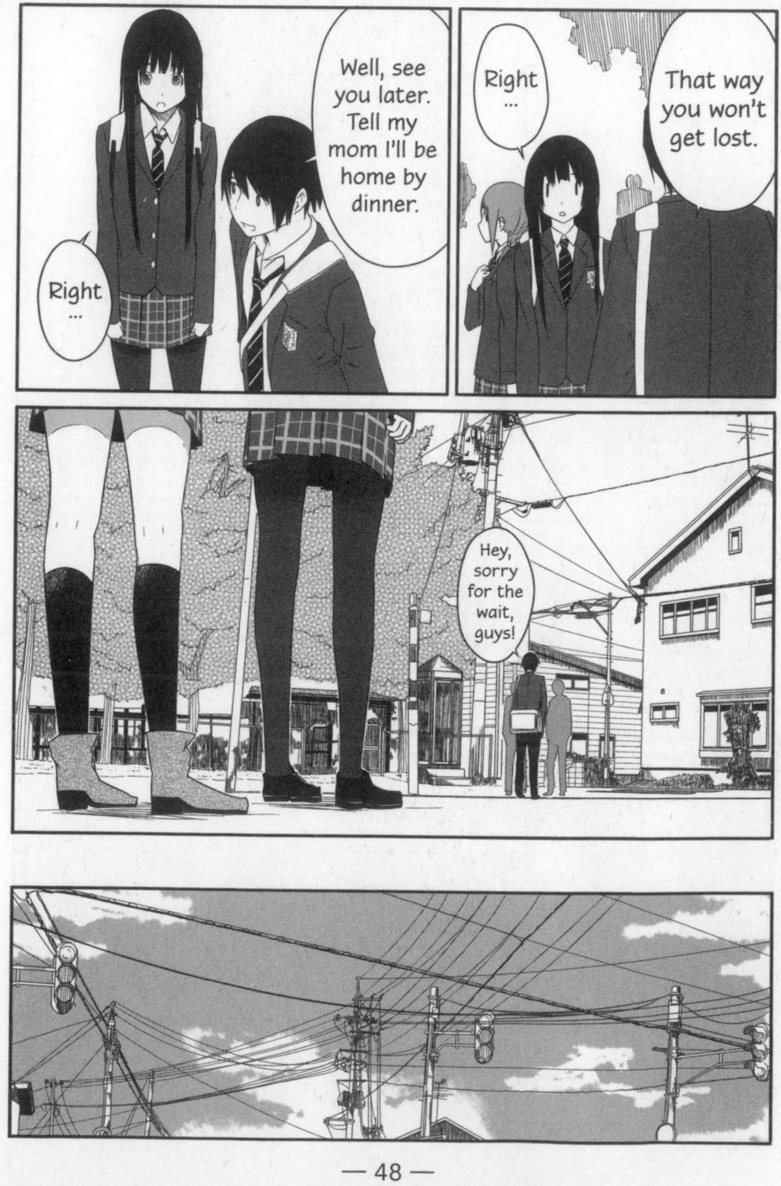
That way you won't get lost.
Right ...
Well, see you later. Tell my mom I'll be home by dinner.
Right ...
Hey, sorry for the wait, guys!

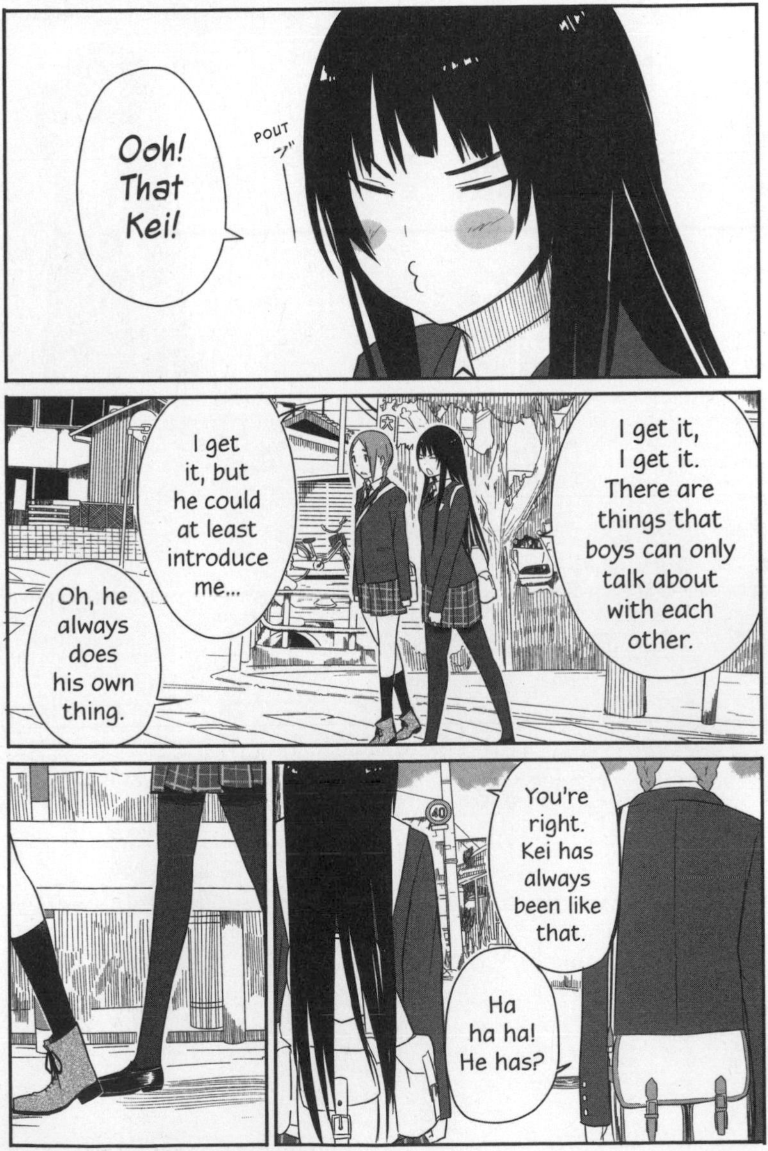
POUT
Ooh! That Kei!
I get it, I get it. There are things that boys can only talk about with each other.
I get it, but he could at least introduce me...
Oh, he always does his own thing.
You're right. Kei has always been like that.
Ha ha ha! He has?

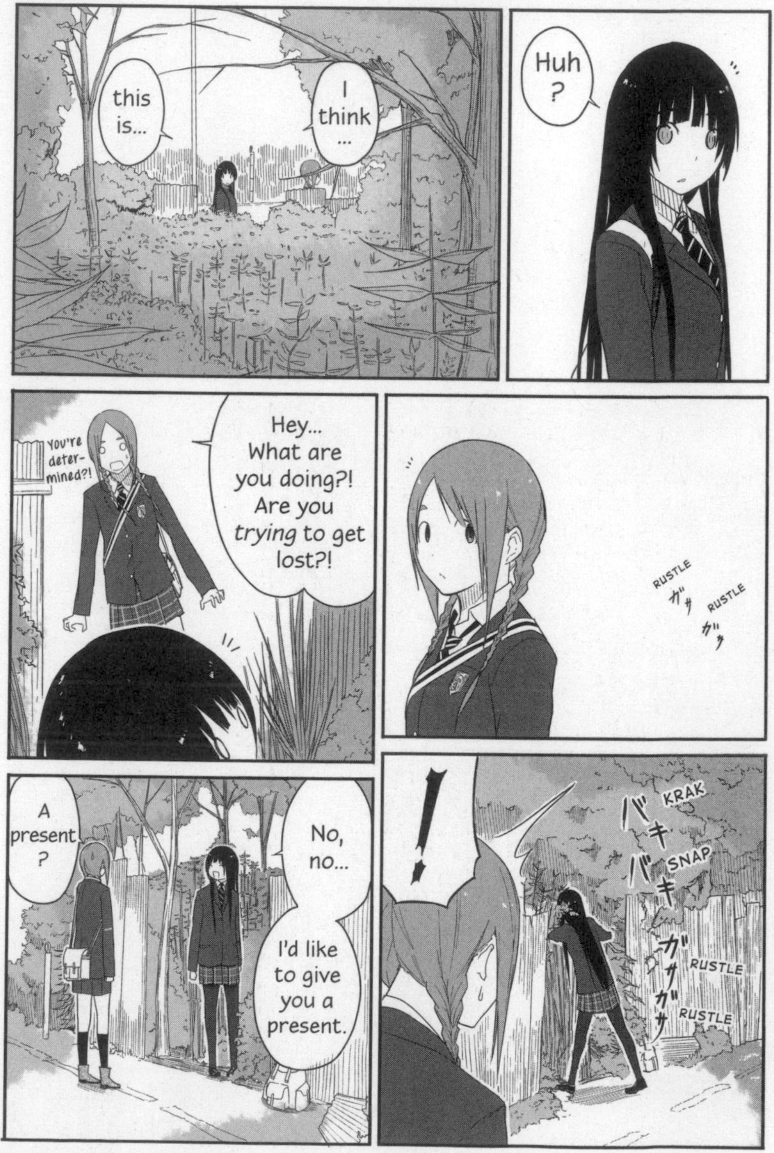
Huh?
I think...
this is...
RUSTLE
ガサ
RUSTLE
ガサ
Hey... What are you doing?! Are you *trying* to get lost?!
You're determined?!
!
KRAK
バキ
SNAP
バキ
ガサガサ
RUSTLE
RUSTLE
No, no...
I'd like to give you a present.
A present?

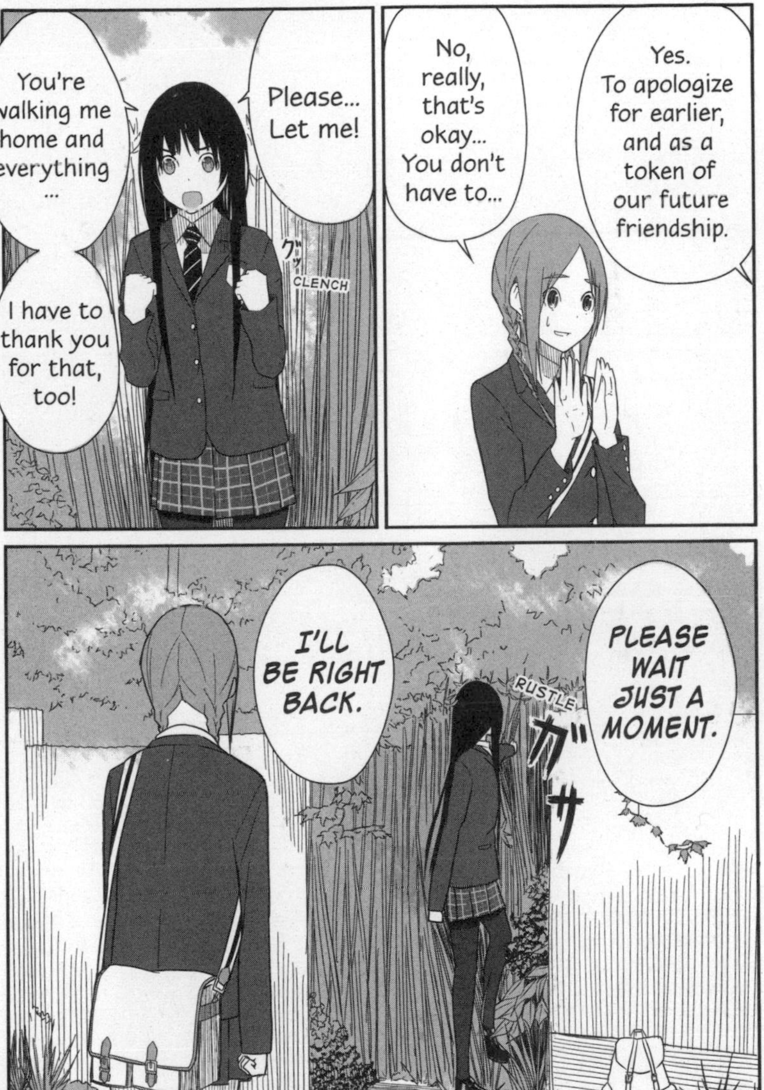
Yes. To apologize for earlier, and as a token of our future friendship.
No, really, that's okay... You don't have to...
Please... Let me!
You're walking me home and everything ...
I have to thank you for that, too!
CLENCH
PLEASE WAIT JUST A MOMENT.
RUSTLE
I'LL BE RIGHT BACK.

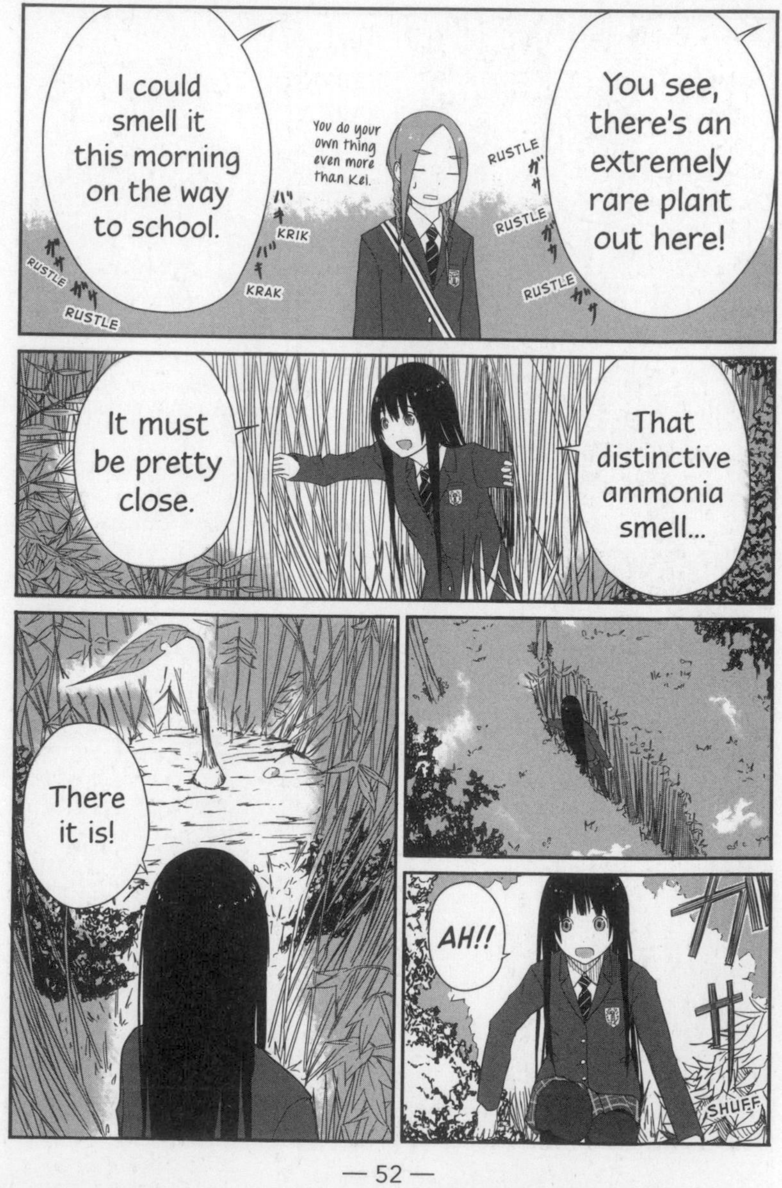
You see, there's an extremely rare plant out here!
RUSTLE
RUSTLE
RUSTLE
You do your own thing even more than Kei.
KRIK
KRAK
I could smell it this morning on the way to school.
RUSTLE
RUSTLE
That distinctive ammonia smell...
It must be pretty close.
AH!!
SHUFF
There it is!

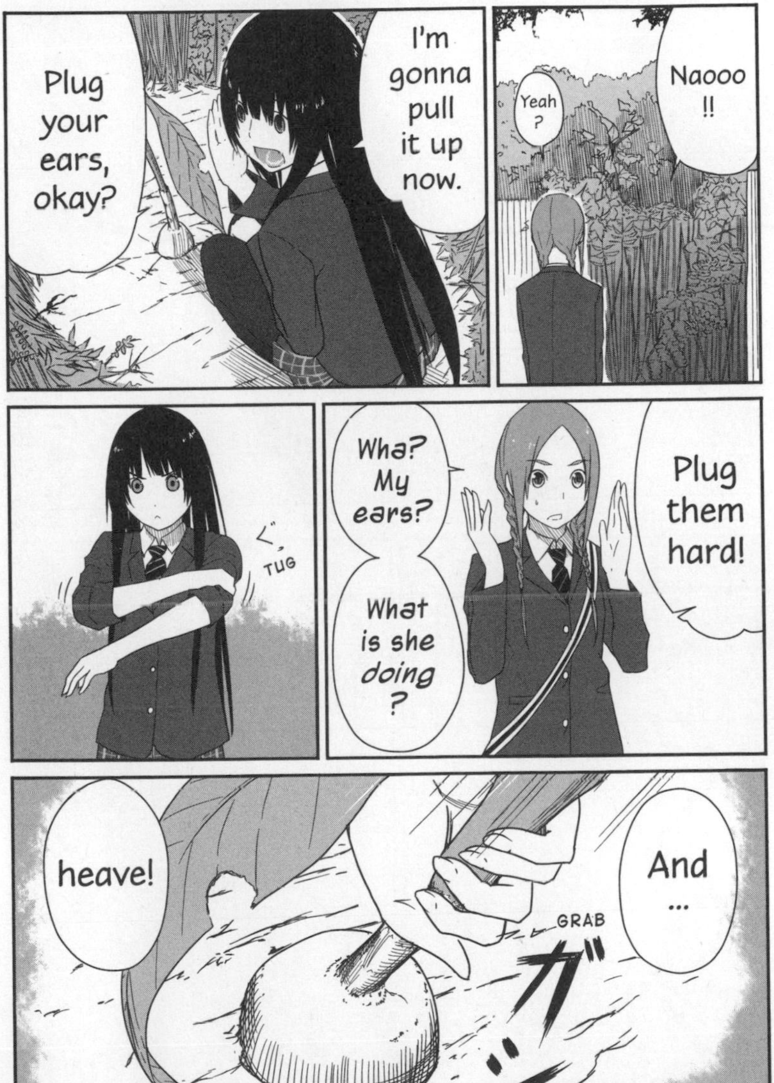
Naooo !!
Yeah ?
I'm gonna pull it up now.
Plug your ears, okay?
Plug them hard!
Wha? My ears?
What is she doing ?
TUG
And ...
GRAB
heave!

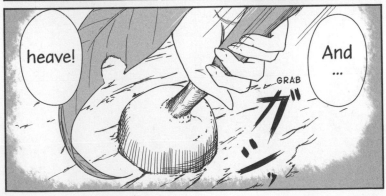

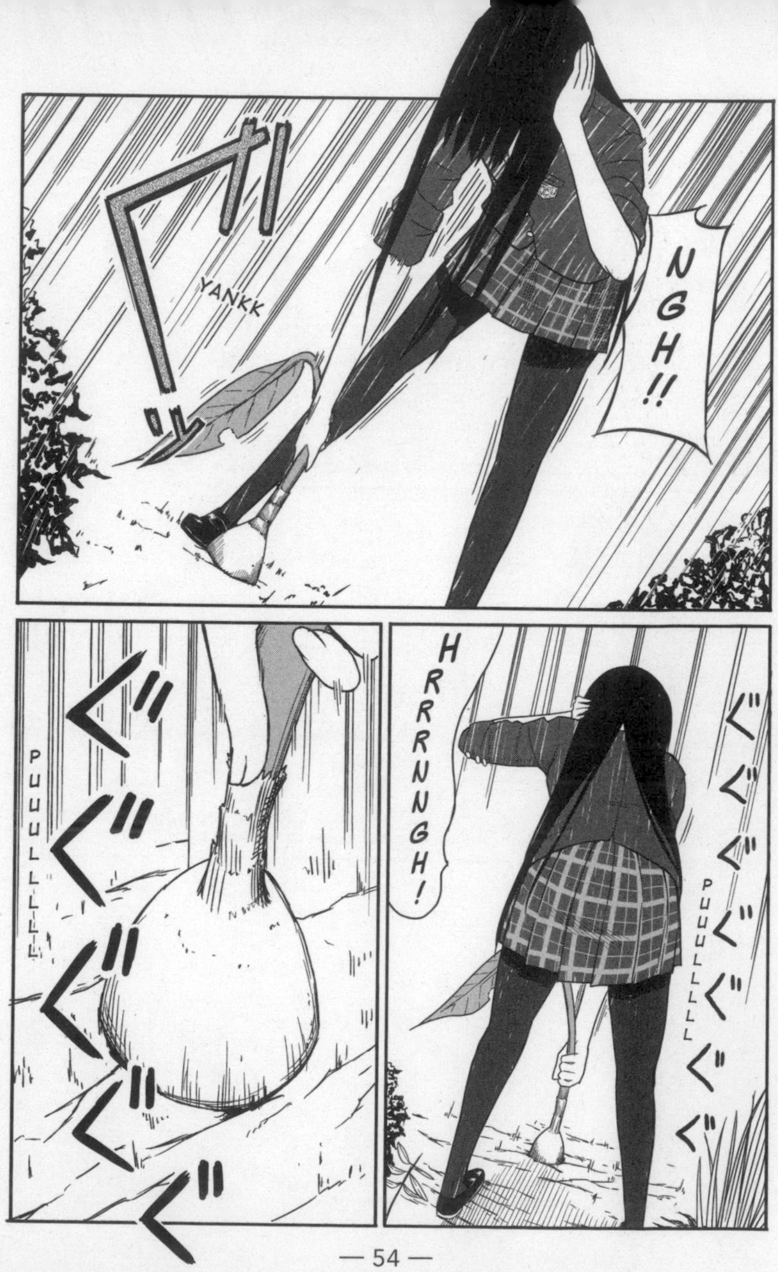
NGH!!
YANKK
HRRRNNGH!
PUUULLLLL
PUUULLLLL

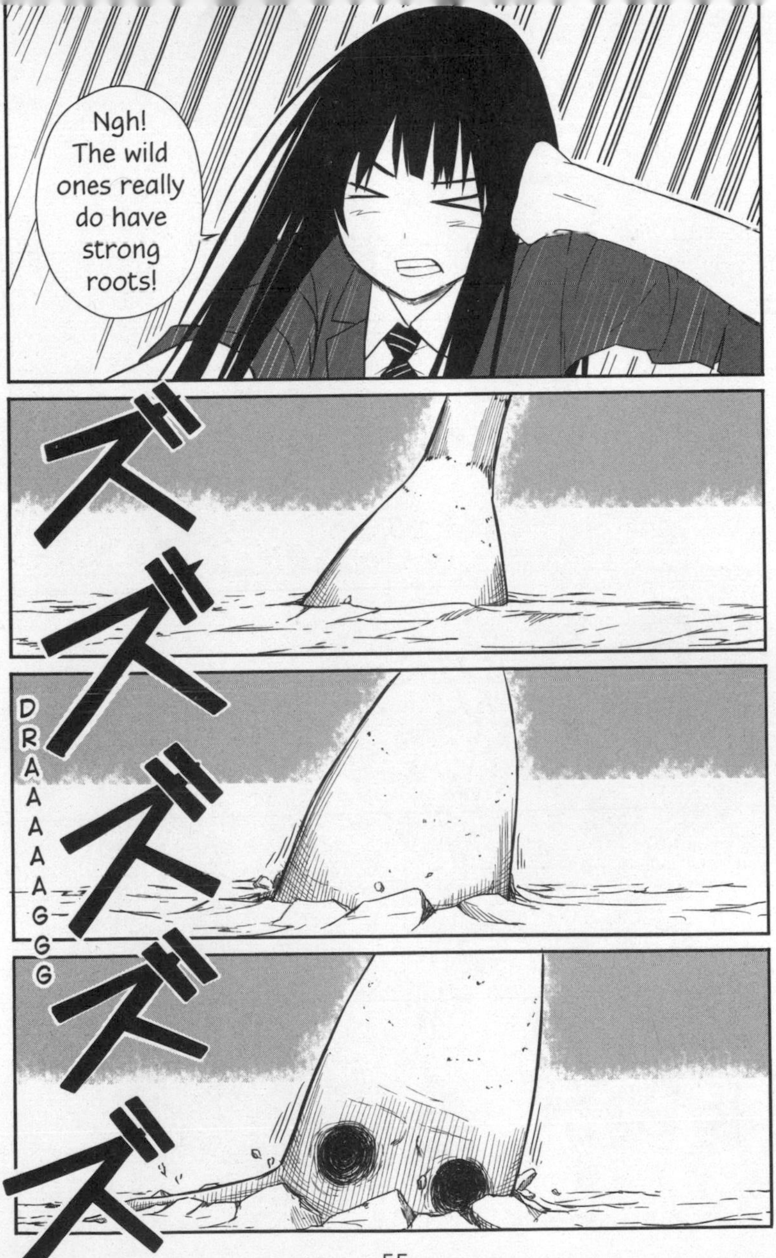
Ngh! The wild ones really do have strong roots!
ズズズズ
DRAAAAAGGG

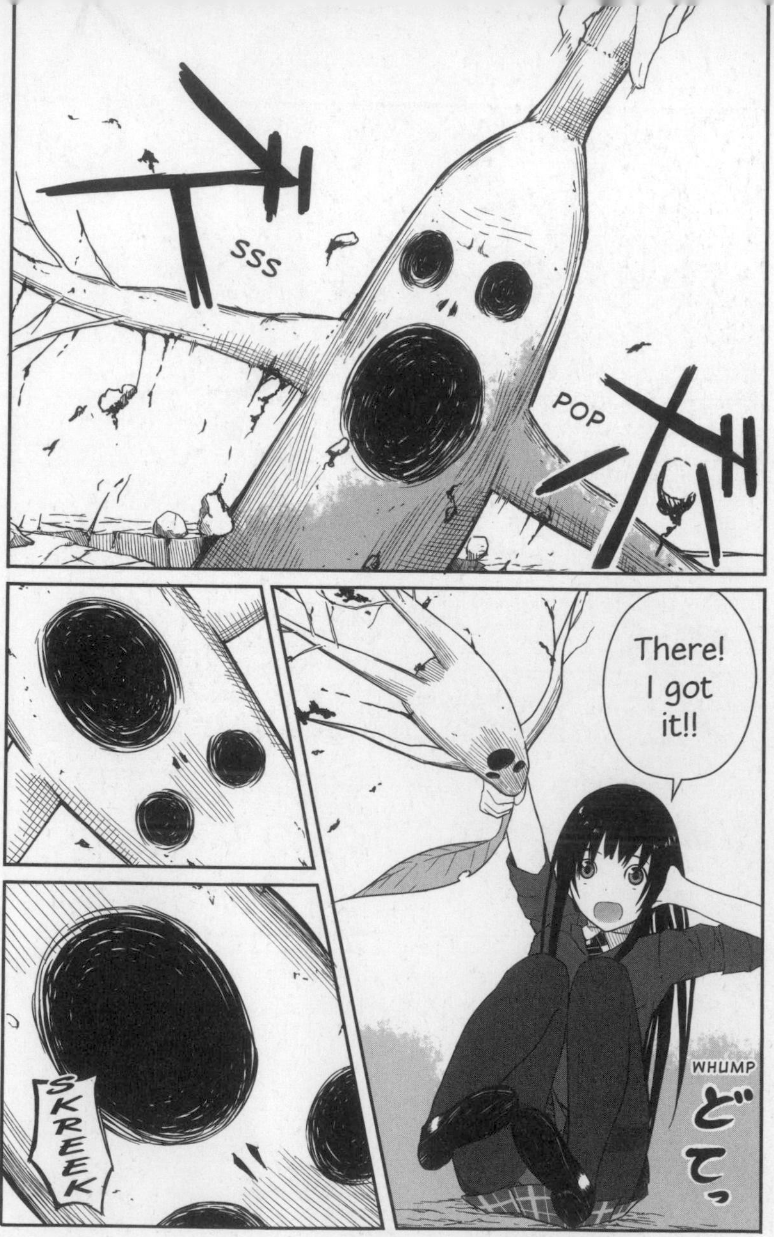
SSS
POP
There! I got it!!
WHUMP
どてっ
SKREEK

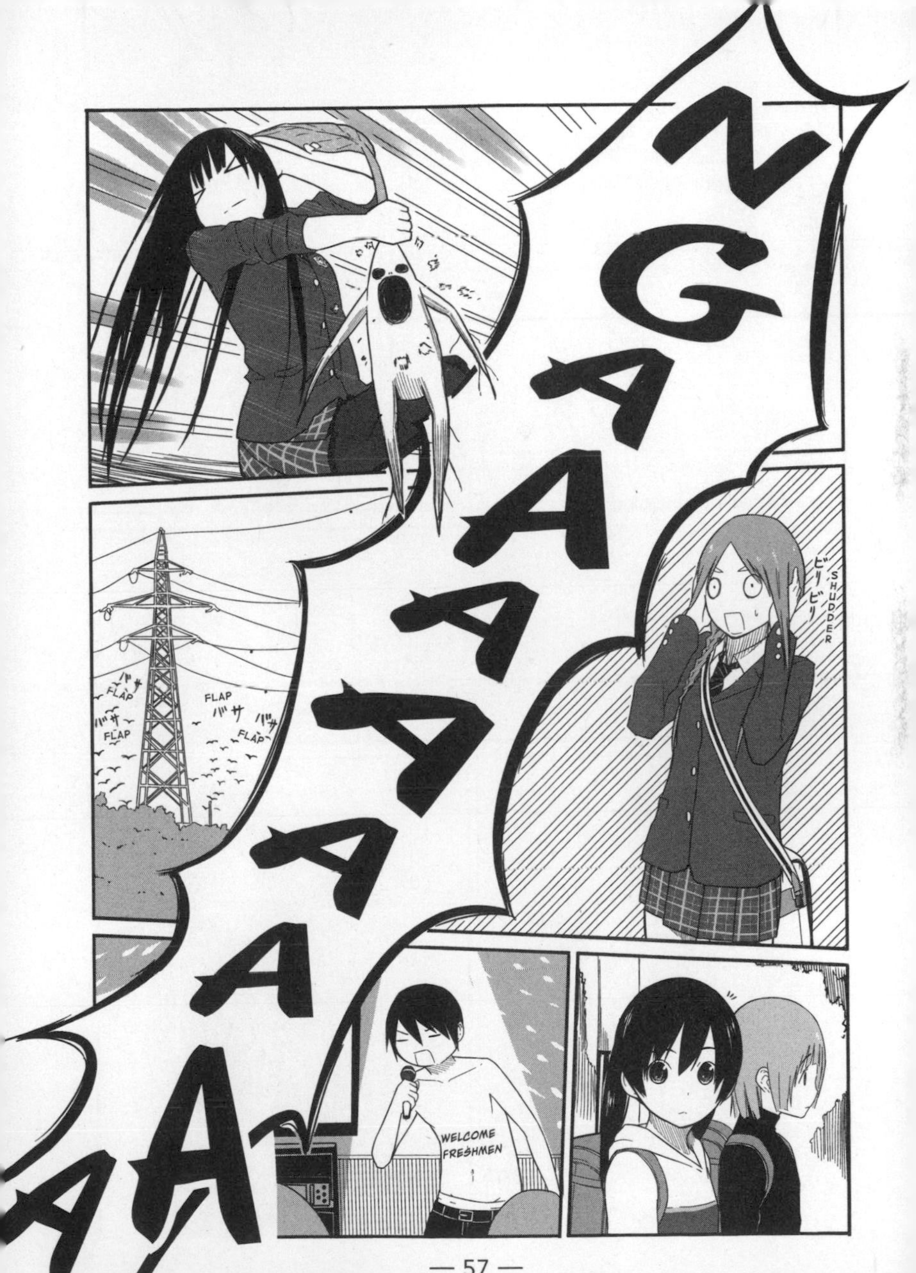
NGAAAAAAAAAA
ビリビリ
SHUDDER
バサ
FLAP
バサ
FLAP
バサ
FLAP
バサ
FLAP
WELCOME FRESHMEN

AAAAA...
What was that...
I got it, Nao!
RUSTLE
Voilà!

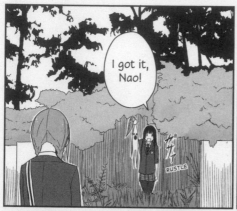

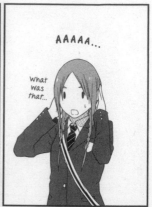

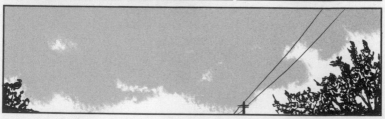

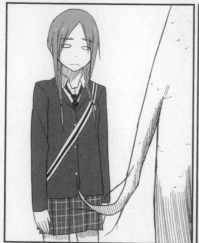

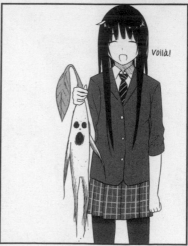

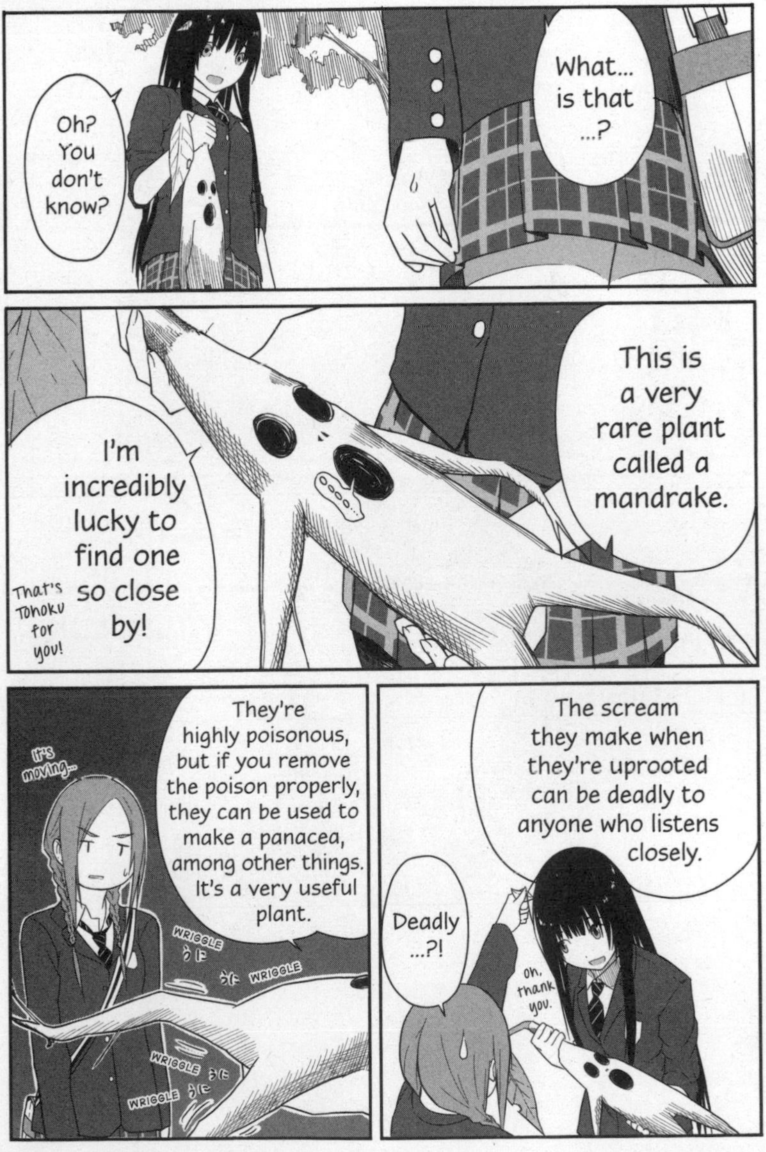
What... is that ...?
Oh? You don't know?
This is a very rare plant called a mandrake.
I'm incredibly lucky to find one so close by!
That's Tohoku for you!
The scream they make when they're uprooted can be deadly to anyone who listens closely.
Deadly ...?!
Oh, thank you.
They're highly poisonous, but if you remove the poison properly, they can be used to make a panacea, among other things. It's a very useful plant.
It's moving...
WRIGGLE うに
うに WRIGGLE
WRIGGLE うに
WRIGGLE うに

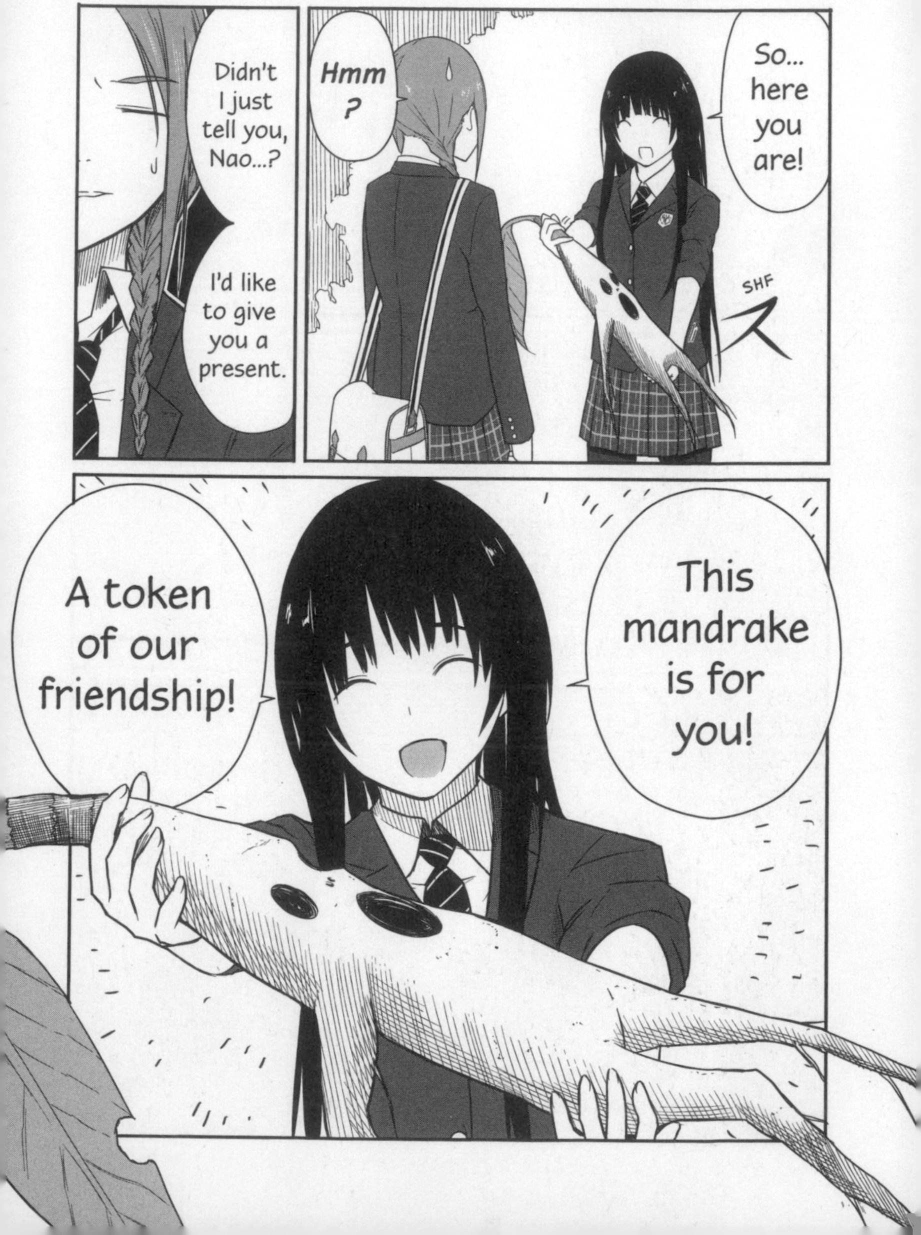
So... here you are!
Hmm?
SHF
Didn't I just tell you, Nao...?
I'd like to give you a present.
This mandrake is for you!
A token of our friendship!

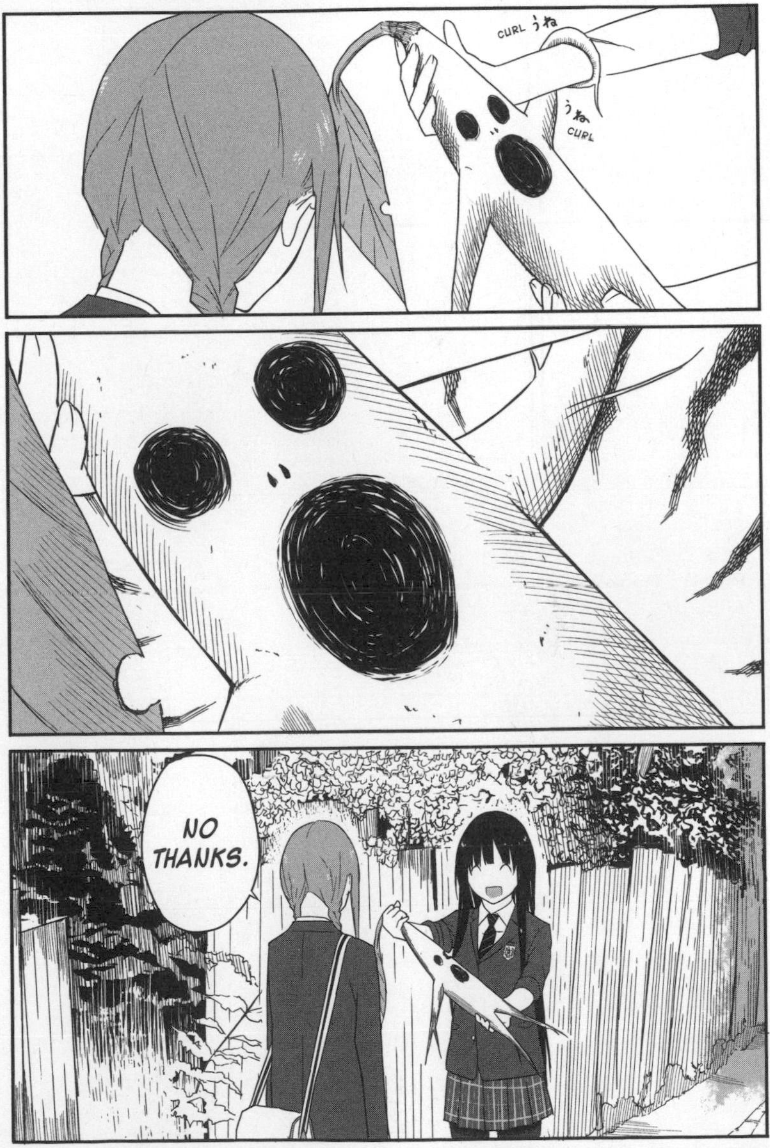
CURL うね
うね CURL
NO THANKS.

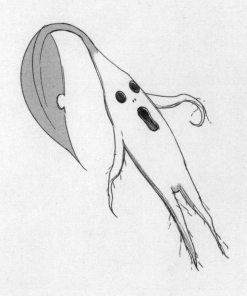

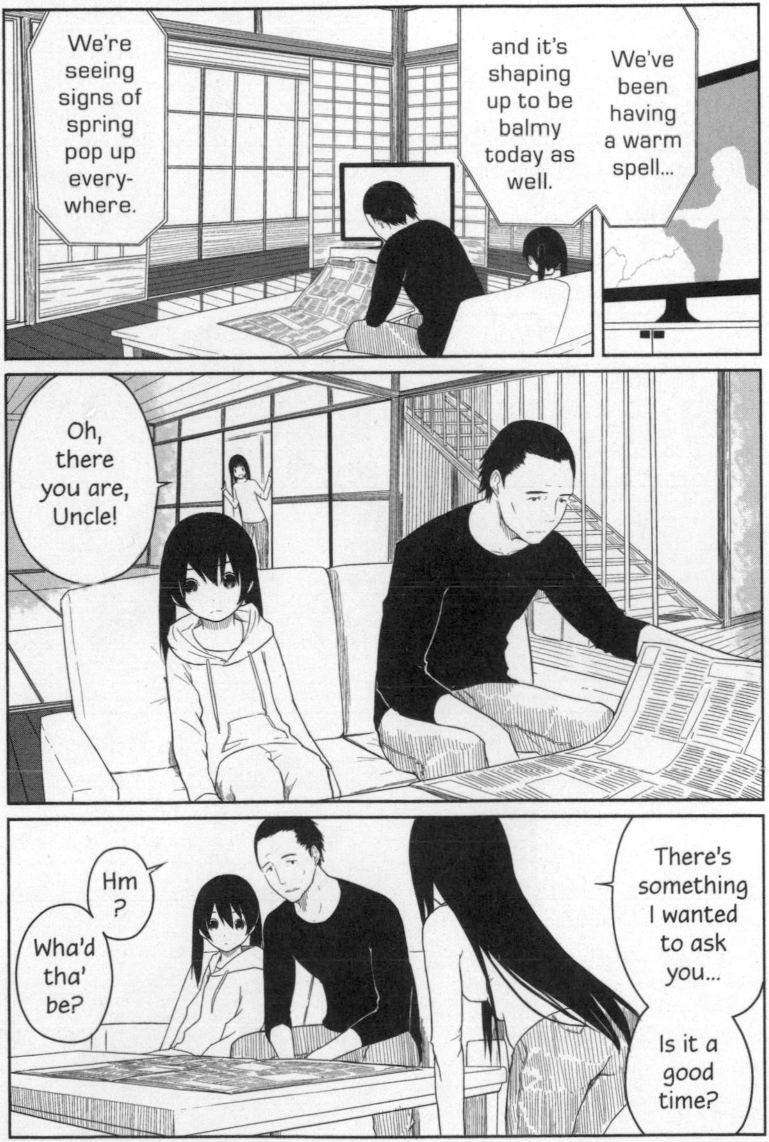
We've been having a warm spell...
and it's shaping up to be balmy today as well.
We're seeing signs of spring pop up every-where.
Oh, there you are, Uncle!
There's something I wanted to ask you...
Is it a good time?
Hm?
Wha'd tha' be?

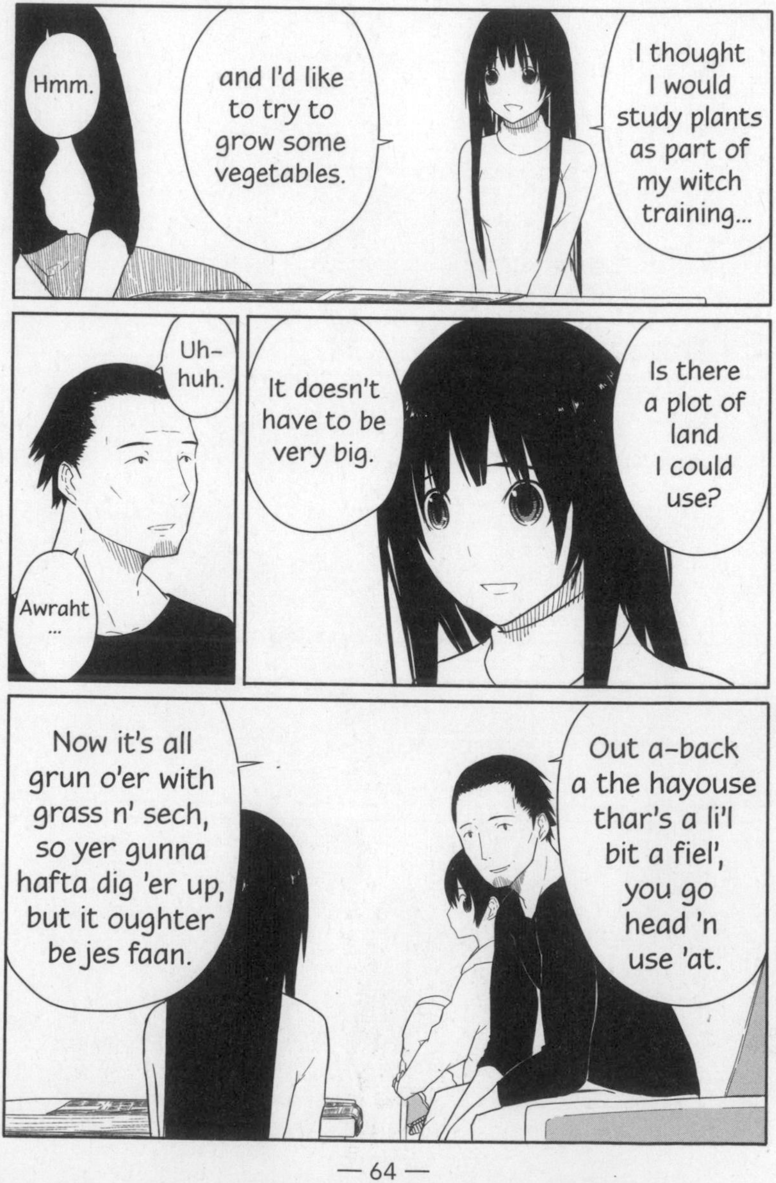
I thought I would study plants as part of my witch training...
and I'd like to try to grow some vegetables.
Hmm.
Is there a plot of land I could use?
It doesn't have to be very big.
Uh-huh.
Awraht ...
Out a-back a the hayouse thar's a li'l bit a fiel', you go head 'n use 'at.
Now it's all grun o'er with grass n' sech, so yer gunna hafta dig 'er up, but it oughter be jes faan.

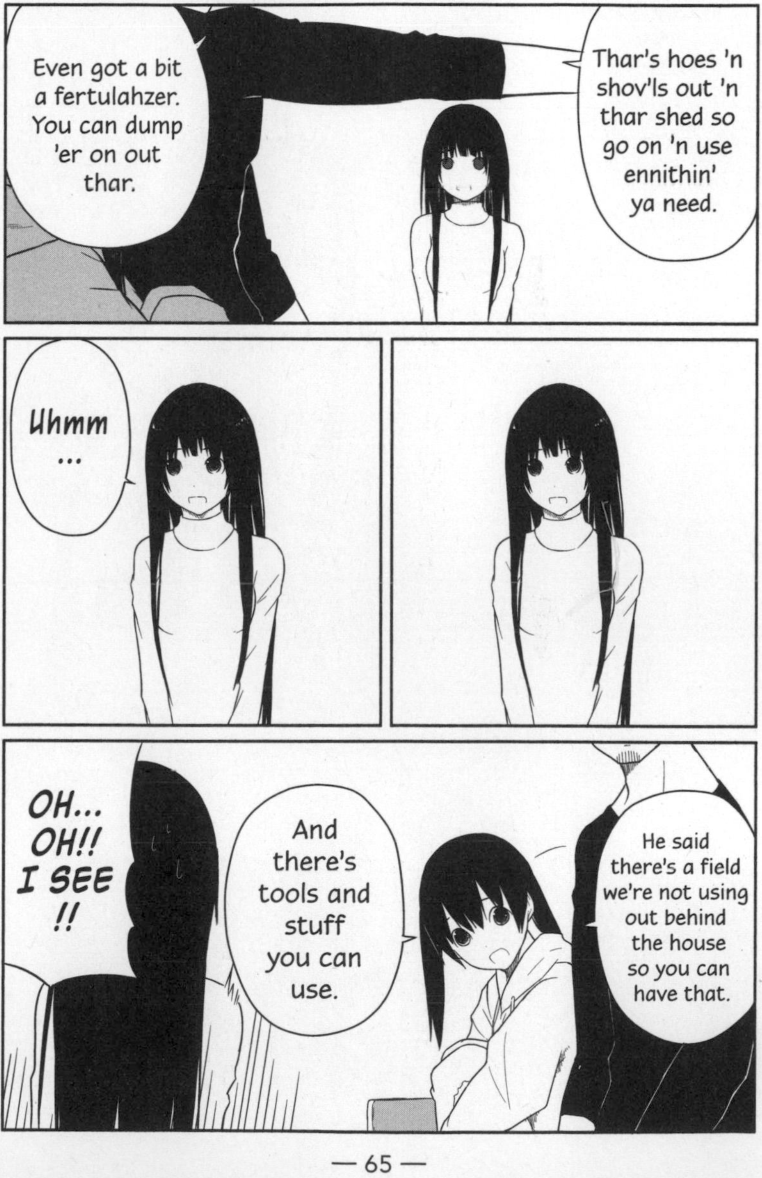
Thar's hoes 'n shov'ls out 'n thar shed so go on 'n use ennithin' ya need.
Even got a bit a fertulahzer. You can dump 'er on out thar.
Uhmm ...
He said there's a field we're not using out behind the house so you can have that.
And there's tools and stuff you can use.
OH... OH!! I SEE !!

Chapter 3
The National Bird's Incessant Call

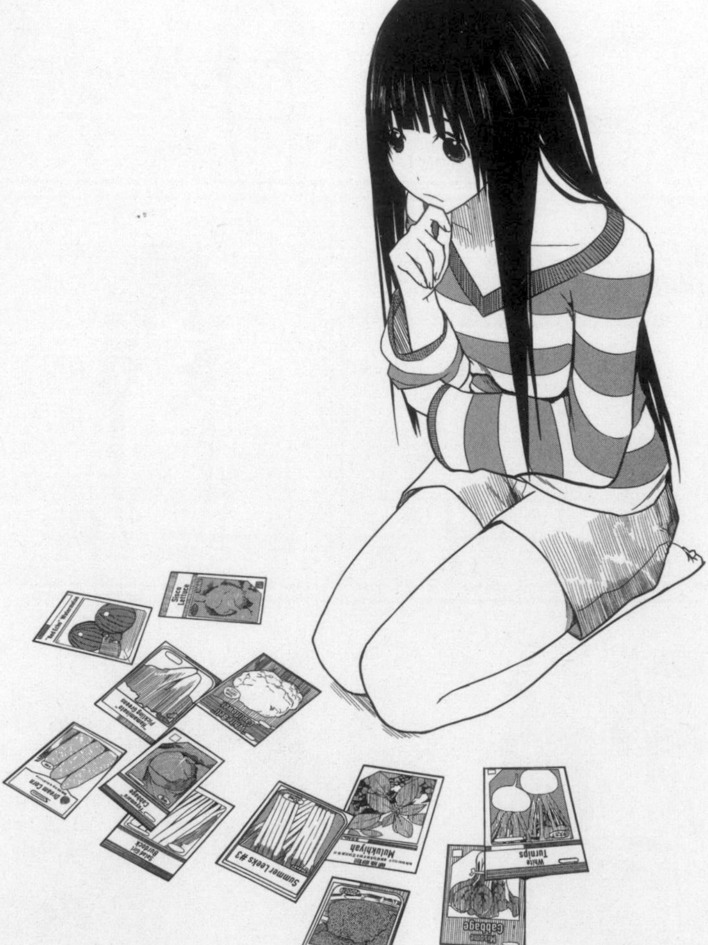

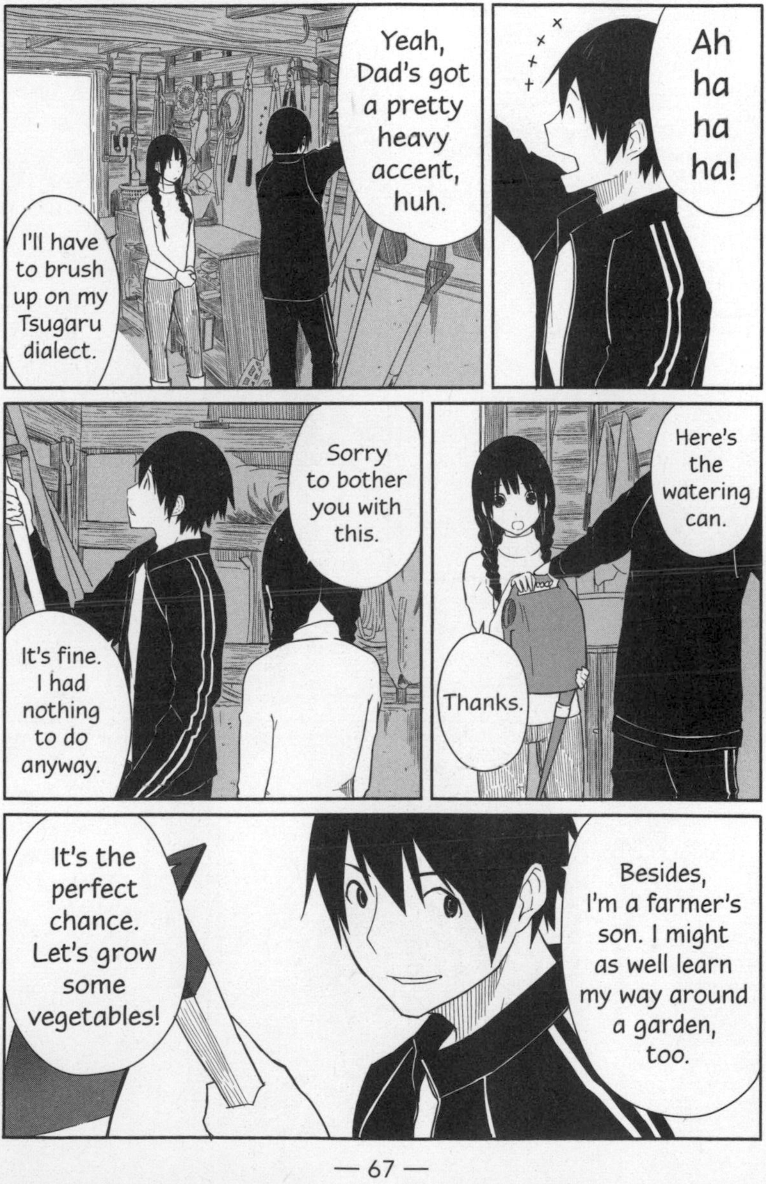
Ah ha ha ha!
Yeah, Dad's got a pretty heavy accent, huh.
I'll have to brush up on my Tsugaru dialect.
Here's the watering can.
Thanks.
Sorry to bother you with this.
It's fine. I had nothing to do anyway.
Besides, I'm a farmer's son. I might as well learn my way around a garden, too.
It's the perfect chance. Let's grow some vegetables!

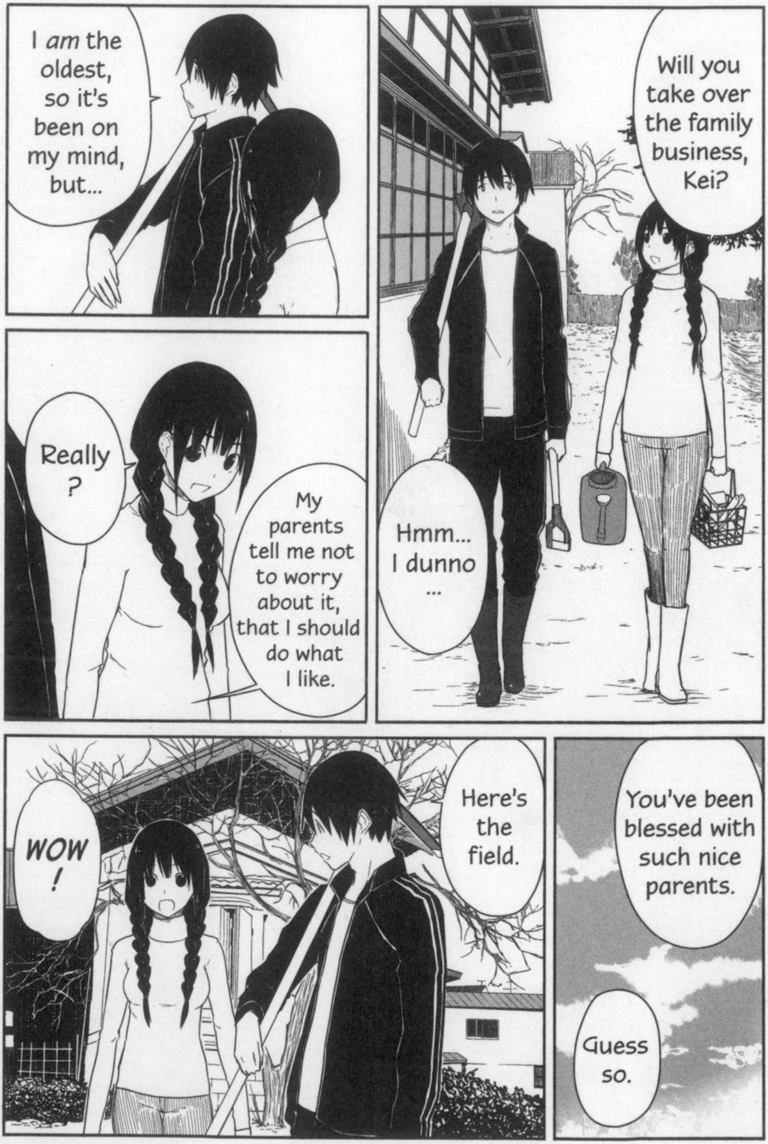
Will you take over the family business, Kei?
Hmm... I dunno ...
I *am* the oldest, so it's been on my mind, but...
My parents tell me not to worry about it, that I should do what I like.
Really ?
You've been blessed with such nice parents.
Guess so.
Here's the field.
WOW !

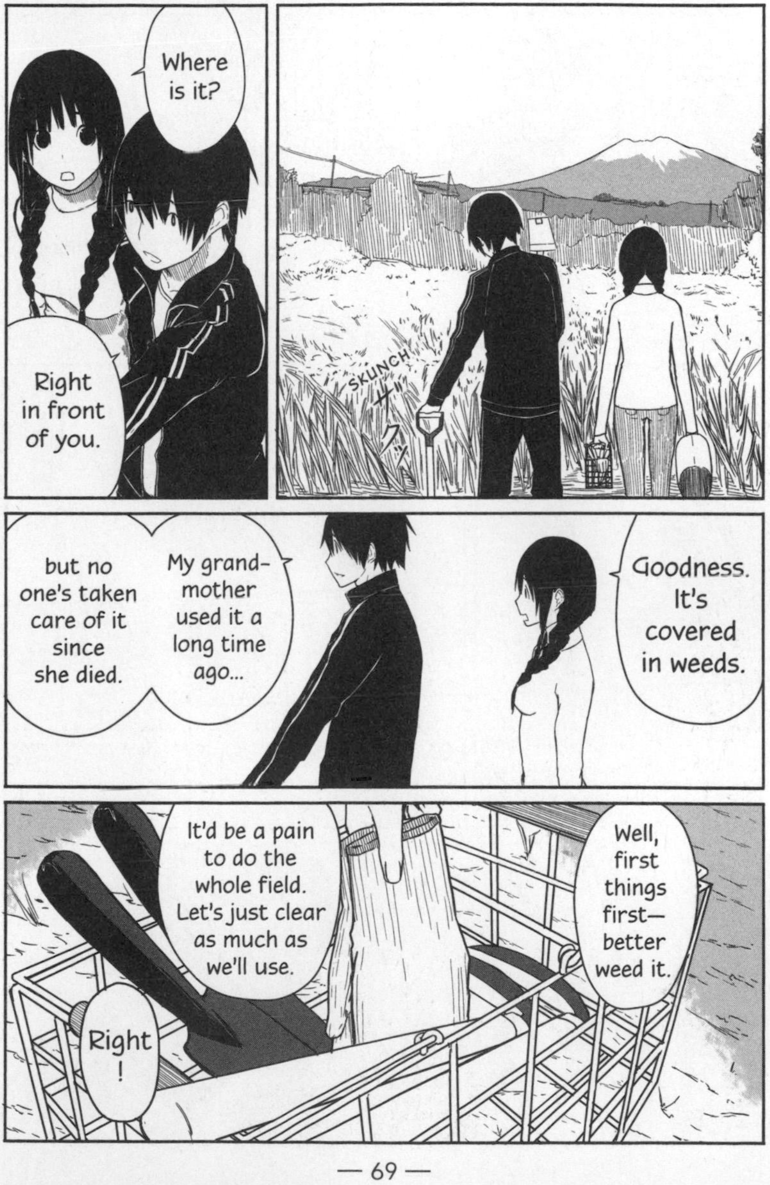
SKUNCH
ザクッ
Where is it?
Right in front of you.
Goodness. It's covered in weeds.
My grand-mother used it a long time ago...
but no one's taken care of it since she died.
Well, first things first—better weed it.
It'd be a pain to do the whole field. Let's just clear as much as we'll use.
Right!

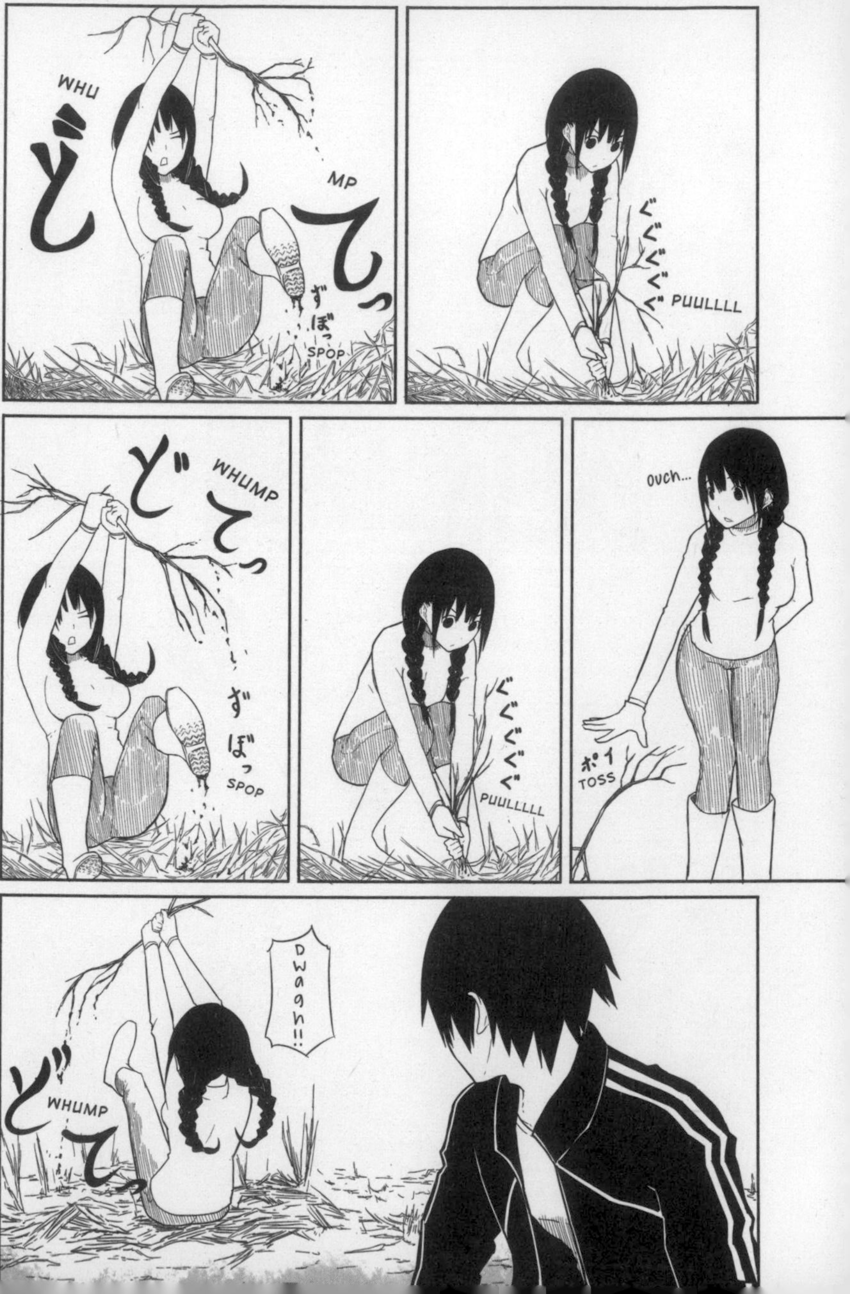
ぐぐぐぐぐ
PUULLLL
どてっ
WHUMP
ずぼっ
SPOP
Ouch...
ポイ
TOSS
ぐぐぐぐぐ
PUULLLLL
どてっ
WHUMP
ずぼっ
SPOP
Dwagh!!
どてっ
WHUMP

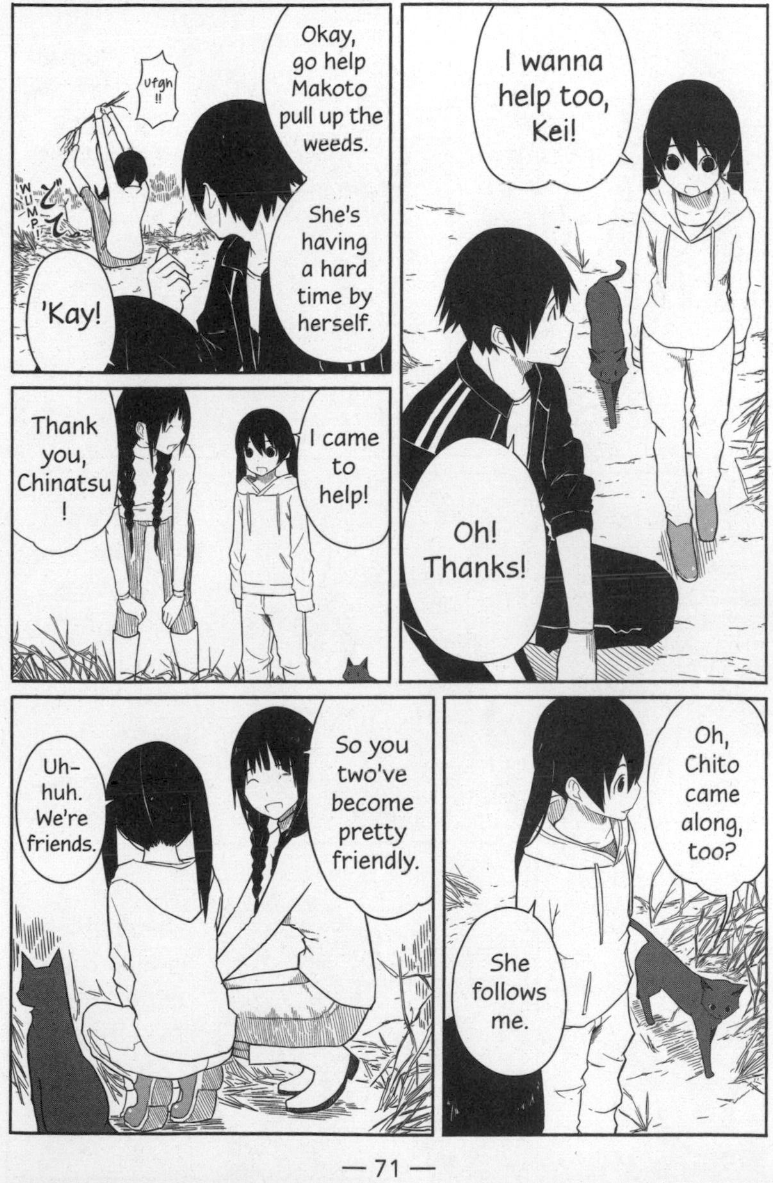
I wanna help too, Kei!
Oh! Thanks!
Okay, go help Makoto pull up the weeds.
She's having a hard time by herself.
Ufgn!!
WUMP!
どて
'Kay!
I came to help!
Thank you, Chinatsu!
Oh, Chito came along, too?
She follows me.
So you two've become pretty friendly.
Uh-huh. We're friends.

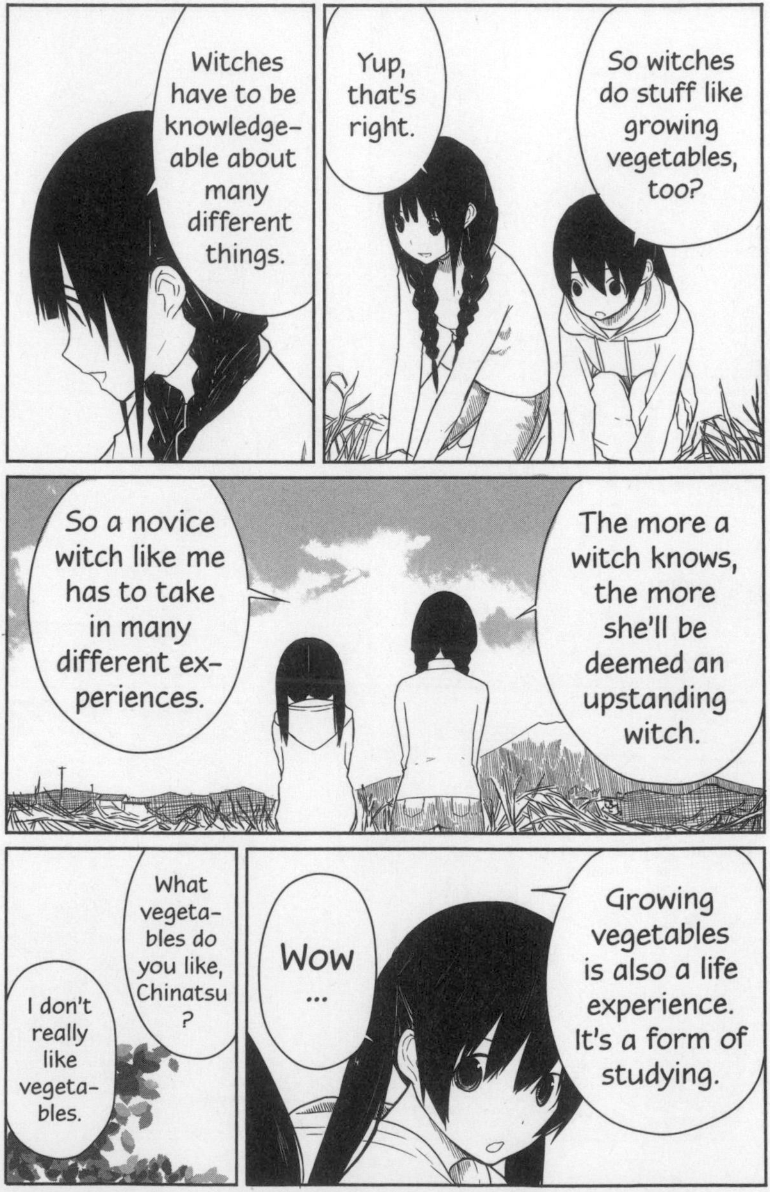
So witches do stuff like growing vegetables, too?
Yup, that's right.
Witches have to be knowledge-able about many different things.
The more a witch knows, the more she'll be deemed an upstanding witch.
So a novice witch like me has to take in many different ex-periences.
Growing vegetables is also a life experience. It's a form of studying.
Wow ...
What vegeta-bles do you like, Chinatsu ?
I don't really like vegeta-bles.

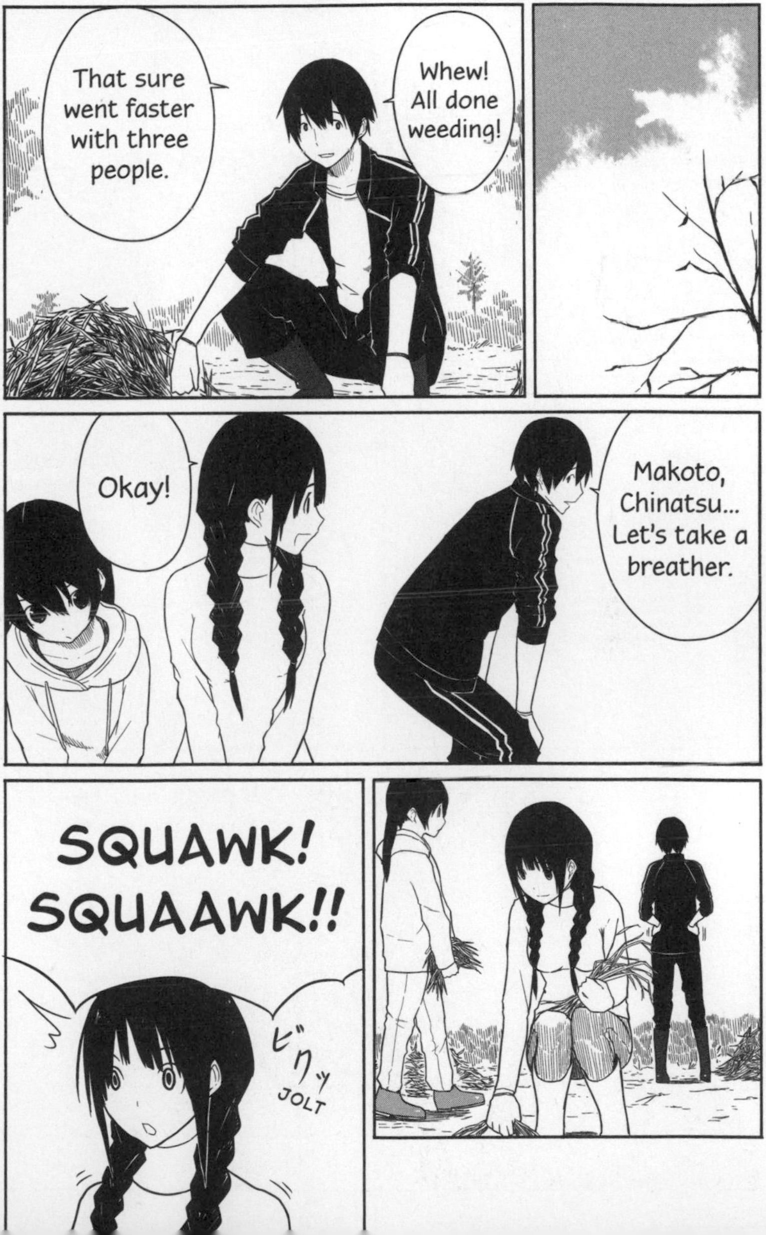
Whew! All done weeding!
That sure went faster with three people.
Makoto, Chinatsu... Let's take a breather.
Okay!
SQUAWK! SQUAAAWK!!
ビクッ
JOLT

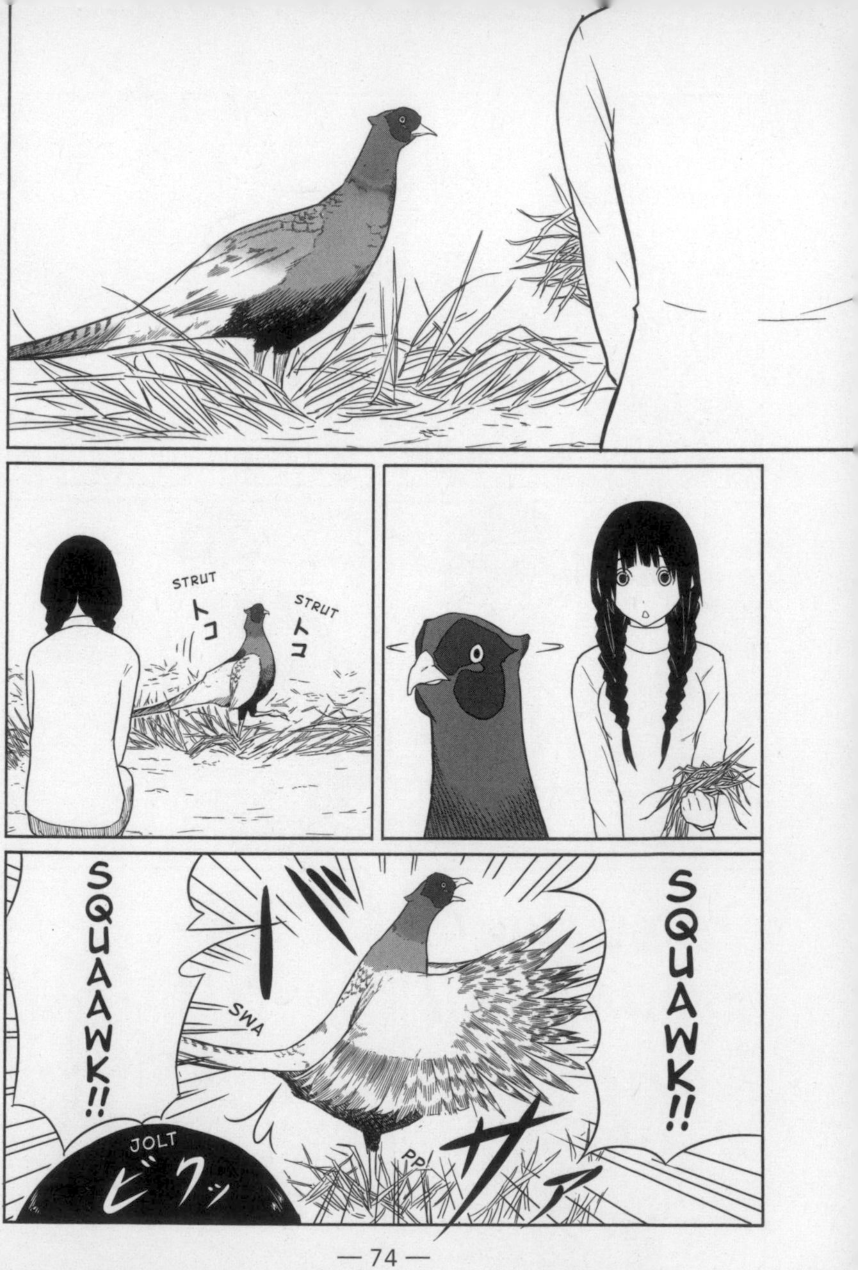
STRUT
トコ
STRUT
トコ
SQUAWK!!
PP!
サァ
SWA
SQUAWK!!
JOLT
ビクッ

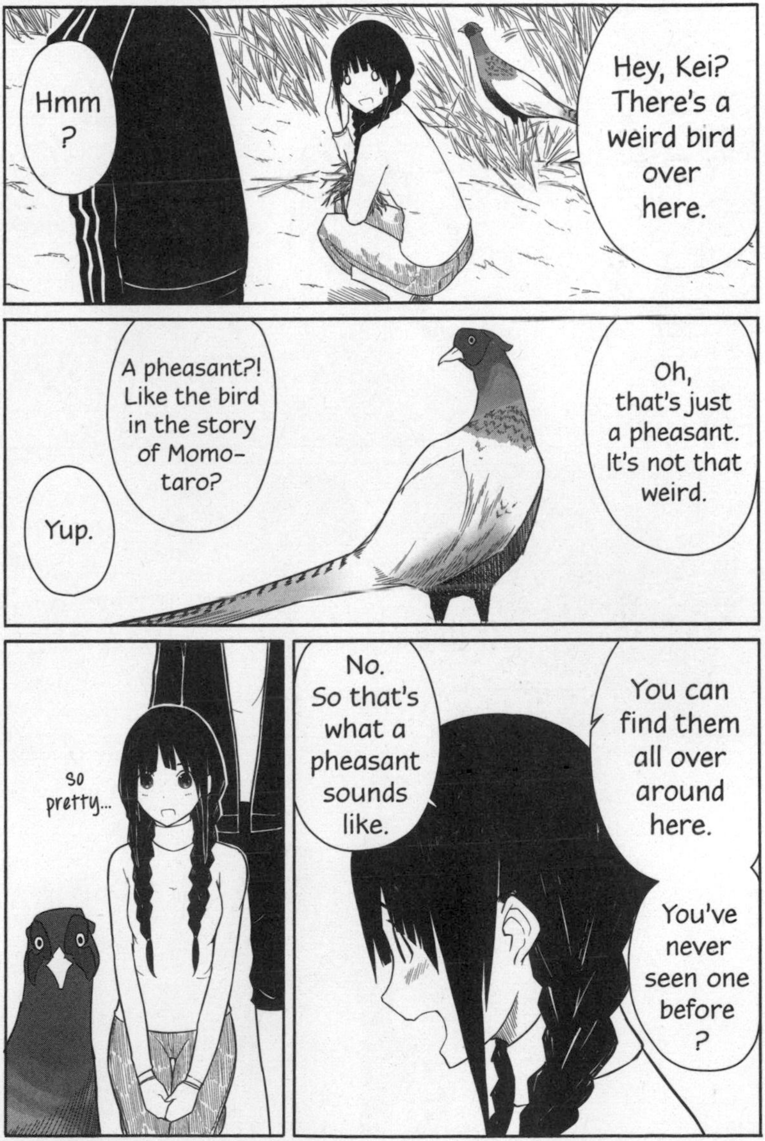
Hey, Kei? There's a weird bird over here.
Hmm?
Oh, that's just a pheasant. It's not that weird.
A pheasant?! Like the bird in the story of Momo-taro?
Yup.
You can find them all over around here.
You've never seen one before?
No. So that's what a pheasant sounds like.
so pretty...

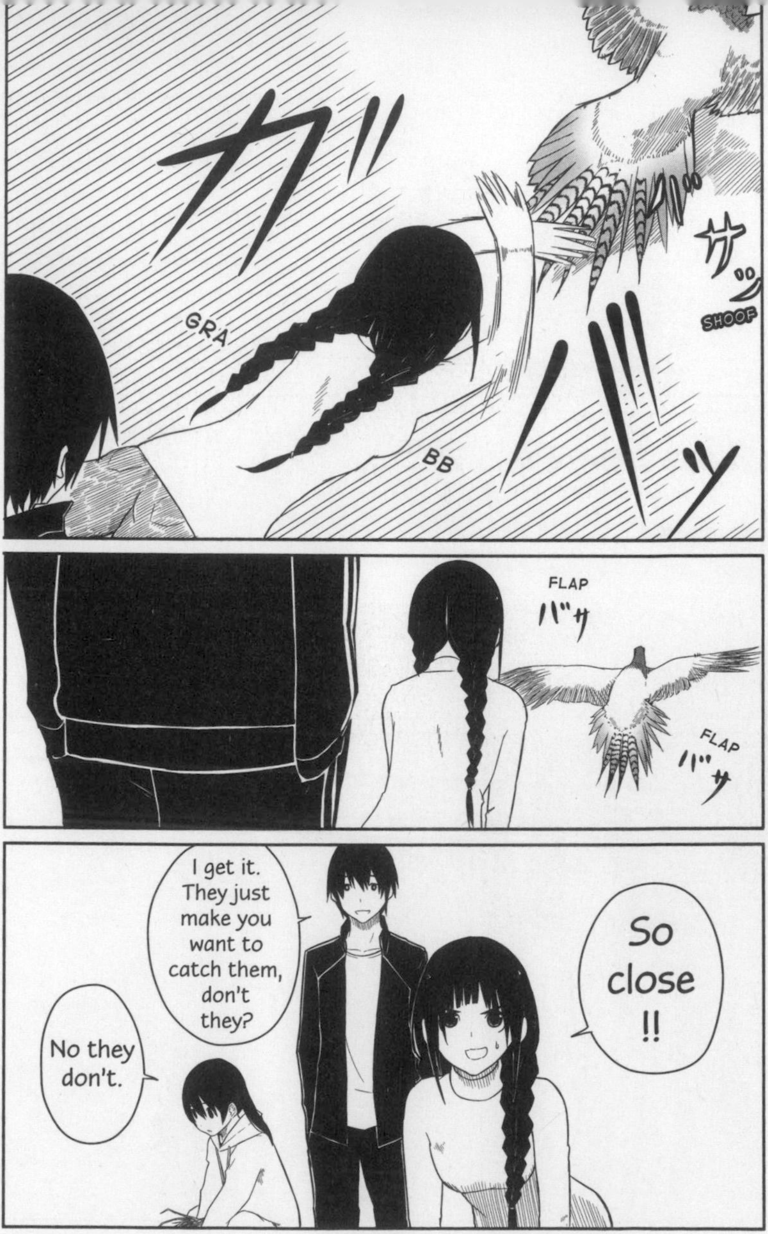
サッ
SHOOF
ガブ
GRA
BB
ッ
FLAP
バサ
FLAP
バサ
So close !!
I get it. They just make you want to catch them, don't they?
No they don't.

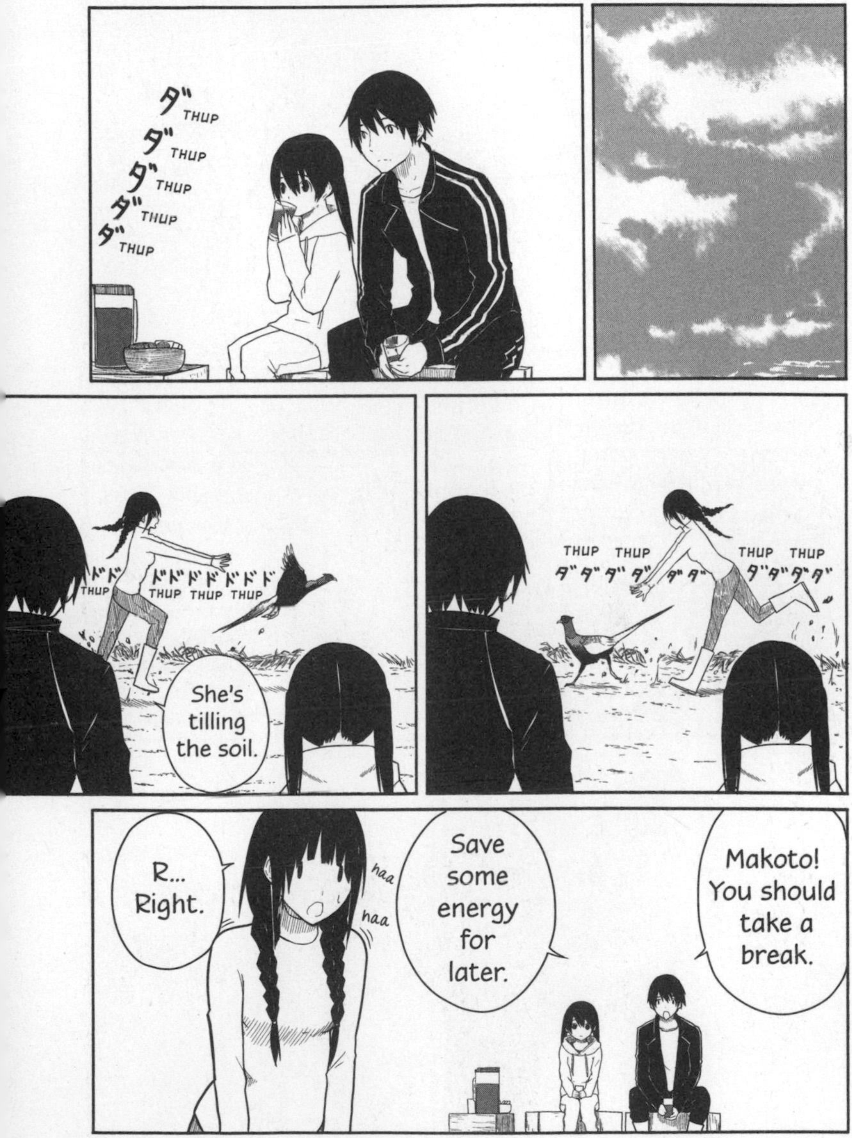

ダ THUP
ダ THUP
ダ THUP
ダ THUP
ダ THUP
THUP THUP
ダダダダ ダダ
THUP THUP
ダダダダ
ドド THUP
ドドドドドド THUP THUP THUP
She's tilling the soil.
Makoto! You should take a break.
Save some energy for later.
haa
haa
R... Right.

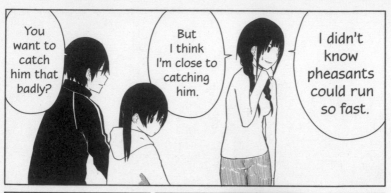

I didn't know pheasants could run so fast.
But I think I'm close to catching him.
You want to catch him that badly?
He's keeping me at a distance where it looks like I can reach him, but I can't.
And he's looking at me as if to say, *"Catch me if you can!"*
Come at me!
No one from around here would try so hard to catch one...
But I've never seen one before! To me, it's rare!
There are none in Yokohama!
Is catching pheasants part of your witch training, too?
Huh?
Oh, no, it has nothing to do with being a witch.
I just want to, that's all.
Whaaat...

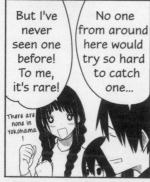

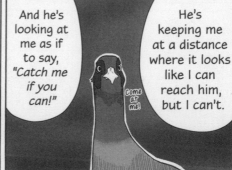

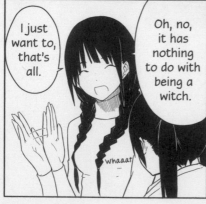

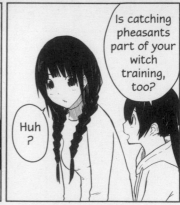

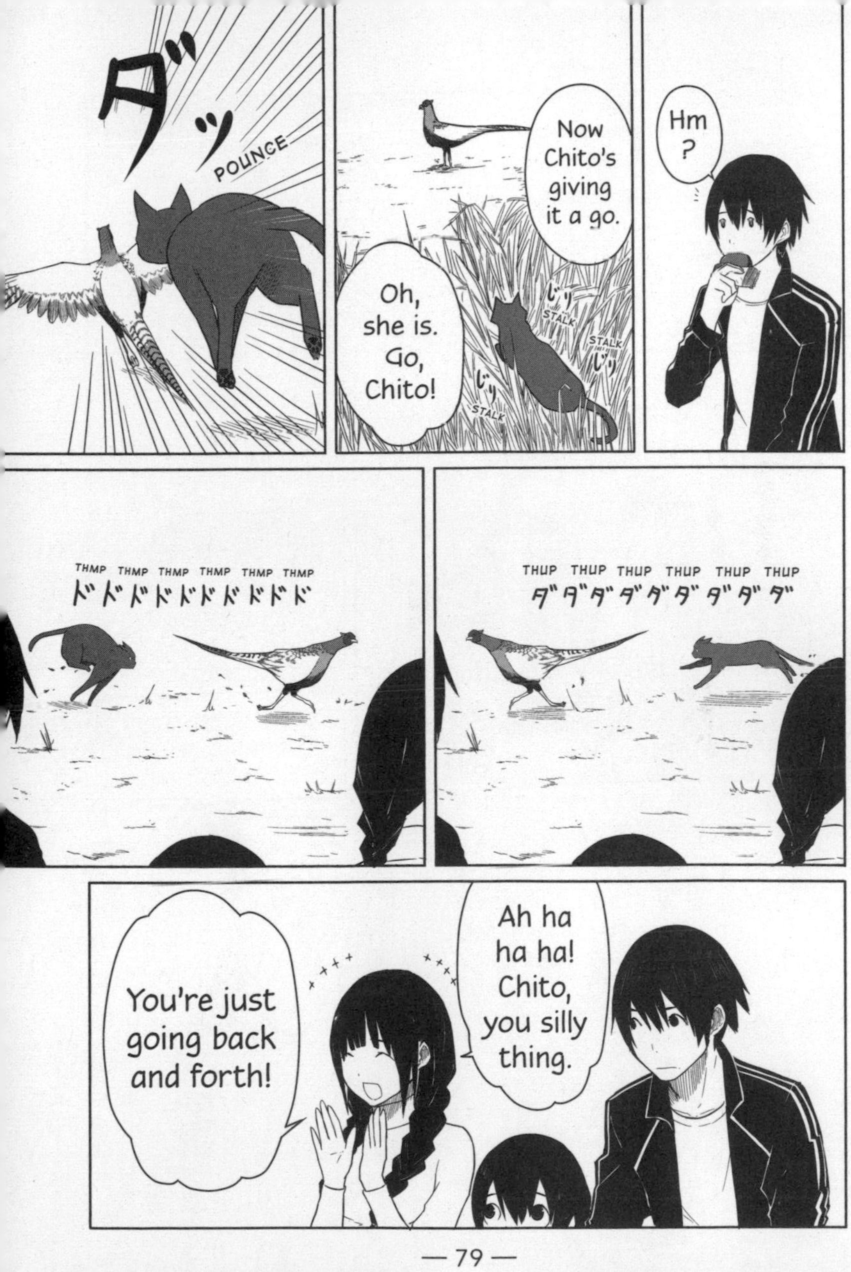
Hm ?
Now Chito's giving it a go.
Oh, she is. Go, Chito!
じり STALK
STALK じり
じり STALK
ダッ
POUNCE
THUP THUP THUP THUP THUP THUP
ダダダダダダダダダ
THMP THMP THMP THMP THMP THMP
ドドドドドドドドド
Ah ha ha ha! Chito, you silly thing.
You're just going back and forth!

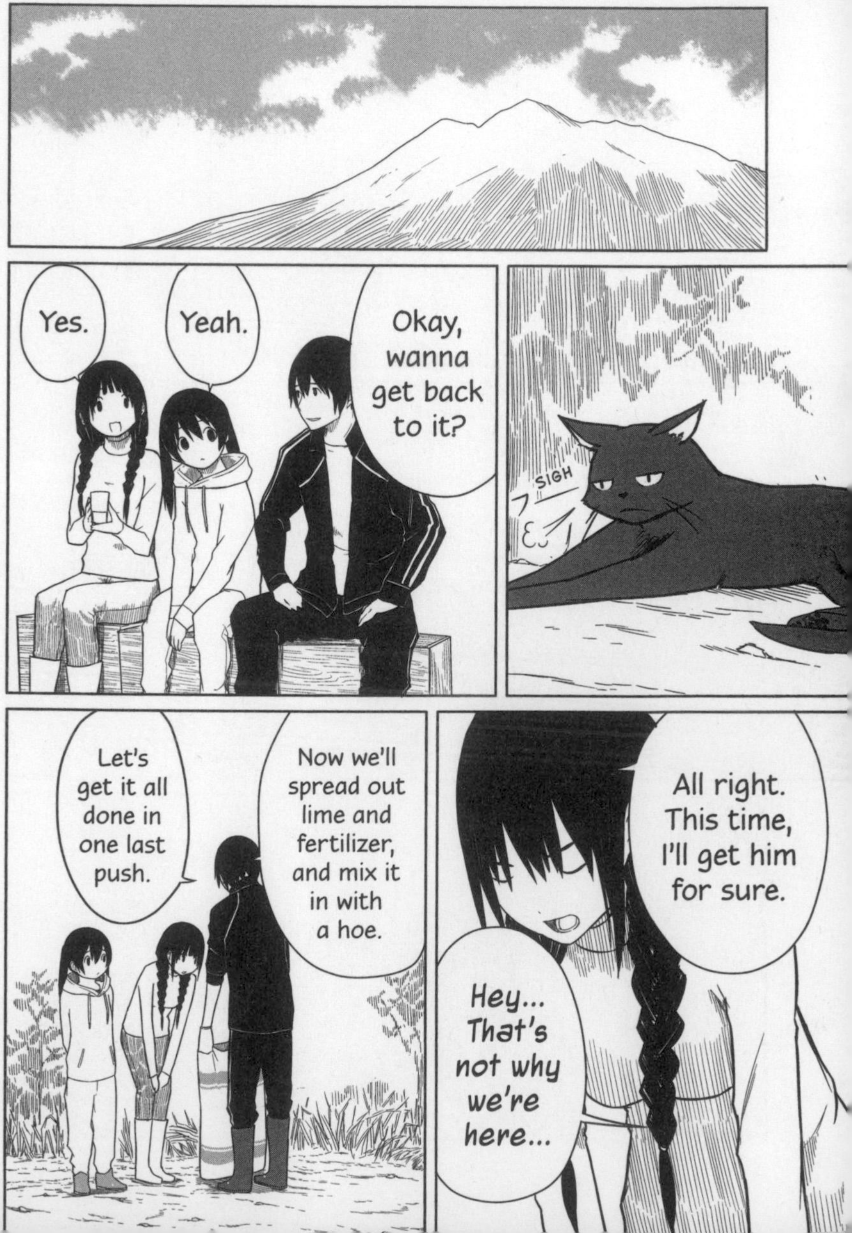
SIGH
Okay, wanna get back to it?
Yeah.
Yes.
All right. This time, I'll get him for sure.
Hey... That's not why we're here...
Now we'll spread out lime and fertilizer, and mix it in with a hoe.
Let's get it all done in one last push.

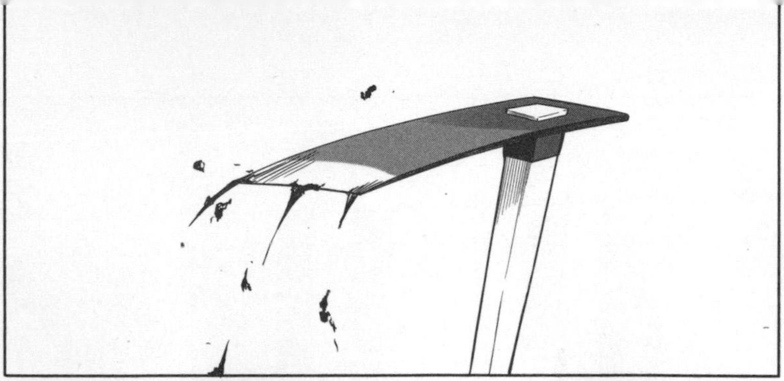

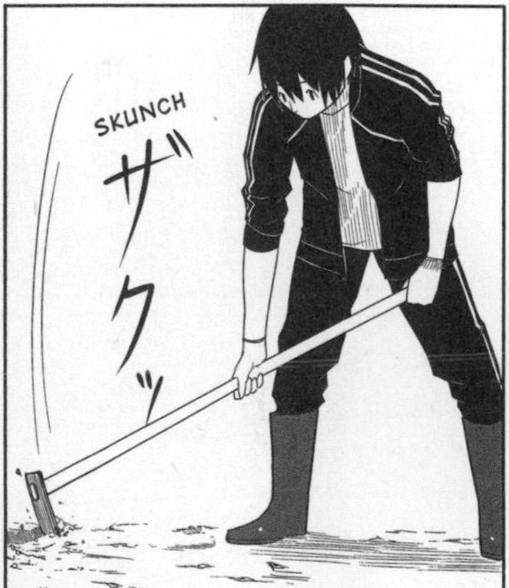
SKUNCH
ザクッ

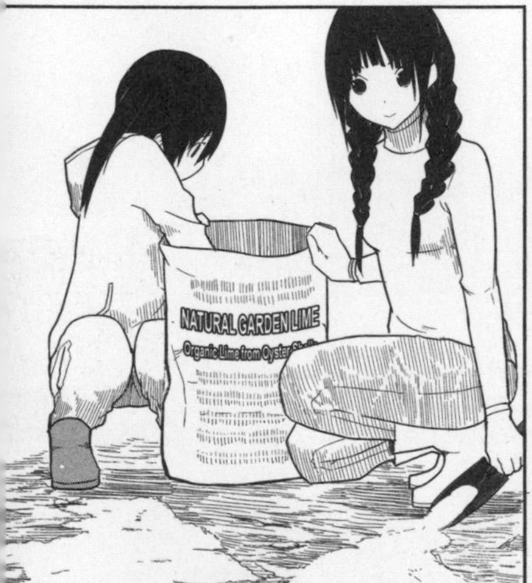
NATURAL GARDEN LIME
Organic Lime from Oyster

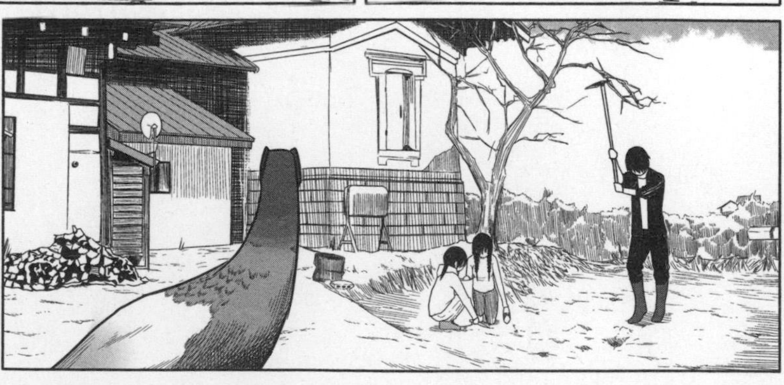

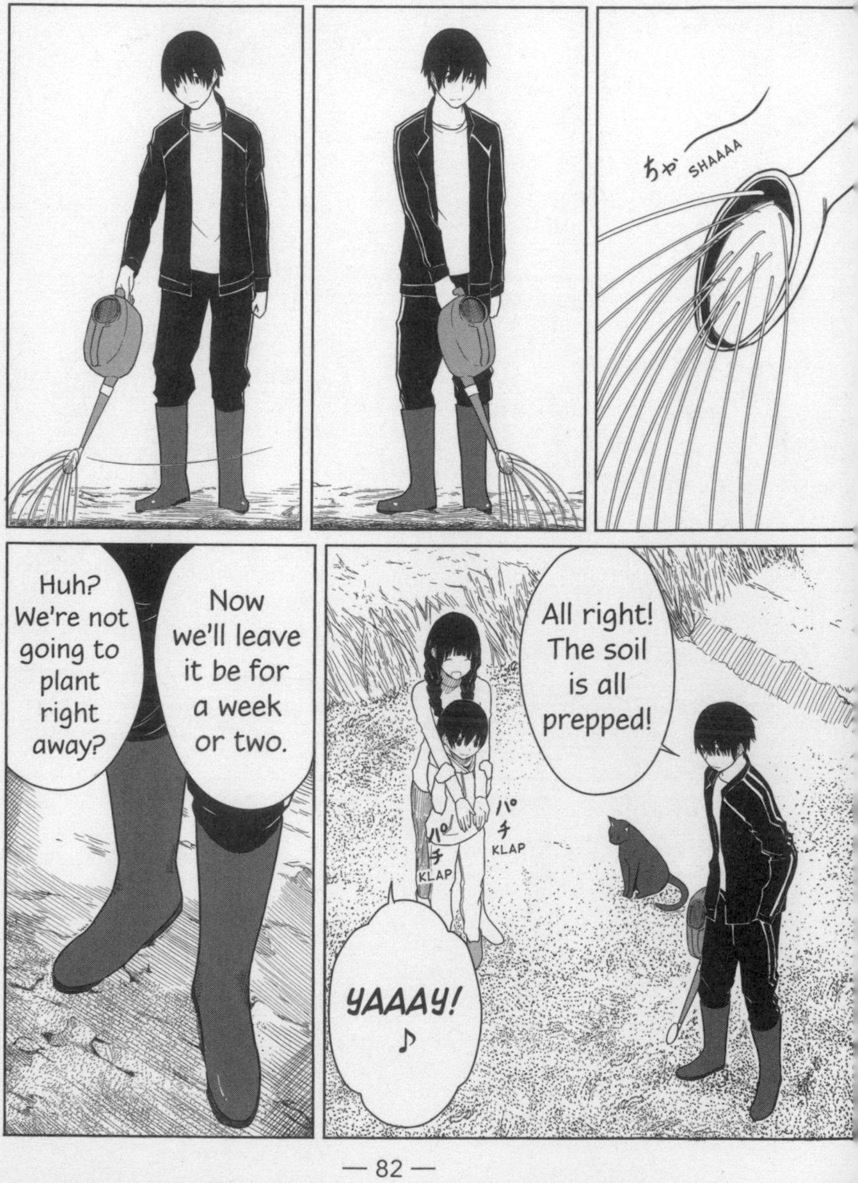
ちゃ SHAAAA
All right! The soil is all prepped!
パチ KLAP
パチ KLAP
YAAAY! ♪
Now we'll leave it be for a week or two.
Huh? We're not going to plant right away?

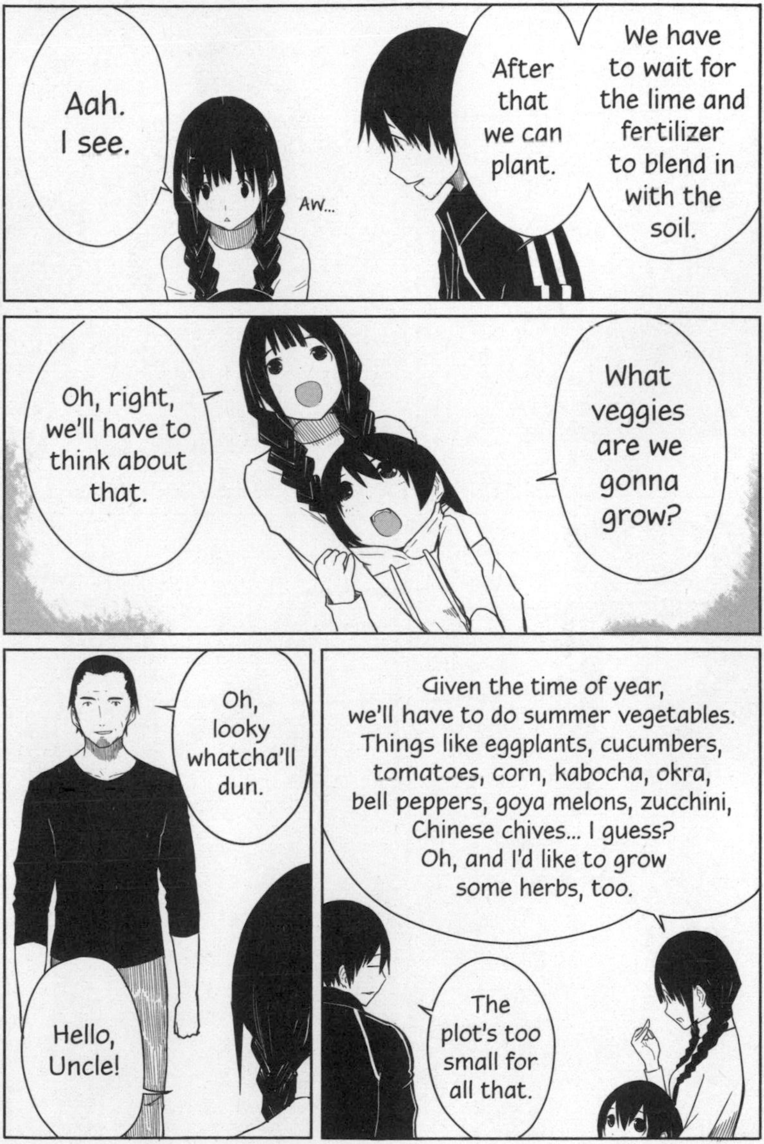
We have to wait for the lime and fertilizer to blend in with the soil.
After that we can plant.
AW...
Aah. I see.
What veggies are we gonna grow?
Oh, right, we'll have to think about that.
Given the time of year, we'll have to do summer vegetables. Things like eggplants, cucumbers, tomatoes, corn, kabocha, okra, bell peppers, goya melons, zucchini, Chinese chives... I guess? Oh, and I'd like to grow some herbs, too.
The plot's too small for all that.
Oh, looky whatcha'll dun.
Hello, Uncle!

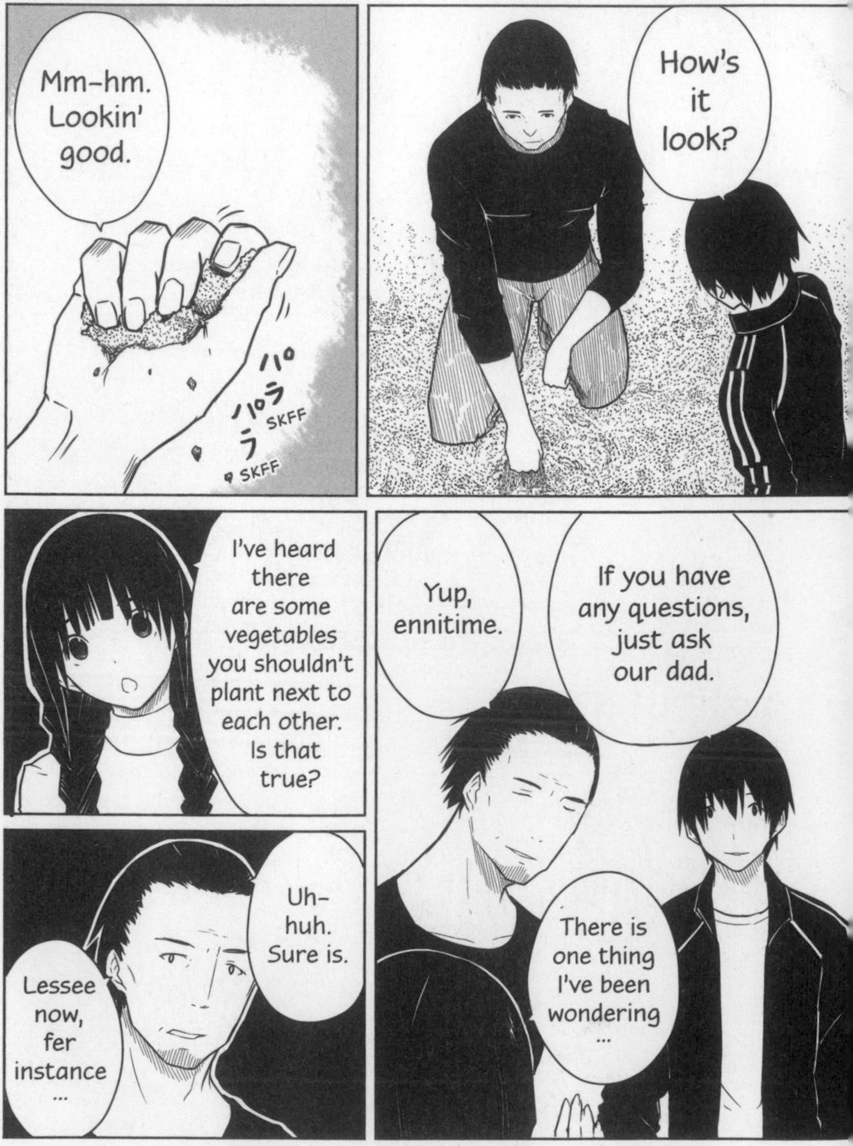
How's it look?
Mm-hm. Lookin' good.
パラパラ
SKFF SKFF
If you have any questions, just ask our dad.
Yup, ennitime.
There is one thing I've been wondering ...
I've heard there are some vegetables you shouldn't plant next to each other. Is that true?
Uh-huh. Sure is.
Lessee now, fer instance ...

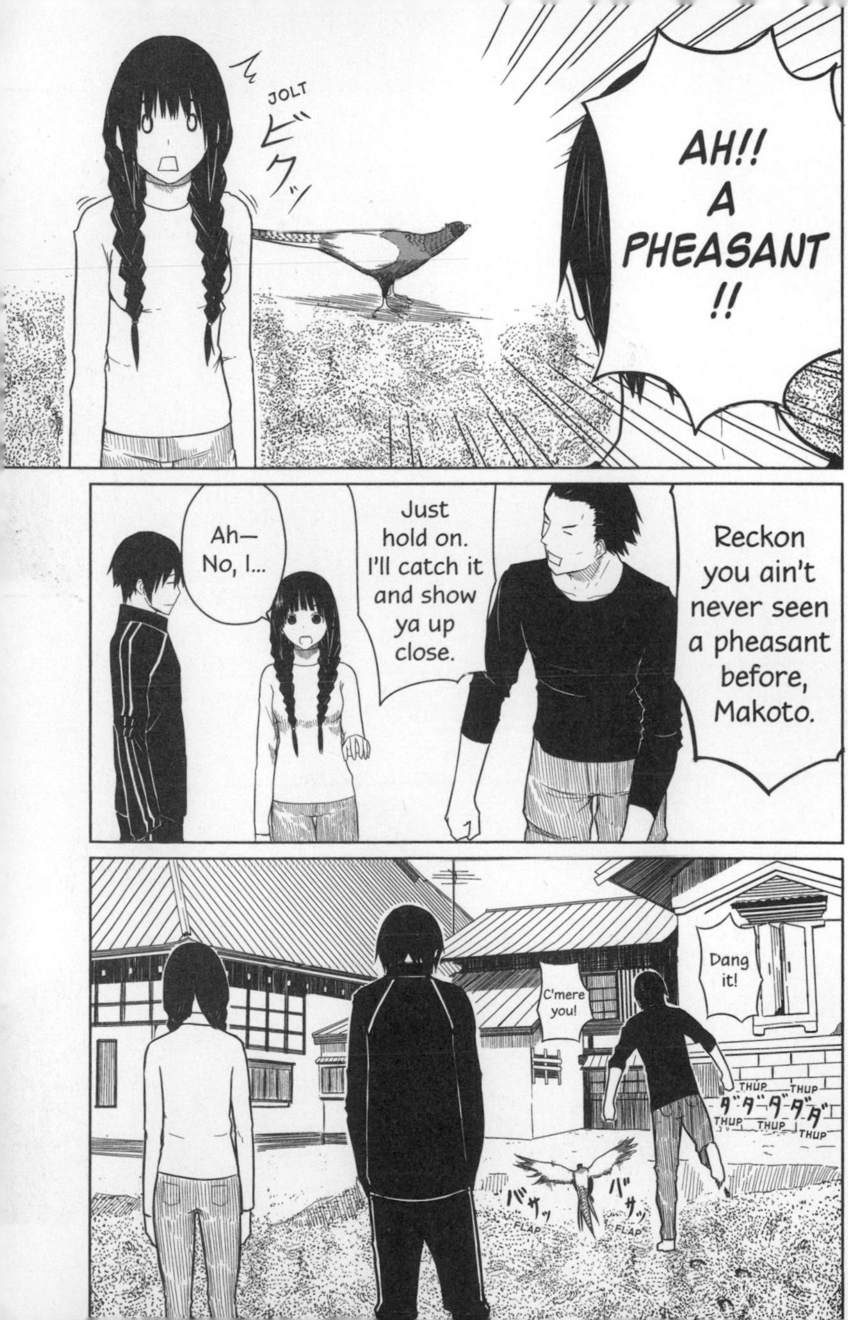
AH!! A PHEASANT !!
JOLT
ビクッ
Reckon you ain't never seen a pheasant before, Makoto.
Just hold on. I'll catch it and show ya up close.
Ah— No, I...
Dang it!
C'mere you!
THUP THUP THUP THUP THUP
ダダダダダ
バサッ
FLAP
バサッ
FLAP

Chapter 4
How Your Familiar Can Help

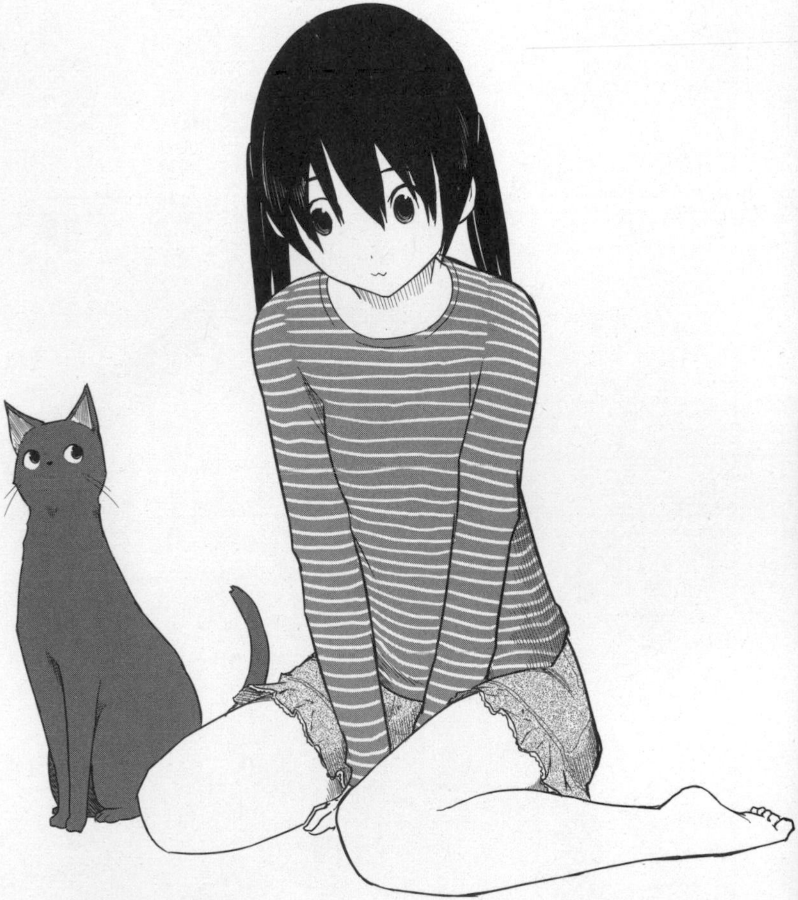

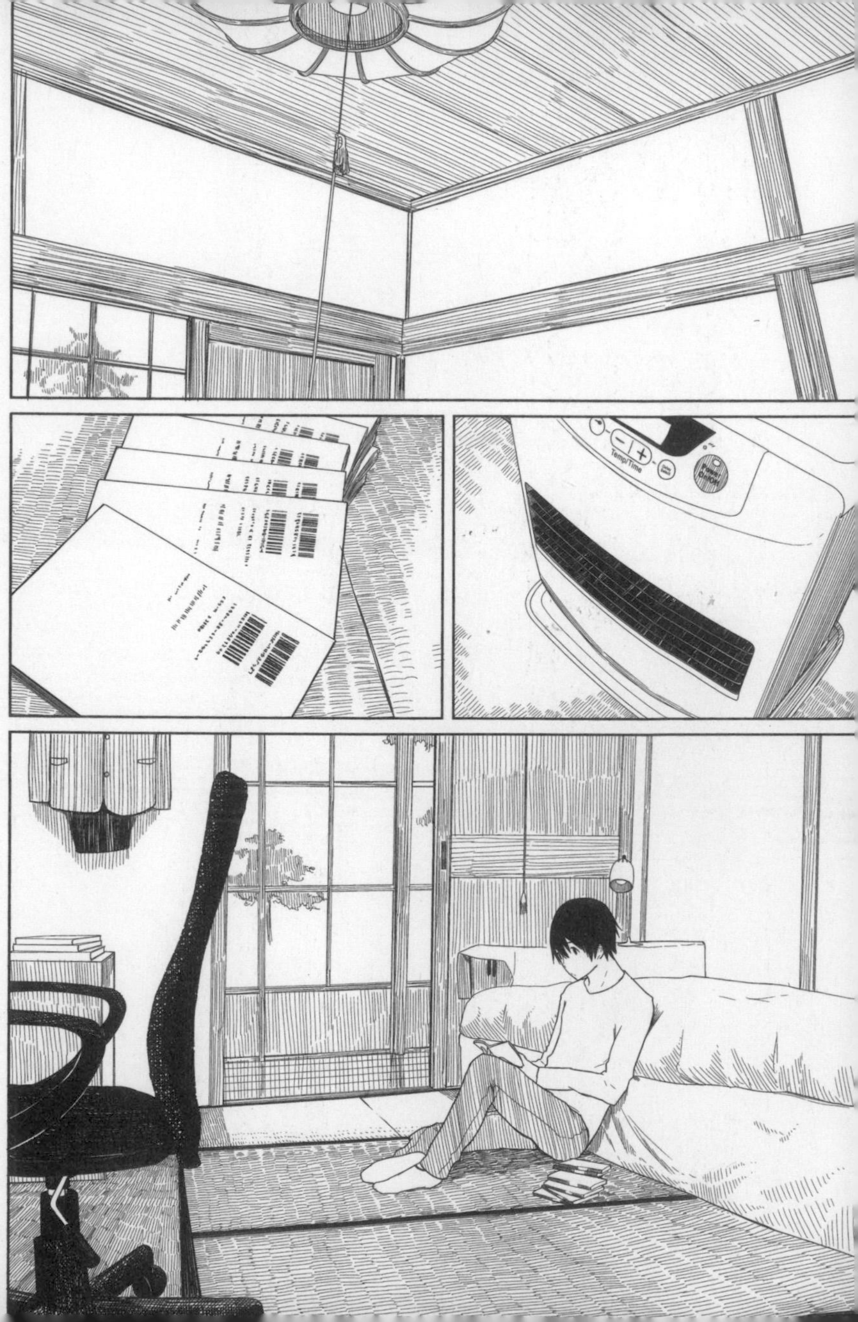
Temp/Time

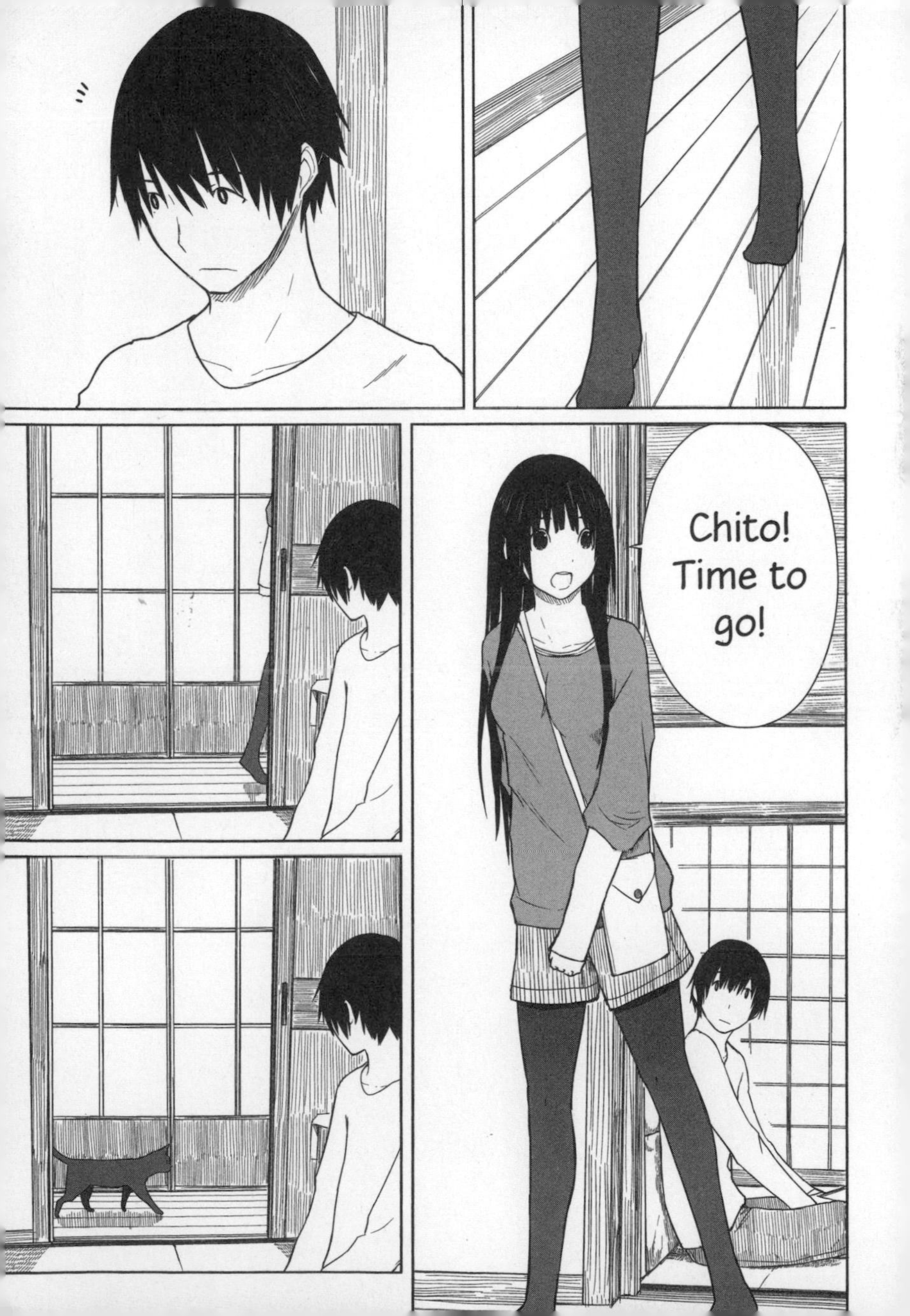
Chito! Time to go!

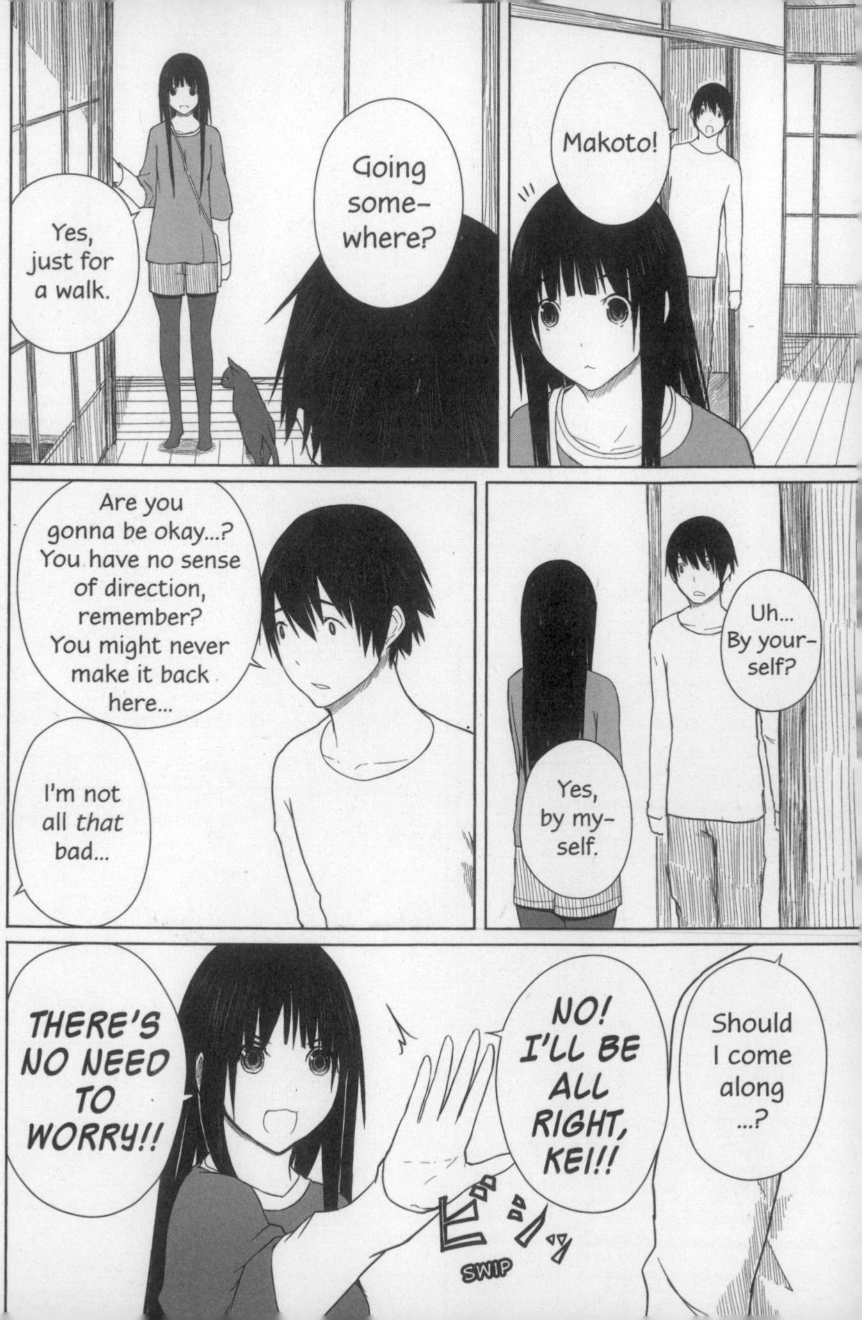
Makoto!
Going somewhere?
Yes, just for a walk.
Uh... By yourself?
Yes, by myself.
Are you gonna be okay...? You have no sense of direction, remember? You might never make it back here...
I'm not all *that* bad...
Should I come along ...?
NO! I'LL BE ALL RIGHT, KEI!!
THERE'S NO NEED TO WORRY!!
SWIP

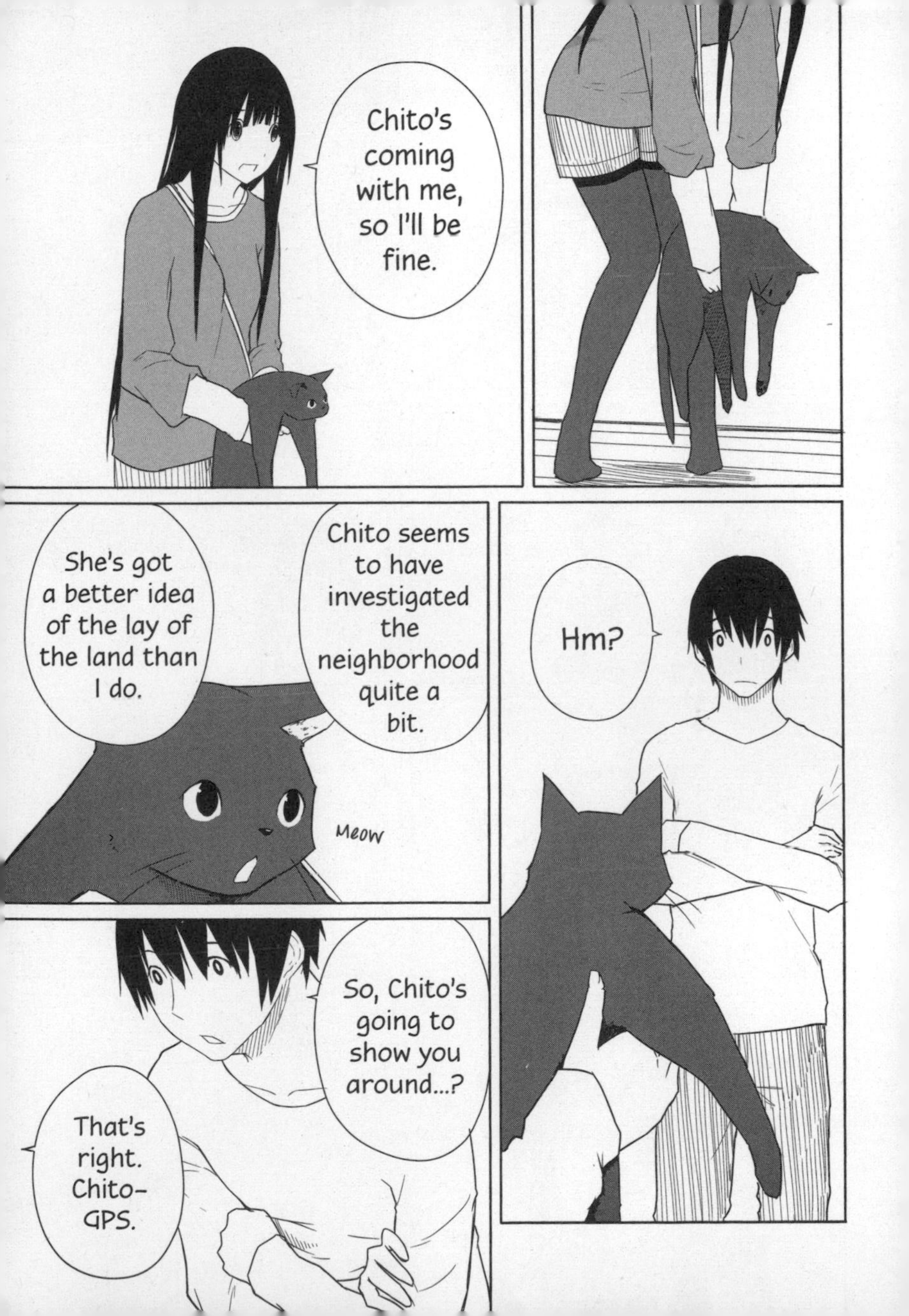
Chito's coming with me, so I'll be fine.
Hm?
Chito seems to have investigated the neighborhood quite a bit.
She's got a better idea of the lay of the land than I do.
Meow
So, Chito's going to show you around...?
That's right. Chito-GPS.

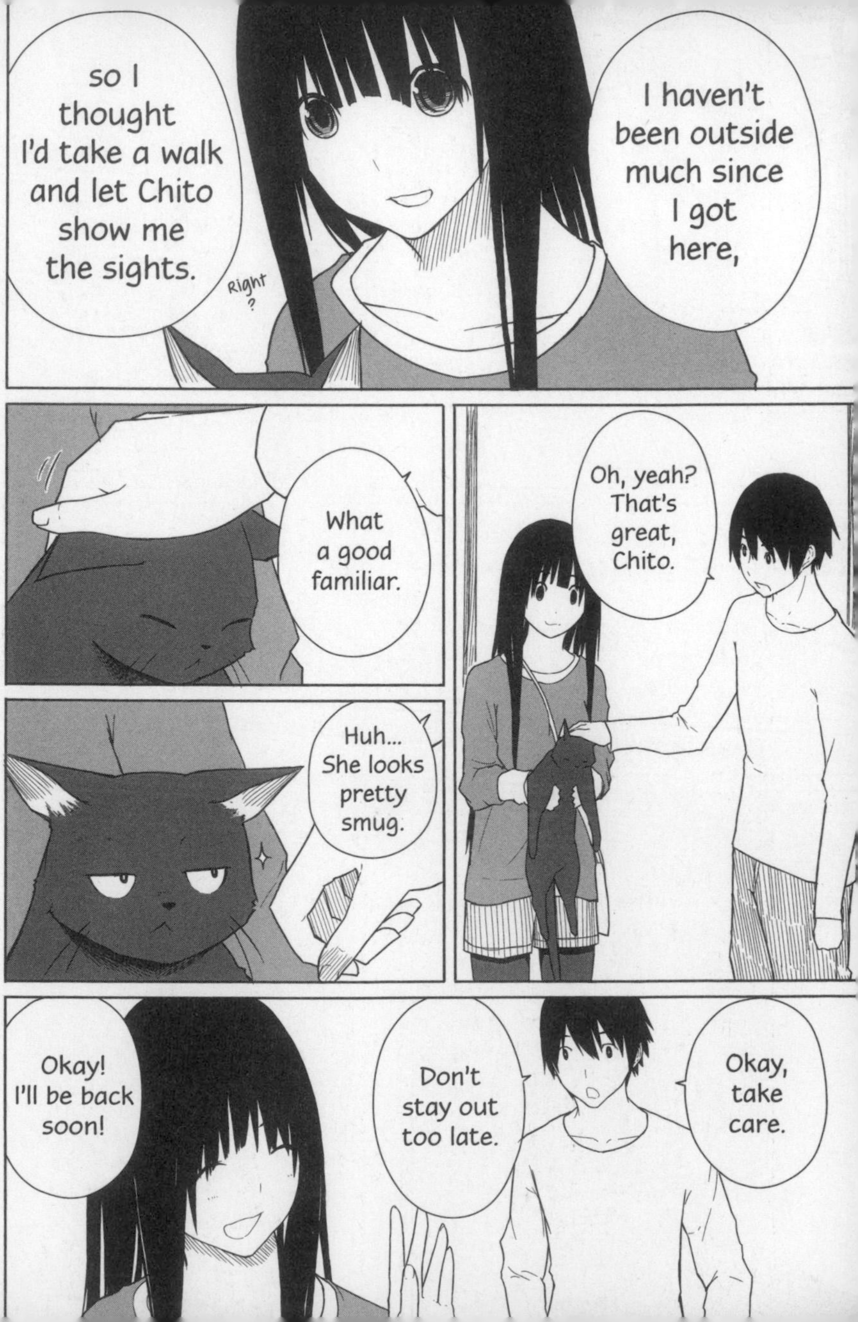
I haven't been outside much since I got here,
so I thought I'd take a walk and let Chito show me the sights.
Right?
Oh, yeah? That's great, Chito.
What a good familiar.
Huh... She looks pretty smug.
Okay, take care.
Don't stay out too late.
Okay! I'll be back soon!

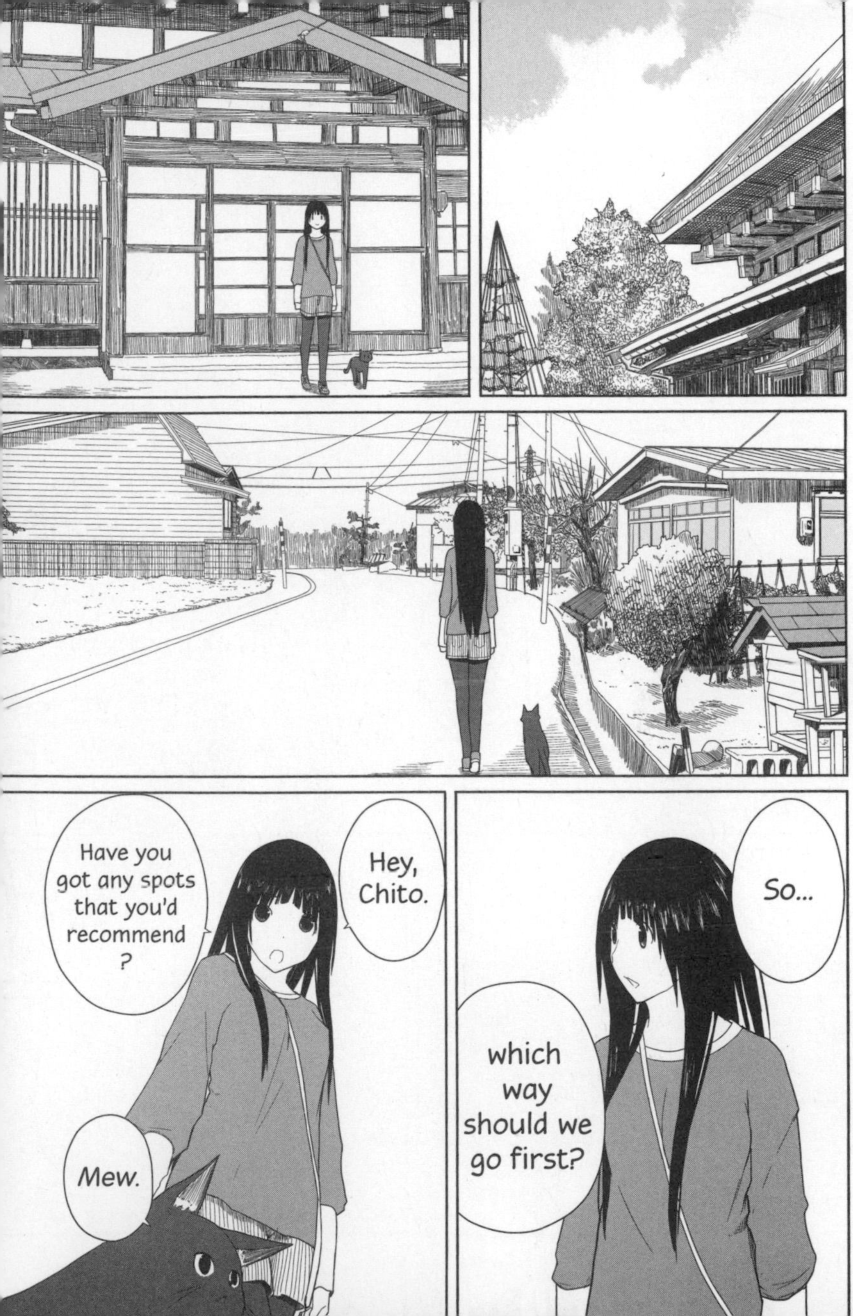
So...
which way should we go first?
Hey, Chito.
Have you got any spots that you'd recommend ?
Mew.

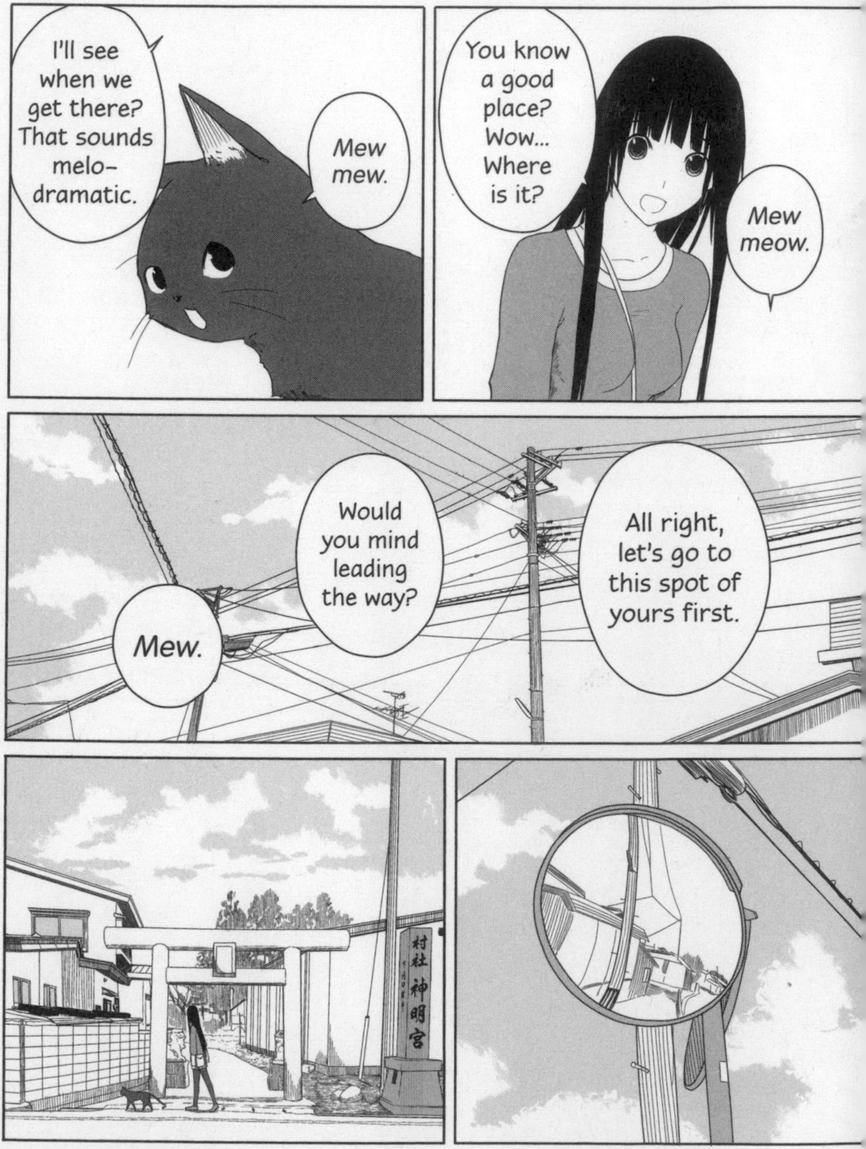
You know a good place? Wow... Where is it?
Mew meow.
Mew mew.
I'll see when we get there? That sounds melo-dramatic.
All right, let's go to this spot of yours first.
Would you mind leading the way?
Mew.
村社神明宮

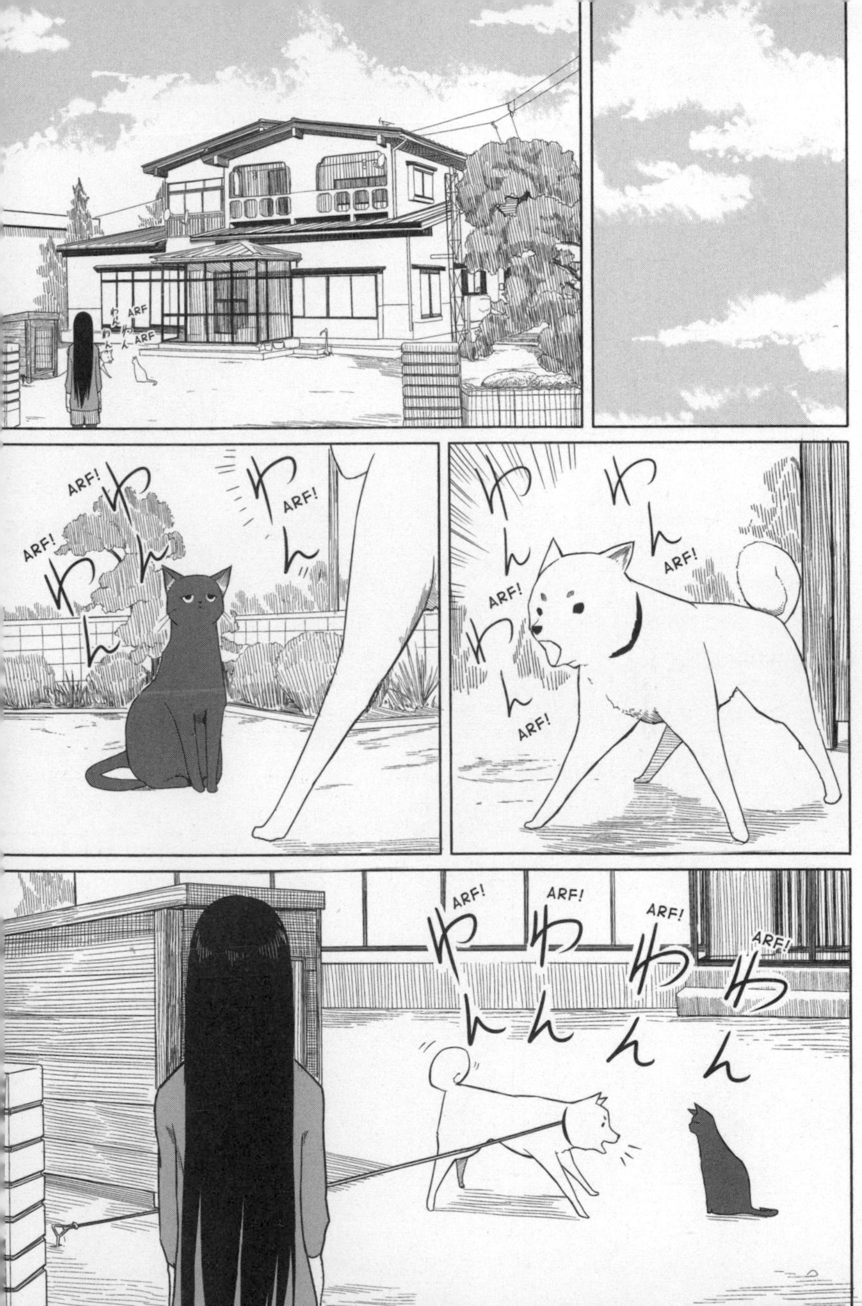
ARF
わん
ARF
わんわん
ARF!
わん
ARF!
わん
ARF!
わん
ARF!
わん
ARF!
わん
ARF!
わん
ARF!
わん
ARF!
わん
ARF!
わん
ARF!
わん

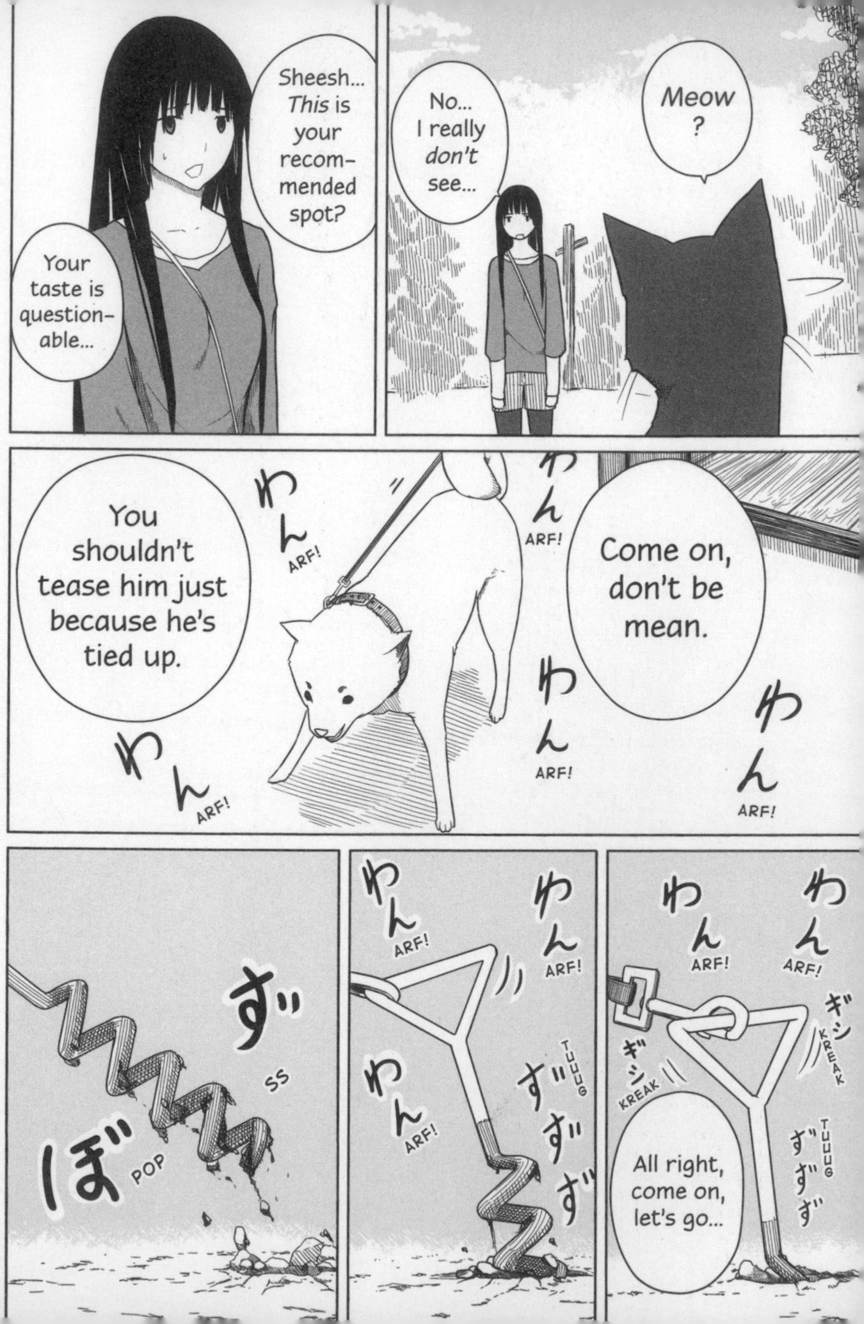
Meow ?
No... I really *don't* see...
Sheesh... *This* is your recom-mended spot?
Your taste is question-able...
わん ARF!
Come on, don't be mean.
わん ARF!
わん ARF!
You shouldn't tease him just because he's tied up.
わん ARF!
わん ARF!
わん ARF!
わん ARF!
ギシ KREAK
ギシ KREAK
ずずず TUUUG
All right, come on, let's go...
わん ARF!
わん ARF!
ずずず TUUUG
わん ARF!
ず SS
ぼ POP

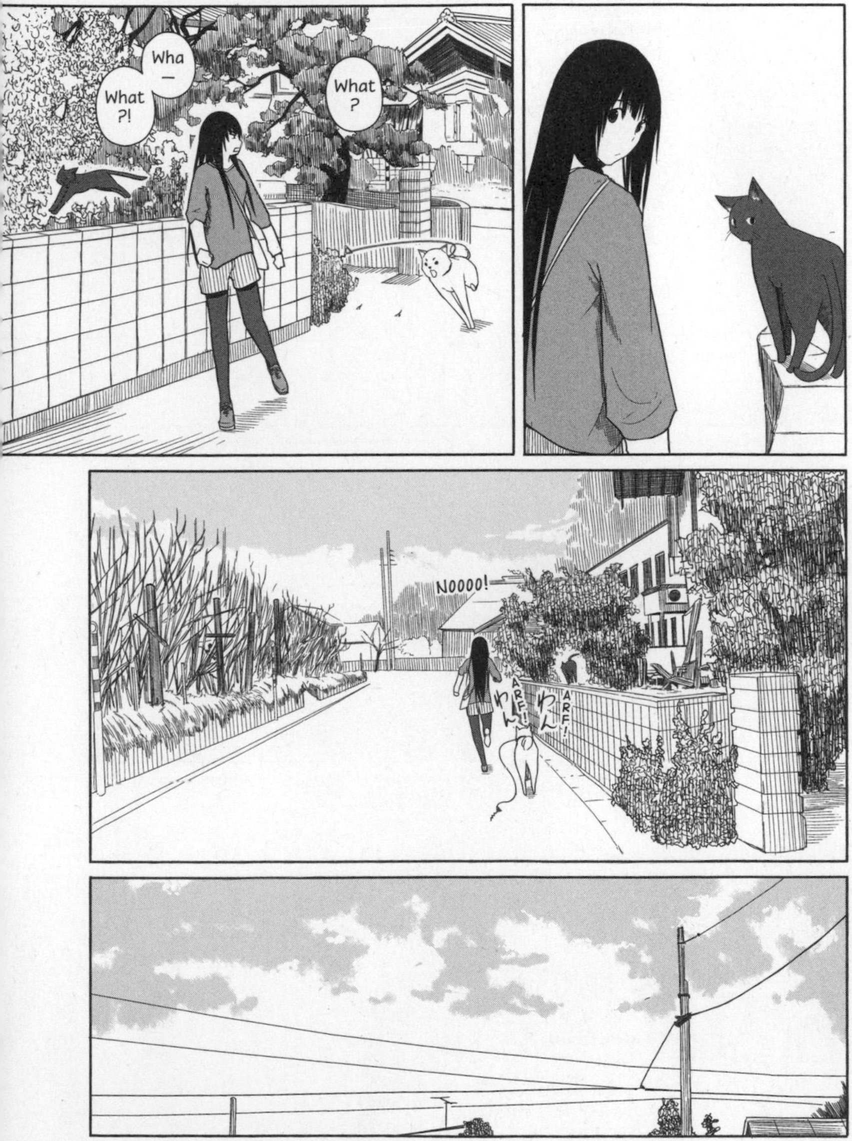
What?
Wha—
What?!
NOOOO!
わん ARF!
わん ARF!

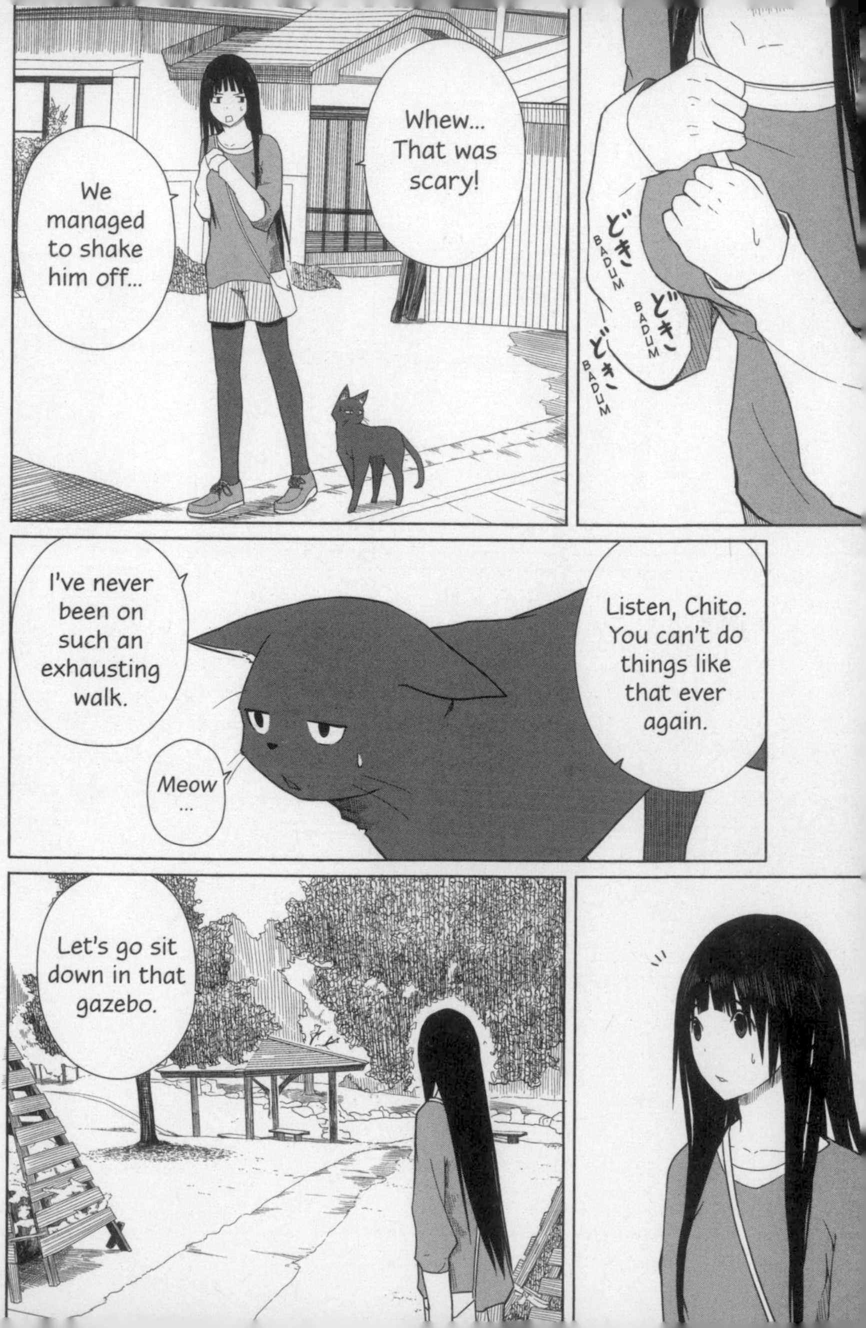
どき
BADUM
どき
BADUM
どき
BADUM
Whew... That was scary!
We managed to shake him off...
Listen, Chito. You can't do things like that ever again.
I've never been on such an exhausting walk.
Meow ...
Let's go sit down in that gazebo.

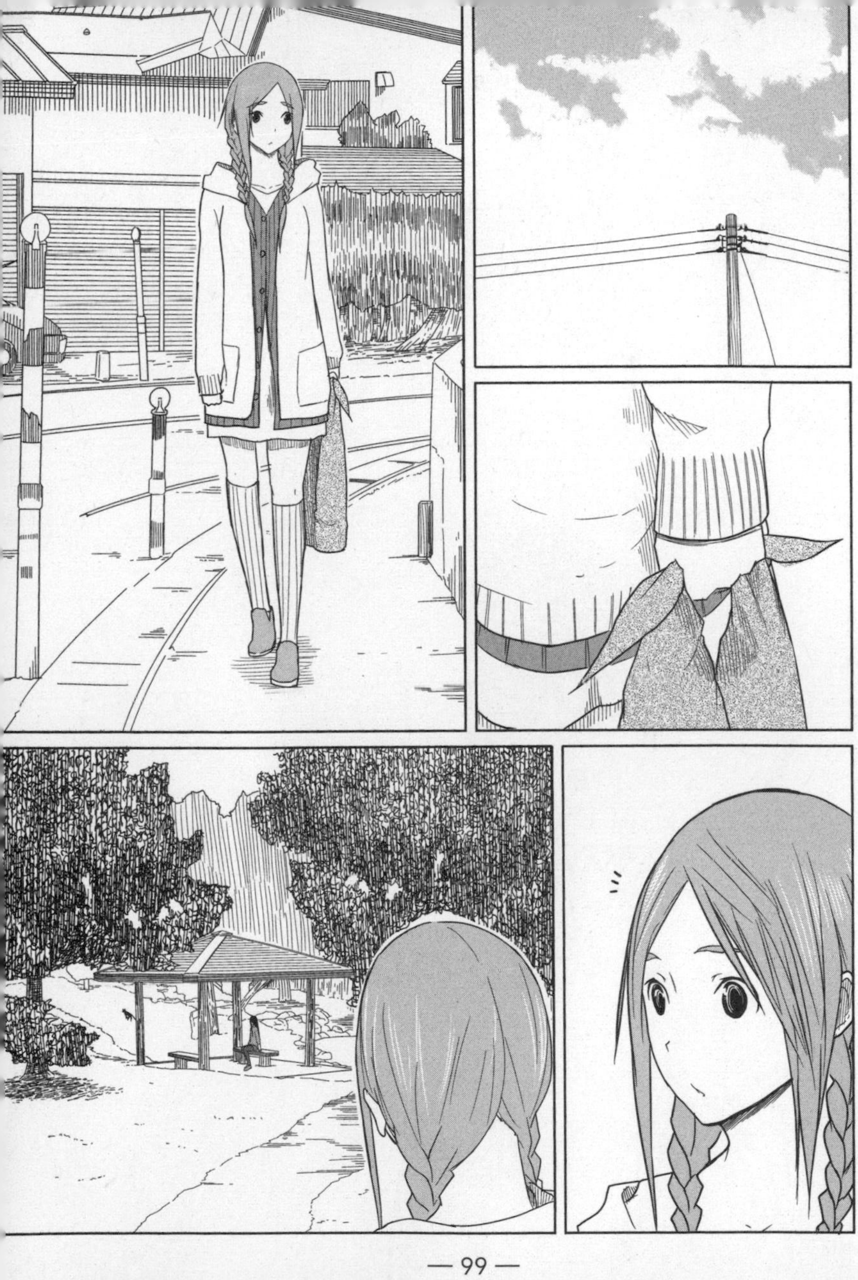

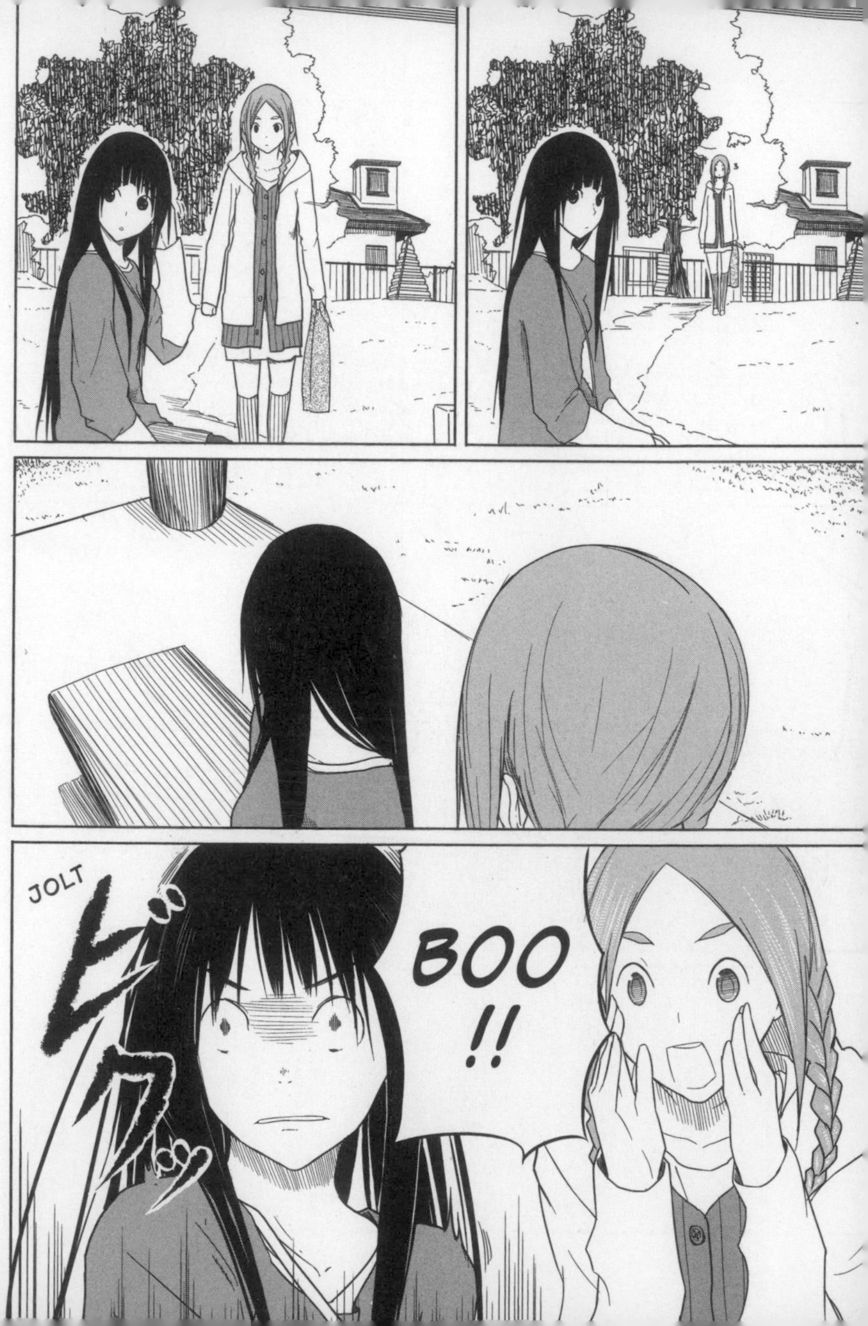
JOLT
BOO
!!

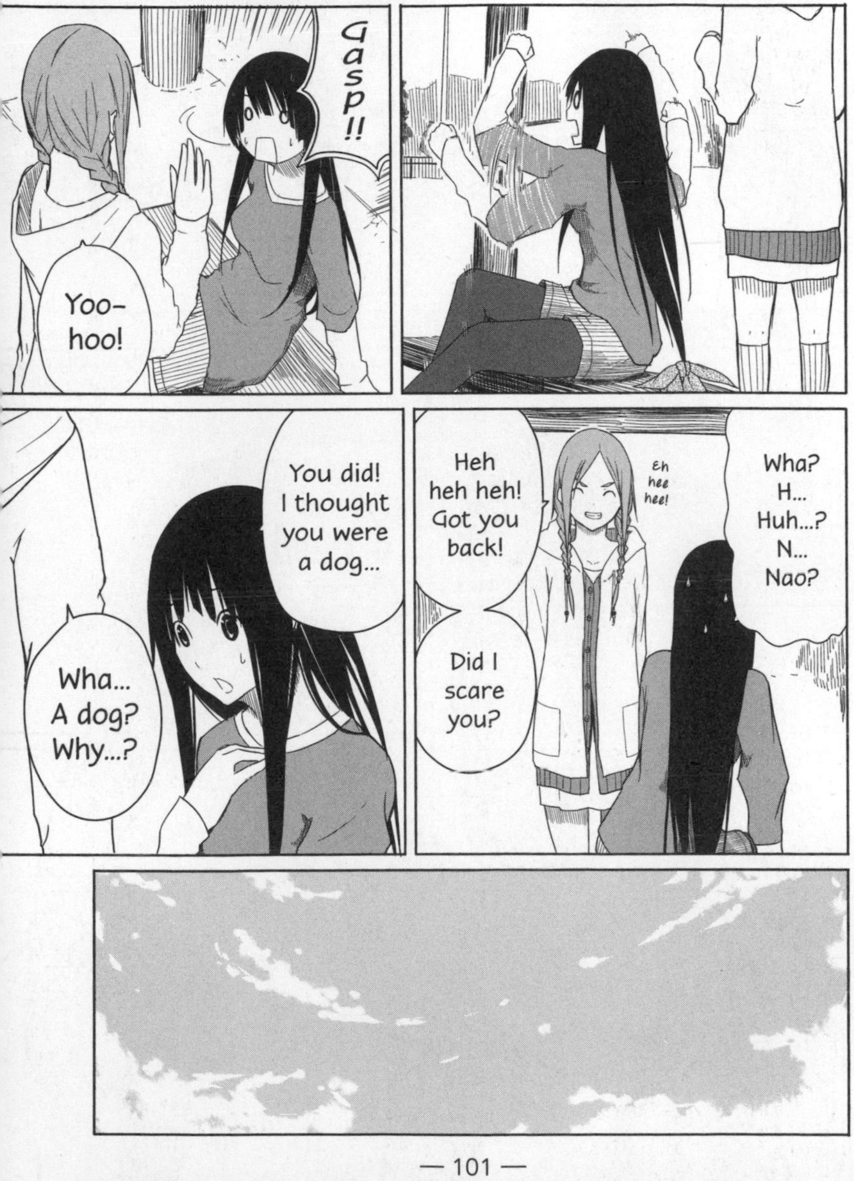
Gasp!!
Yoo-hoo!
Wha? H... Huh...? N... Nao?
Eh hee hee!
Heh heh heh! Got you back!
Did I scare you?
You did! I thought you were a dog...
Wha... A dog? Why...?

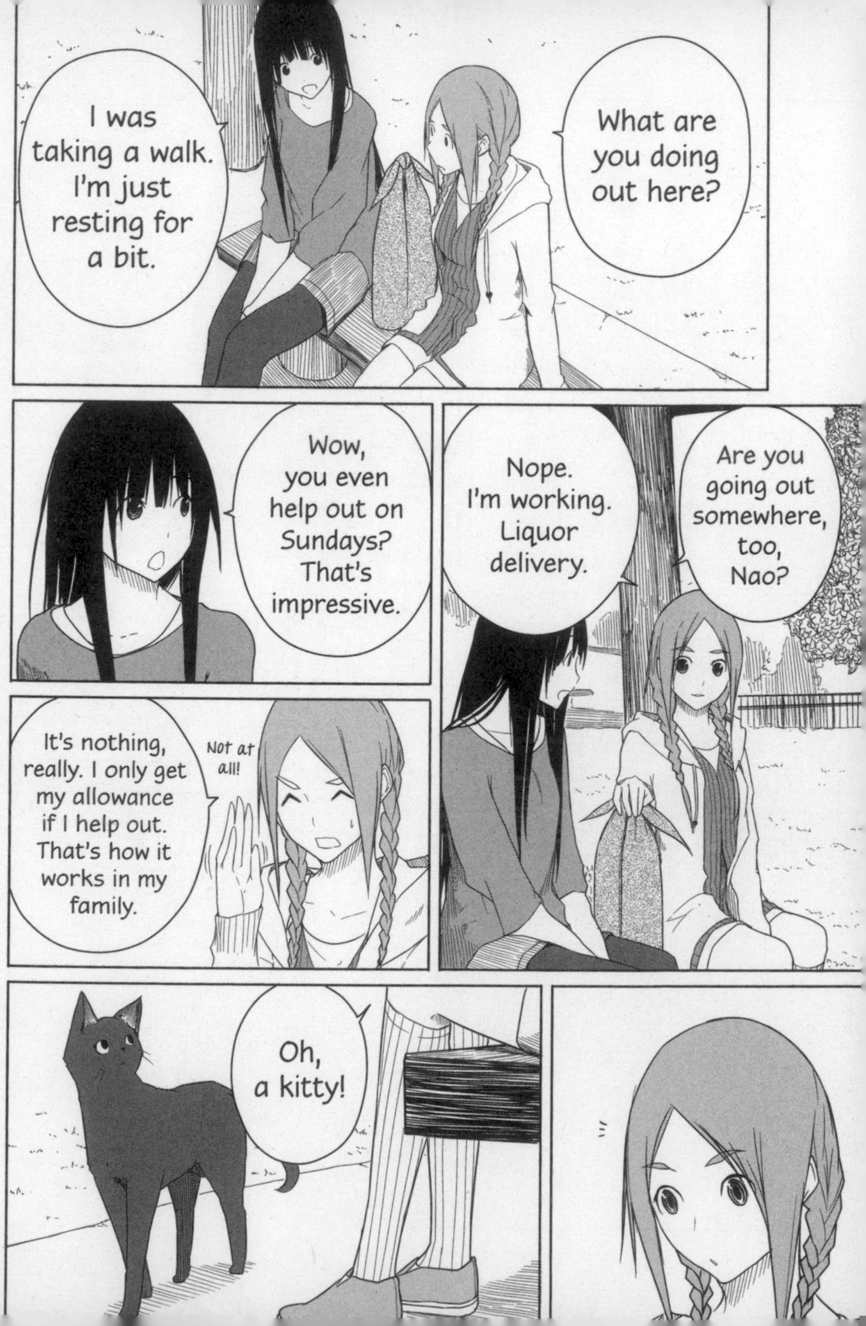
What are you doing out here?
I was taking a walk. I'm just resting for a bit.
Are you going out somewhere, too, Nao?
Nope. I'm working. Liquor delivery.
Wow, you even help out on Sundays? That's impressive.
Not at all!
It's nothing, really. I only get my allowance if I help out. That's how it works in my family.
Oh, a kitty!

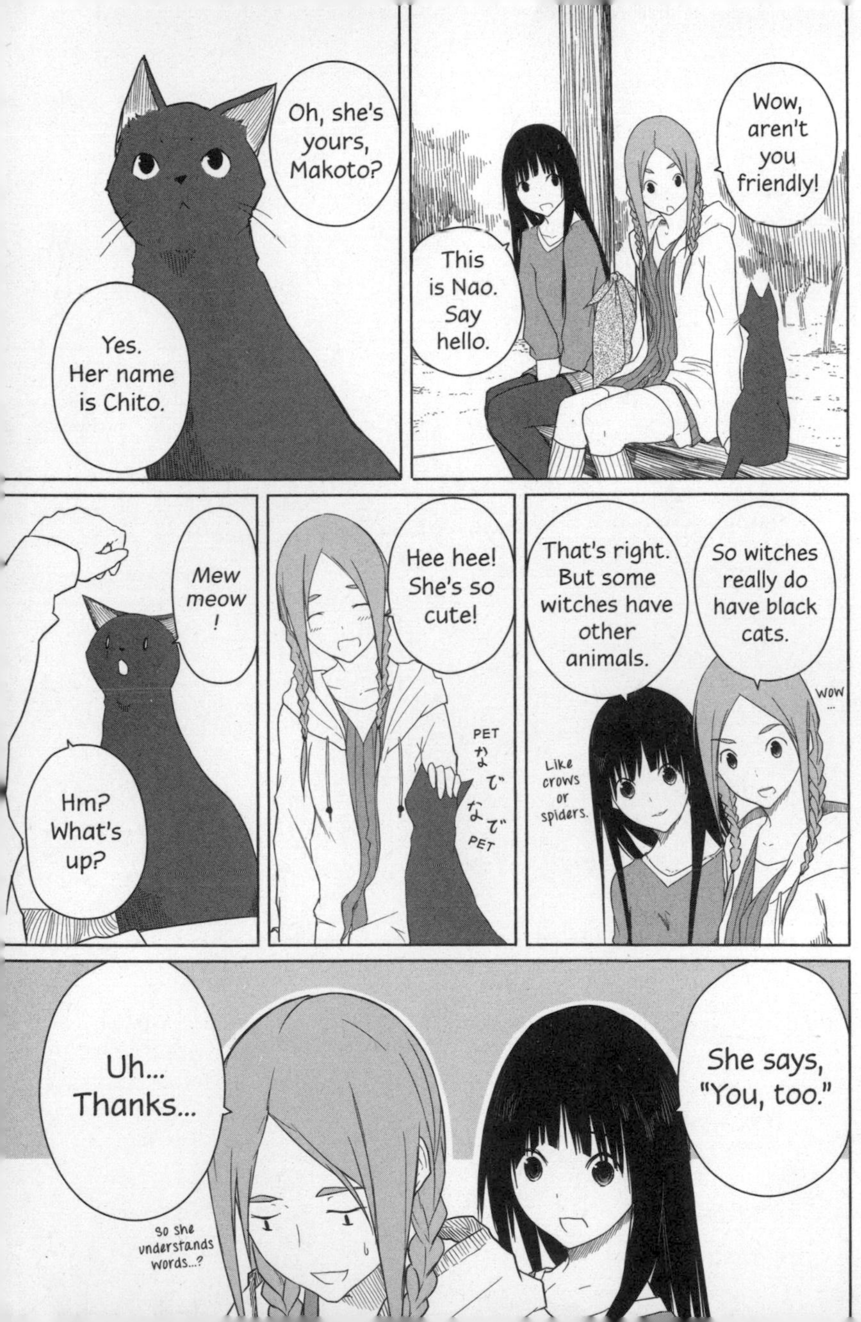
Wow, aren't you friendly!
This is Nao. Say hello.
Oh, she's yours, Makoto?
Yes. Her name is Chito.
So witches really do have black cats.
WOW...
That's right. But some witches have other animals.
Like crows or spiders.
Hee hee! She's so cute!
PET なで
なで PET
Mew meow!
Hm? What's up?
She says, "You, too."
Uh... Thanks...
So she understands words...?

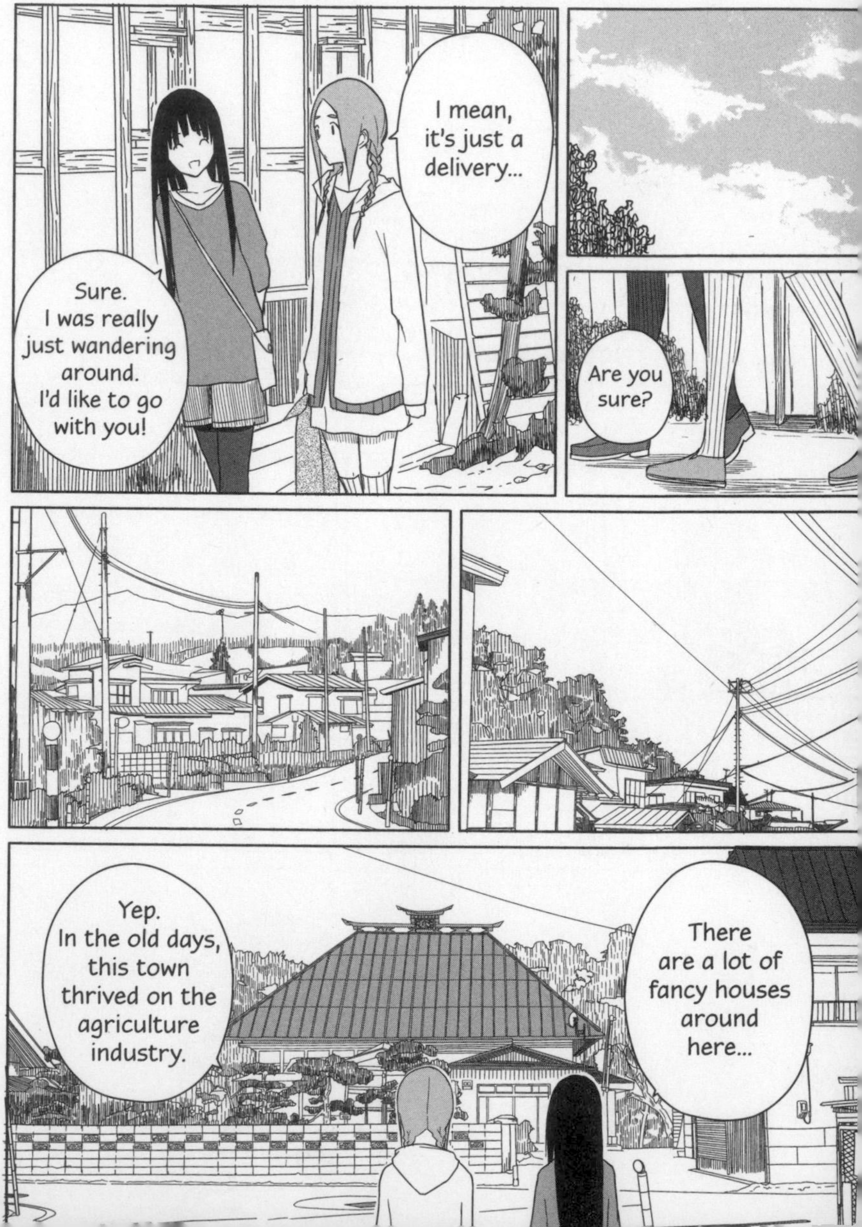
Are you sure?
I mean, it's just a delivery...
Sure. I was really just wandering around. I'd like to go with you!
There are a lot of fancy houses around here...
Yep. In the old days, this town thrived on the agriculture industry.

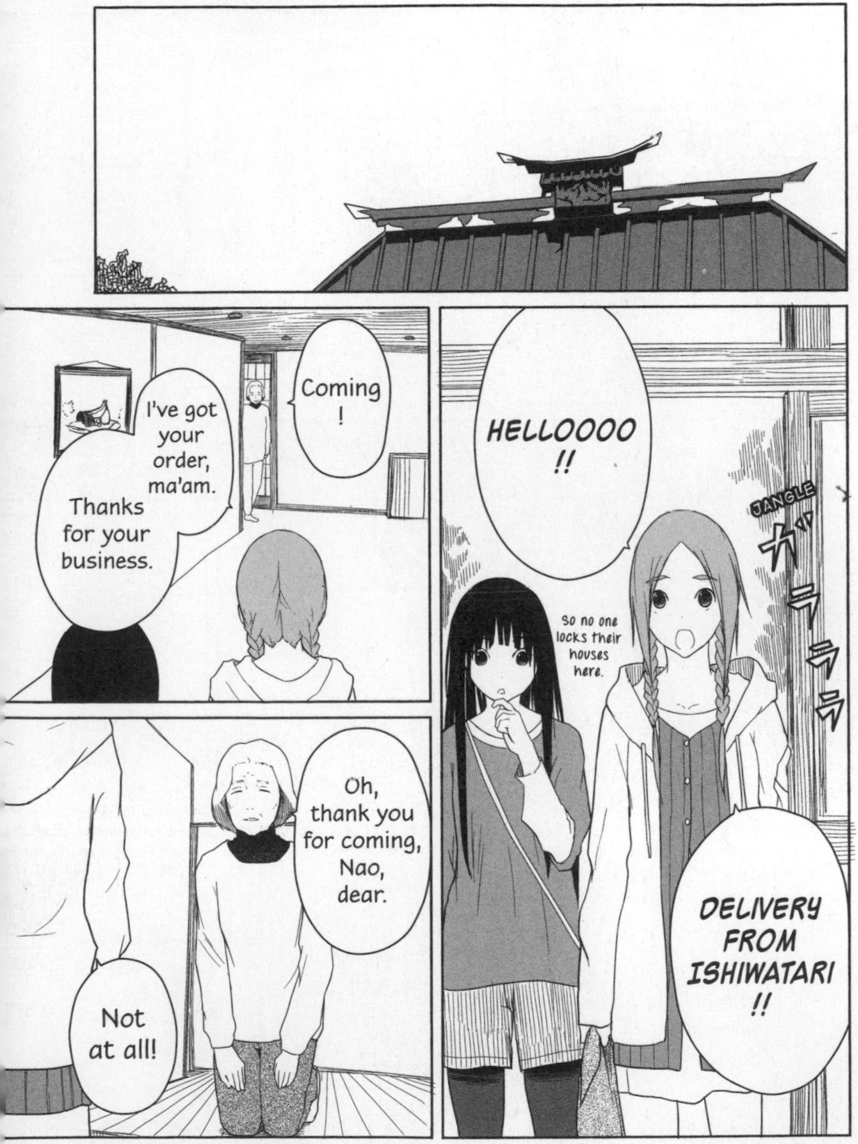
HELLOOOO!!
JANGLE
So no one locks their houses here.
DELIVERY FROM ISHIWATARI!!
Coming!
I've got your order, ma'am.
Thanks for your business.
Oh, thank you for coming, Nao, dear.
Not at all!

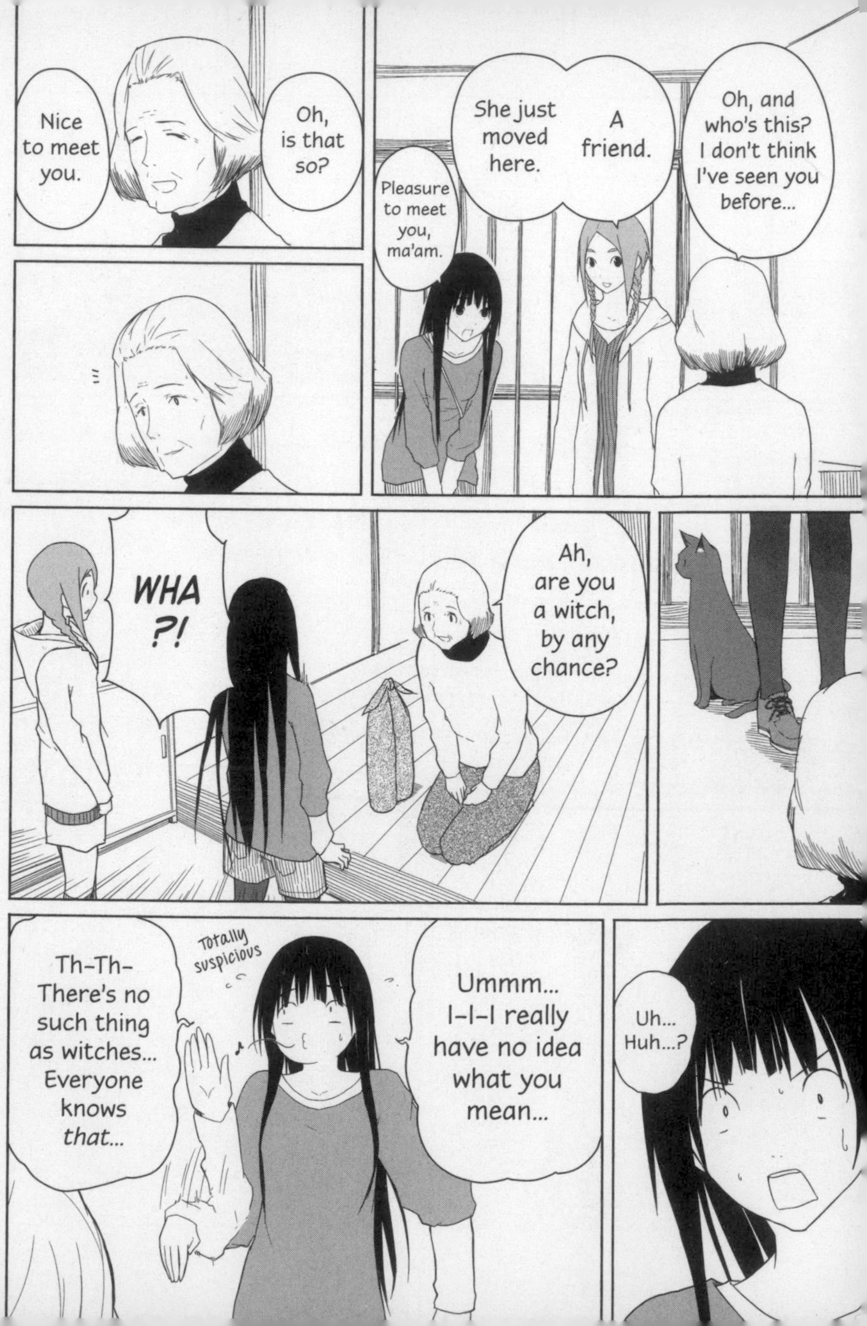
Oh, and who's this? I don't think I've seen you before...
A friend.
She just moved here.
Pleasure to meet you, ma'am.
Oh, is that so?
Nice to meet you.
Ah, are you a witch, by any chance?
WHA ?!
Uh... Huh...?
Ummm... I-I-I really have no idea what you mean...
Totally suspicious
Th-Th- There's no such thing as witches... Everyone knows *that*...

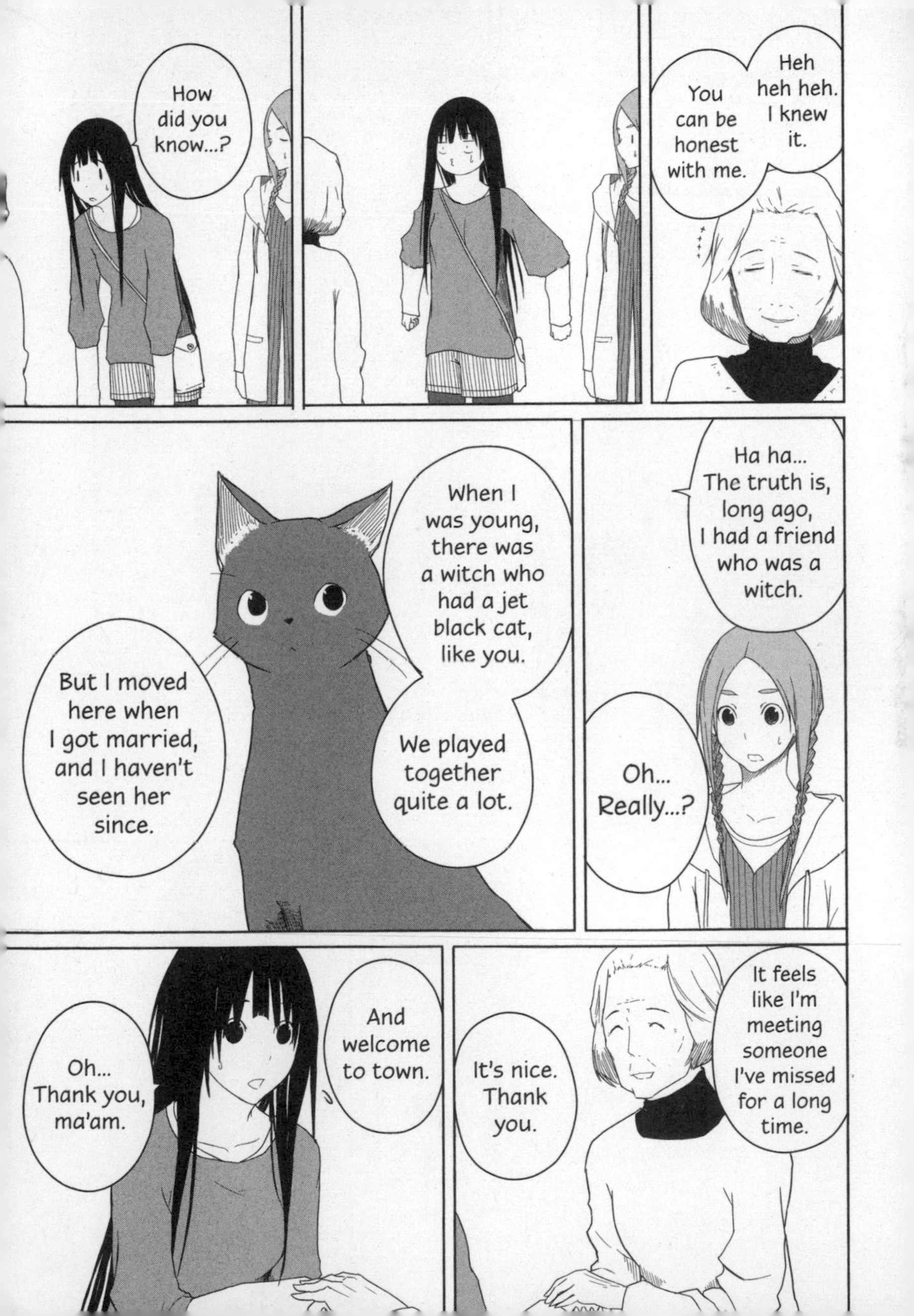
Heh heh heh. I knew it.
You can be honest with me.
How did you know...?
Ha ha... The truth is, long ago, I had a friend who was a witch.
Oh... Really...?
When I was young, there was a witch who had a jet black cat, like you.
We played together quite a lot.
But I moved here when I got married, and I haven't seen her since.
It feels like I'm meeting someone I've missed for a long time.
It's nice. Thank you.
And welcome to town.
Oh... Thank you, ma'am.

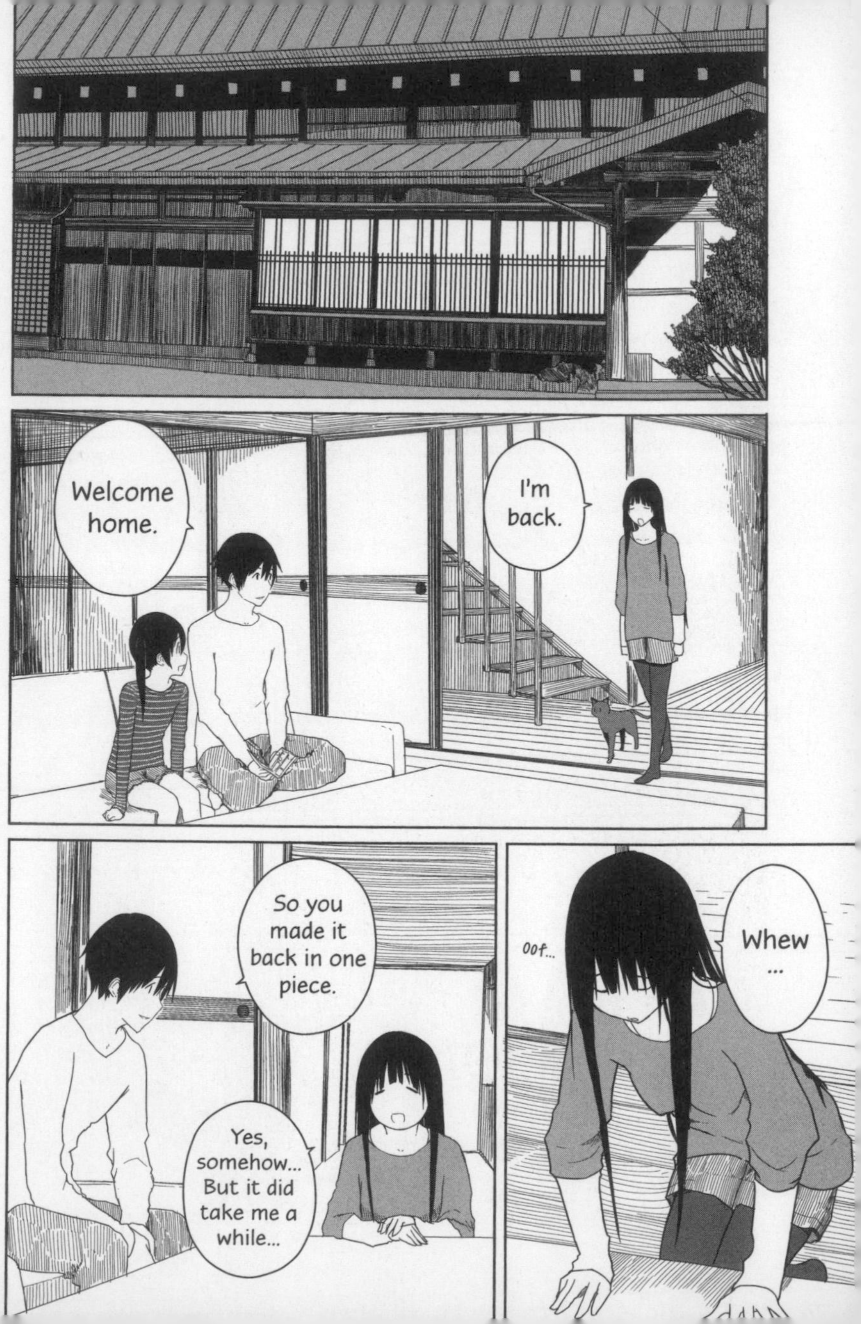
I'm back.
Welcome home.
Whew ...
Oof...
So you made it back in one piece.
Yes, somehow... But it did take me a while...

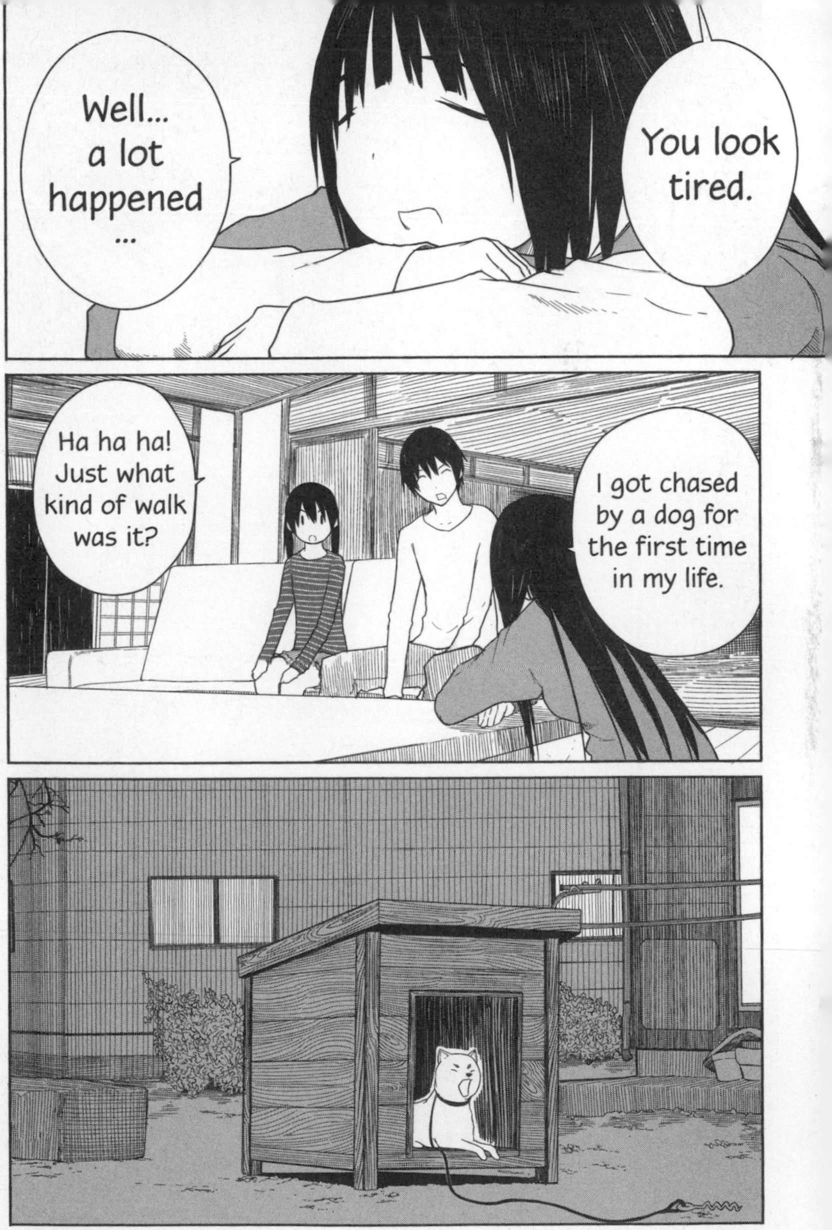
You look tired.
Well... a lot happened...
I got chased by a dog for the first time in my life.
Ha ha ha! Just what kind of walk was it?

Chapter 5
A Visitor for the Witch

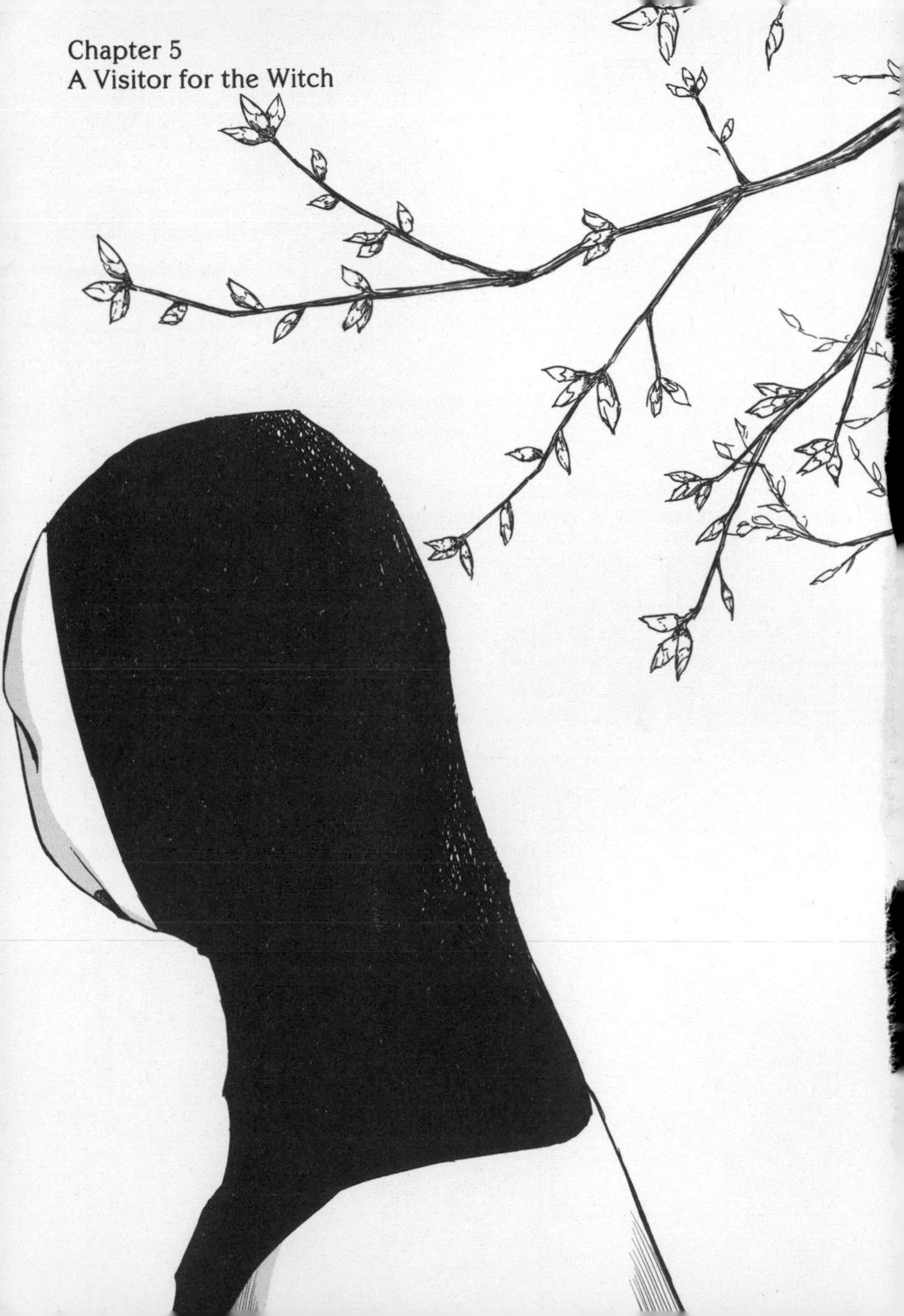

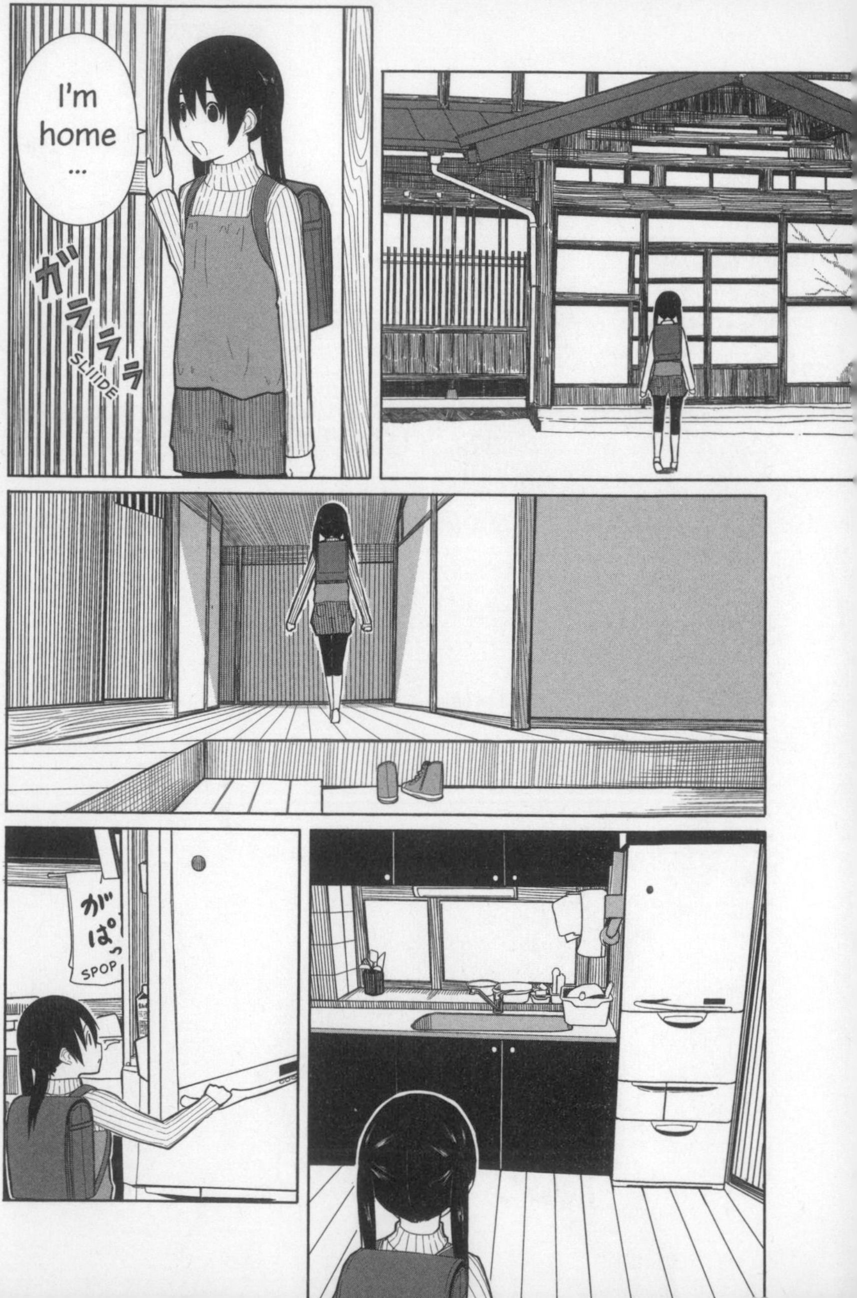
I'm home ...
ガラララ
SLIIIDE
がぱっ
SPOP

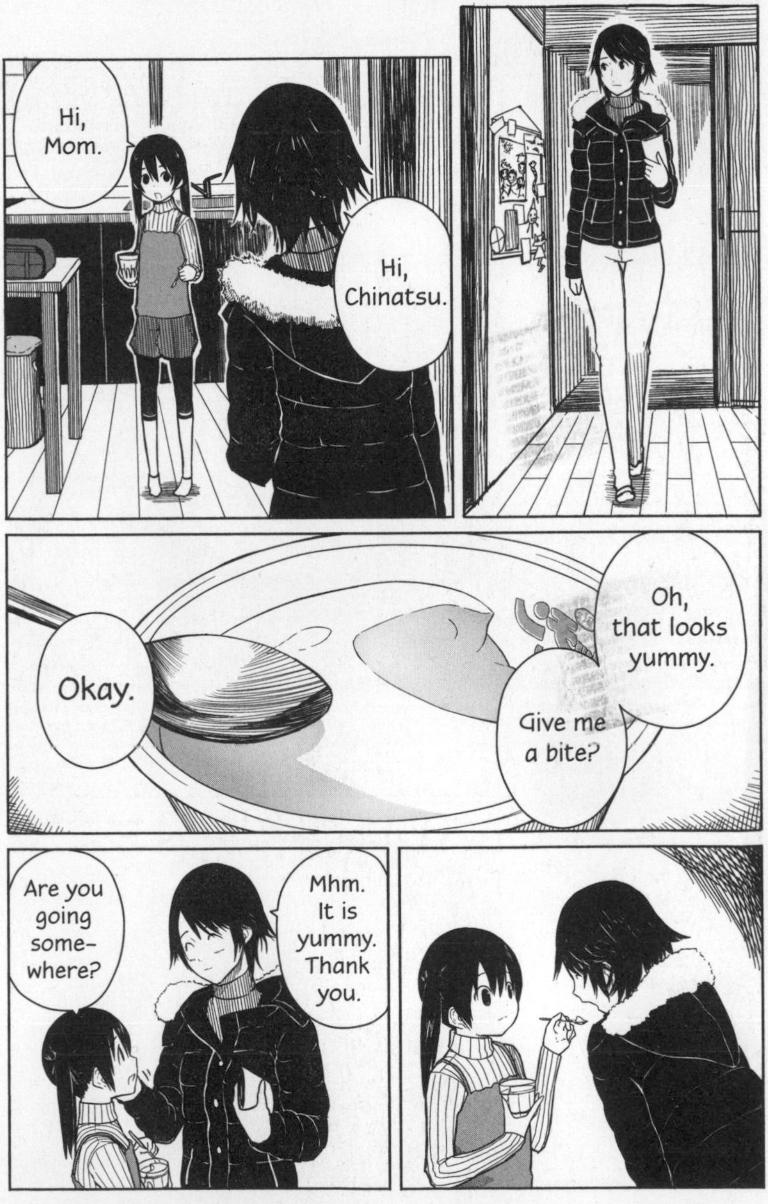
Hi, Mom.
Hi, Chinatsu.
Oh, that looks yummy.
Give me a bite?
Okay.
Mhm. It is yummy. Thank you.
Are you going some-where?

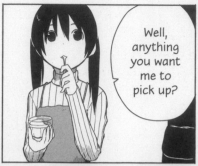

Yup. Groceries for dinner.
Want to come, Chinatsu?
Nah. I'll stay in. There's a show I wanna watch.
Well, anything you want me to pick up?
Uhm...
Ah! Pudding!
What? Aren't you eating some right now?
For Kei and Makoto!
Oh, I see!
Isn't that sweet of you!

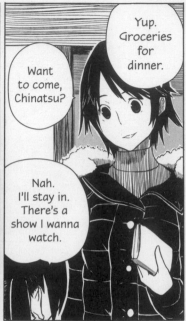

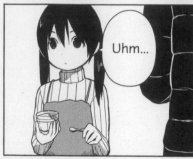

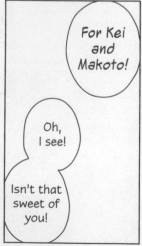

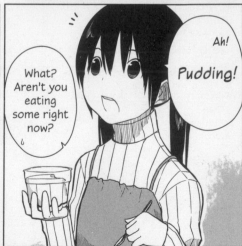

I'M BACK!

ガラララ
SLIII-DE

...Hi.

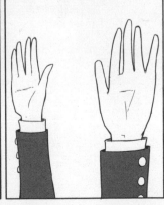

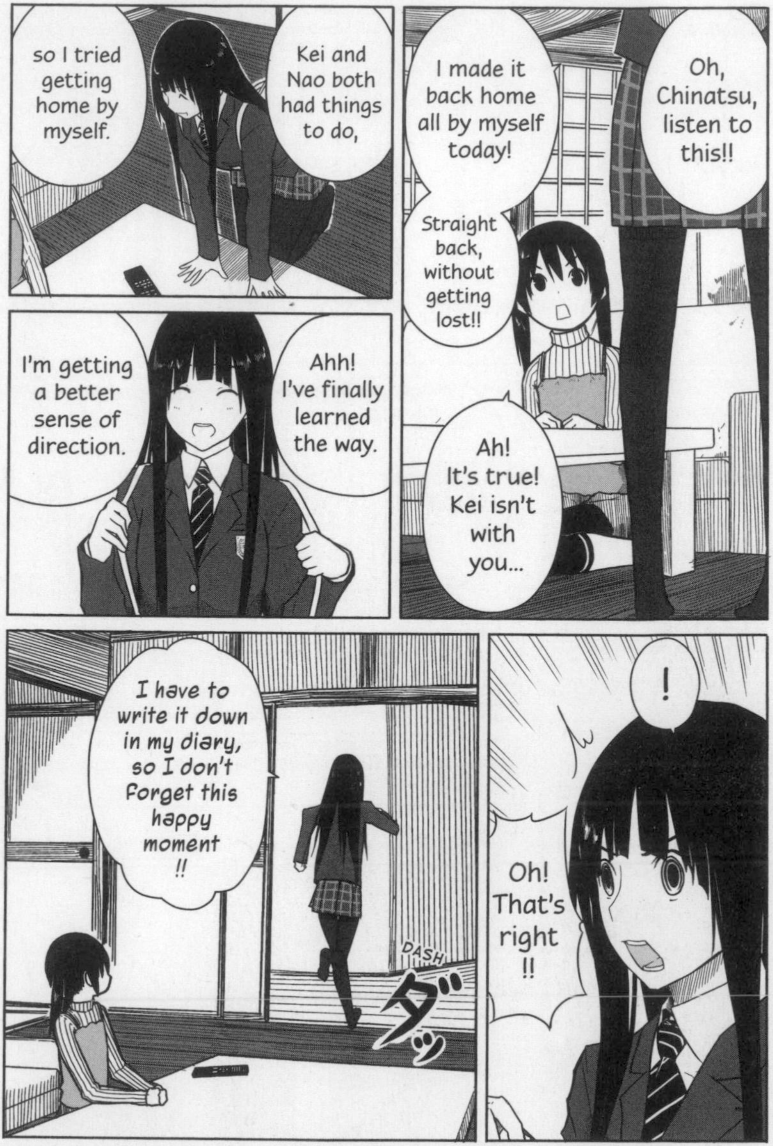
Oh, Chinatsu, listen to this!!
I made it back home all by myself today!
Straight back, without getting lost!!
Ah! It's true! Kei isn't with you...
Kei and Nao both had things to do,
so I tried getting home by myself.
Ahh! I've finally learned the way.
I'm getting a better sense of direction.
!
Oh! That's right !!
I have to write it down in my diary, so I don't forget this happy moment !!
DASH

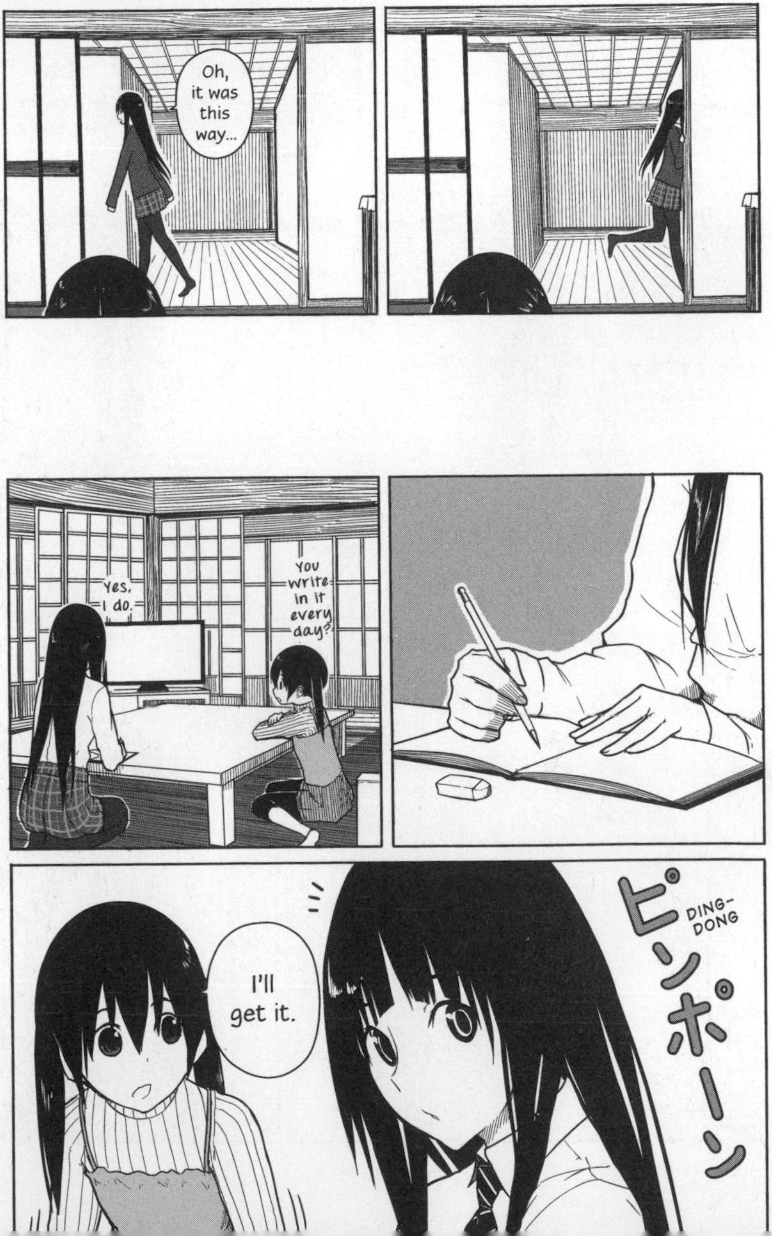
Oh, it was this way...
You write in it every day?
Yes, I do.
ピンポーン
DING-DONG
I'll get it.

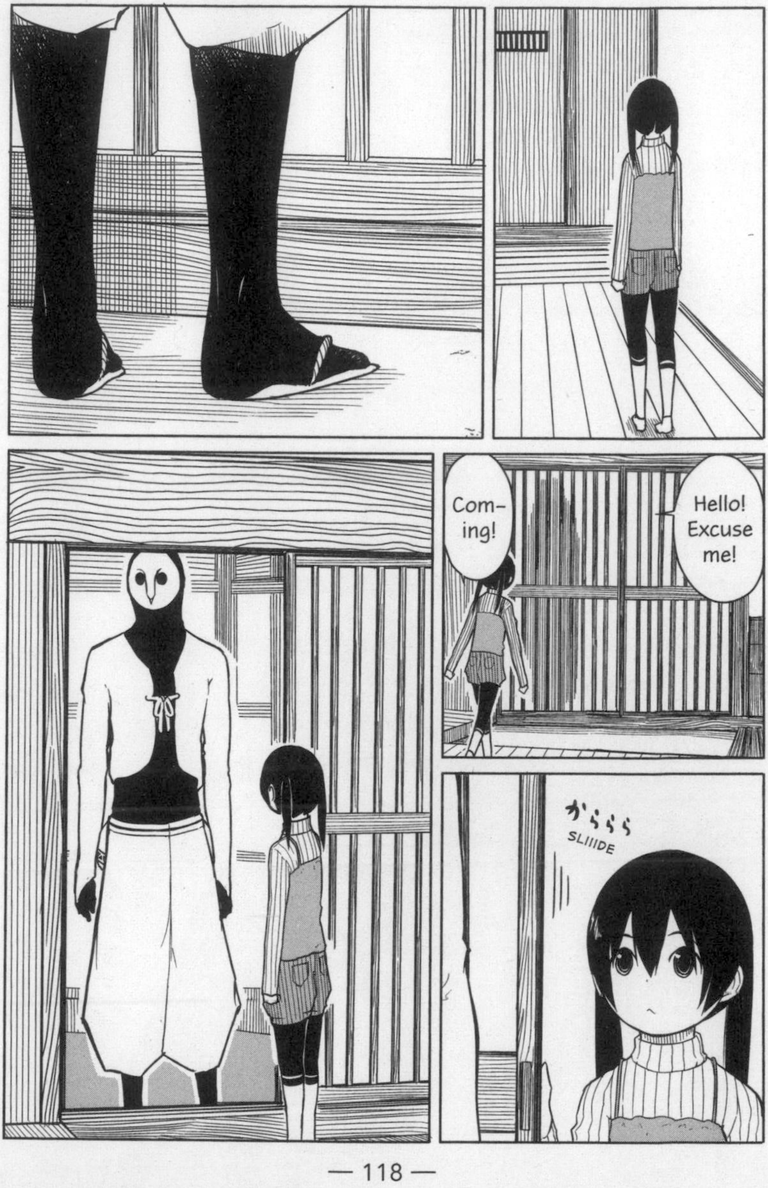
Hello! Excuse me!
Com-ing!
からららら
SLIIIDE

Hello there.

Oh.

SLAM

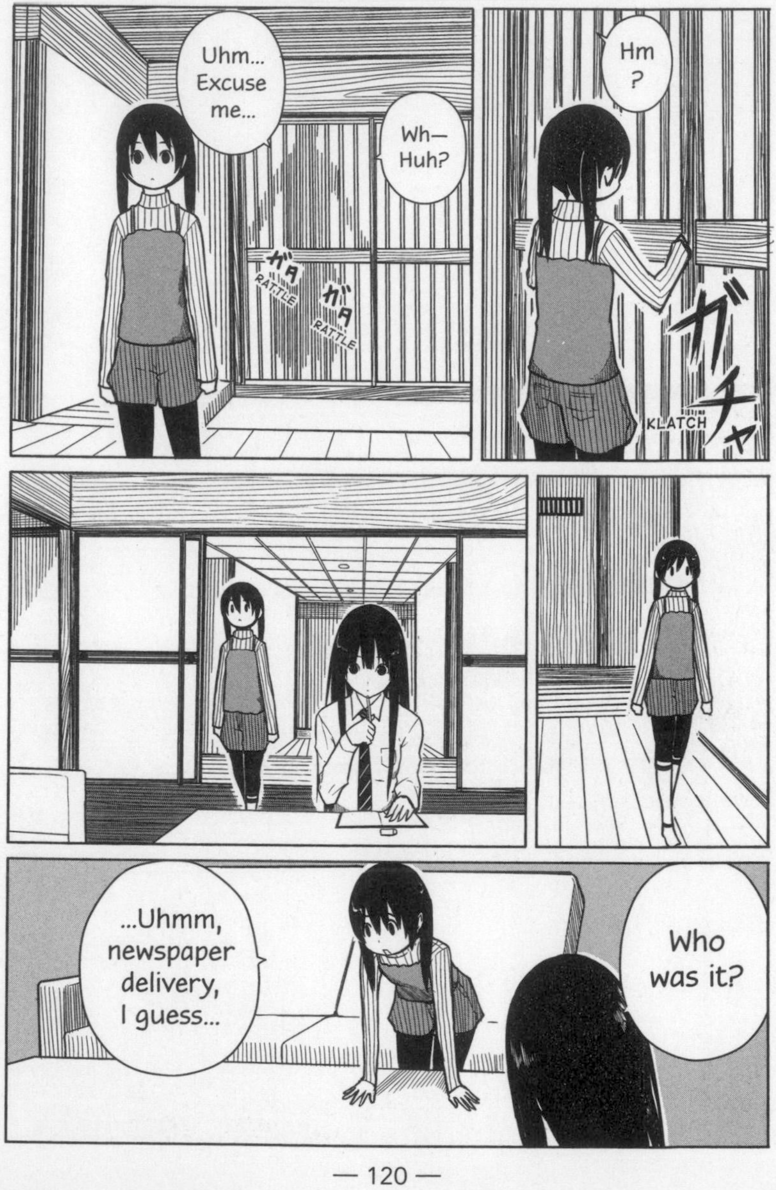
Hm ?
ガチャ
KLATCH
Uhm... Excuse me...
Wh— Huh?
ガタ
RATTLE
ガタ
RATTLE
Who was it?
...Uhmm, newspaper delivery, I guess...

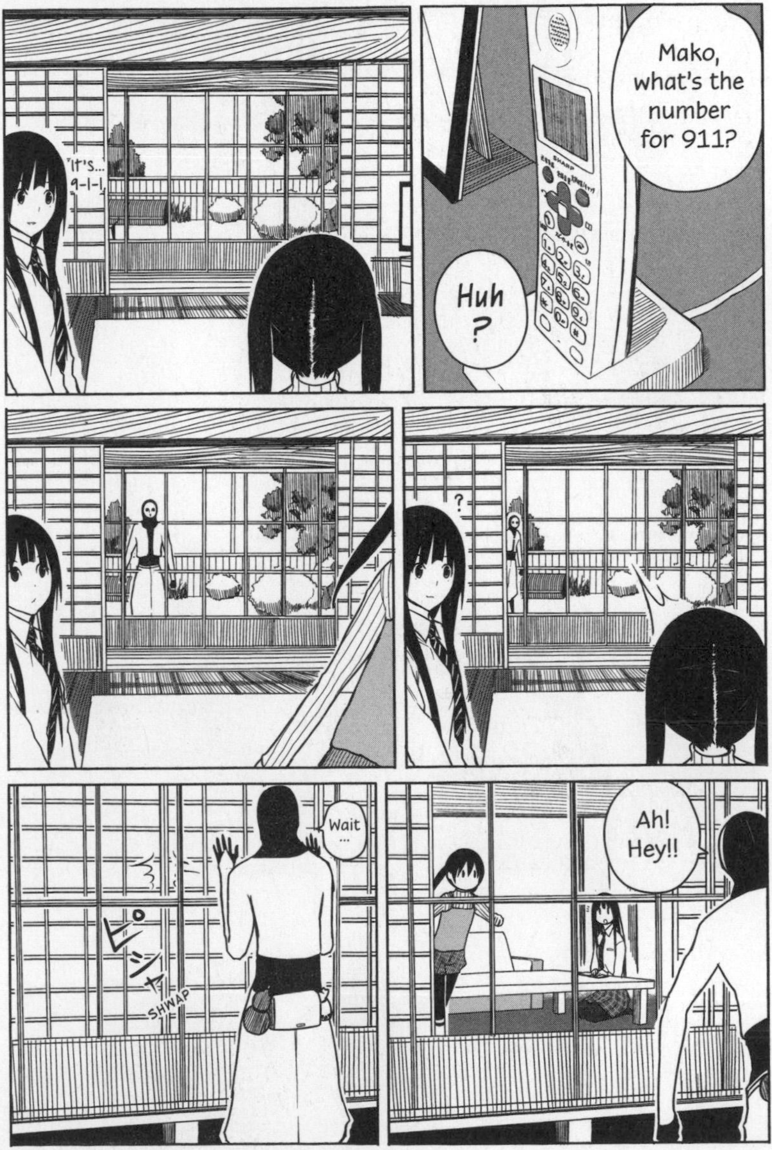
Mako, what's the number for 911?
Huh?
It's... 9-1-1.
?
Ah! Hey!!
Wait...
ピシャ
SHWAP

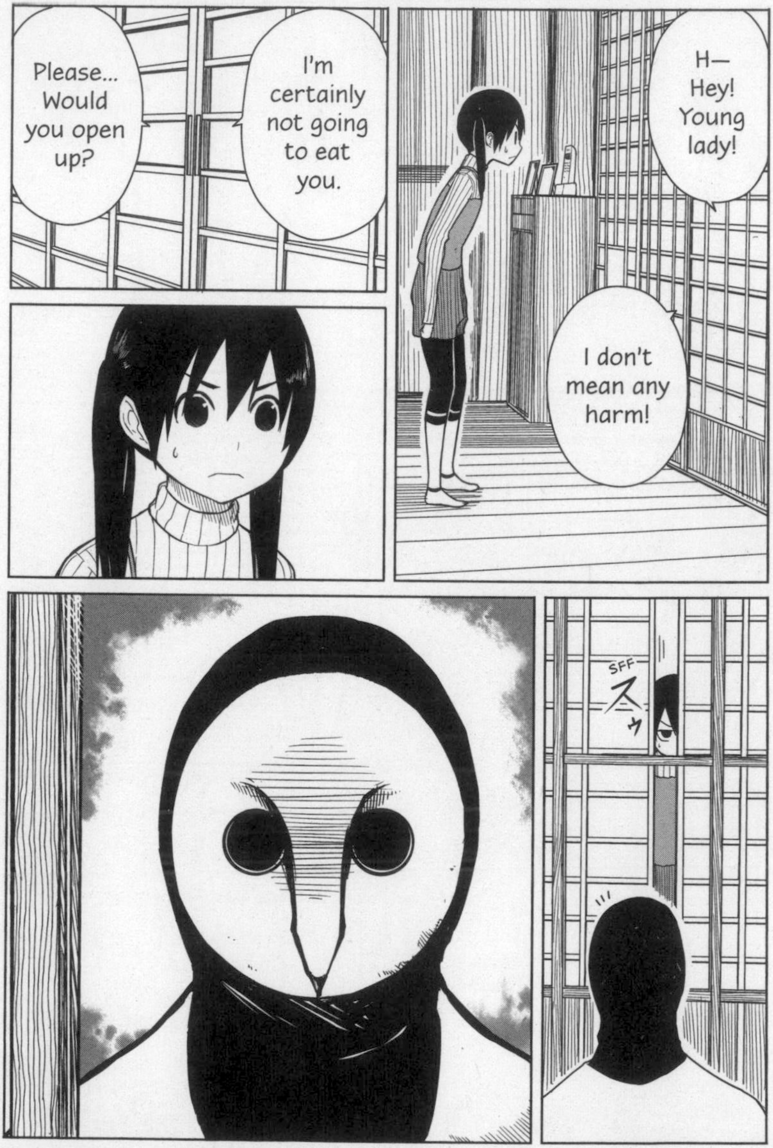
H—
Hey! Young lady!
I don't mean any harm!
I'm certainly not going to eat you.
Please... Would you open up?
SFF
スゥ

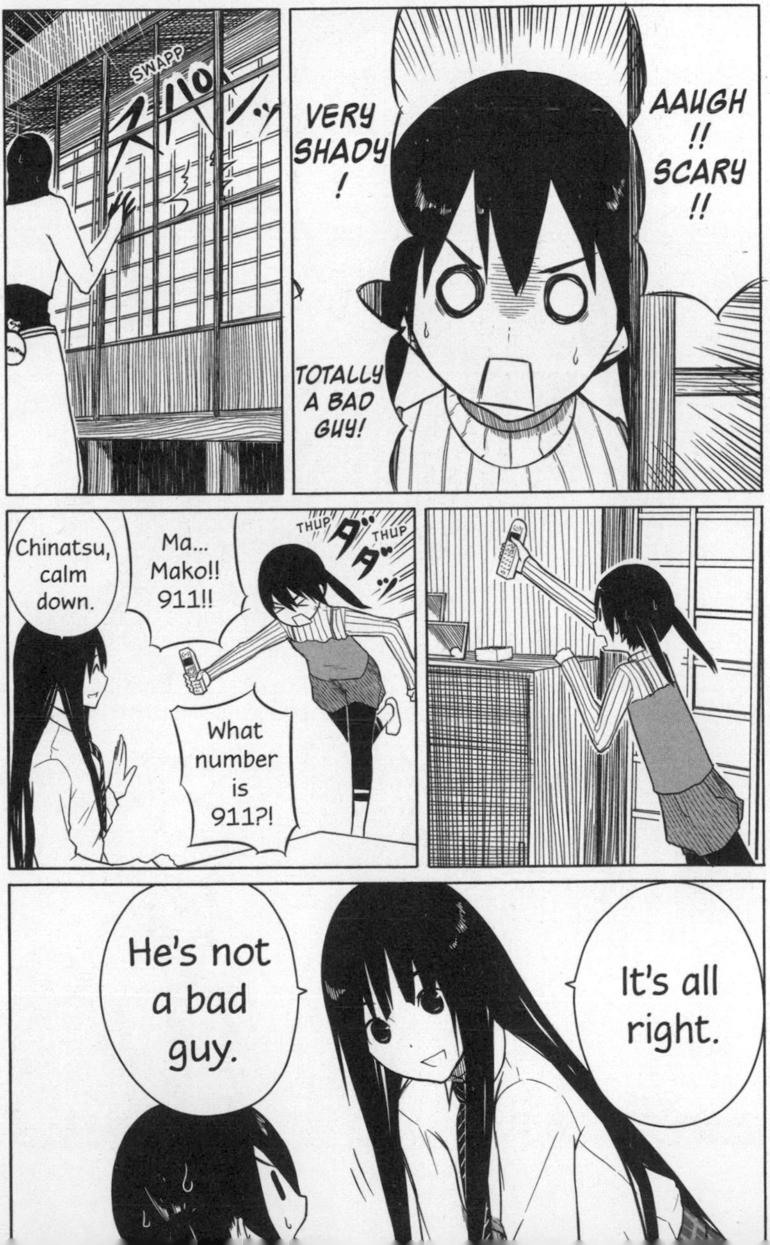
AAUGH!! SCARY!!
VERY SHADY!
TOTALLY A BAD GUY!
SWAPP
THUP THUP
Ma... Mako!! 911!!
Chinatsu, calm down.
What number is 911?!
It's all right.
He's not a bad guy.

Huh?
Now what do I do...
I heard this was the place, but...
カララ
SLIDE
Oh, I thought so.
Hello!
Oh!
You're the Harbinger, right?
Yeah! That's me!
So if you know who I am, you must be the witch who moved here not too long ago, right?
Yes, that's right.

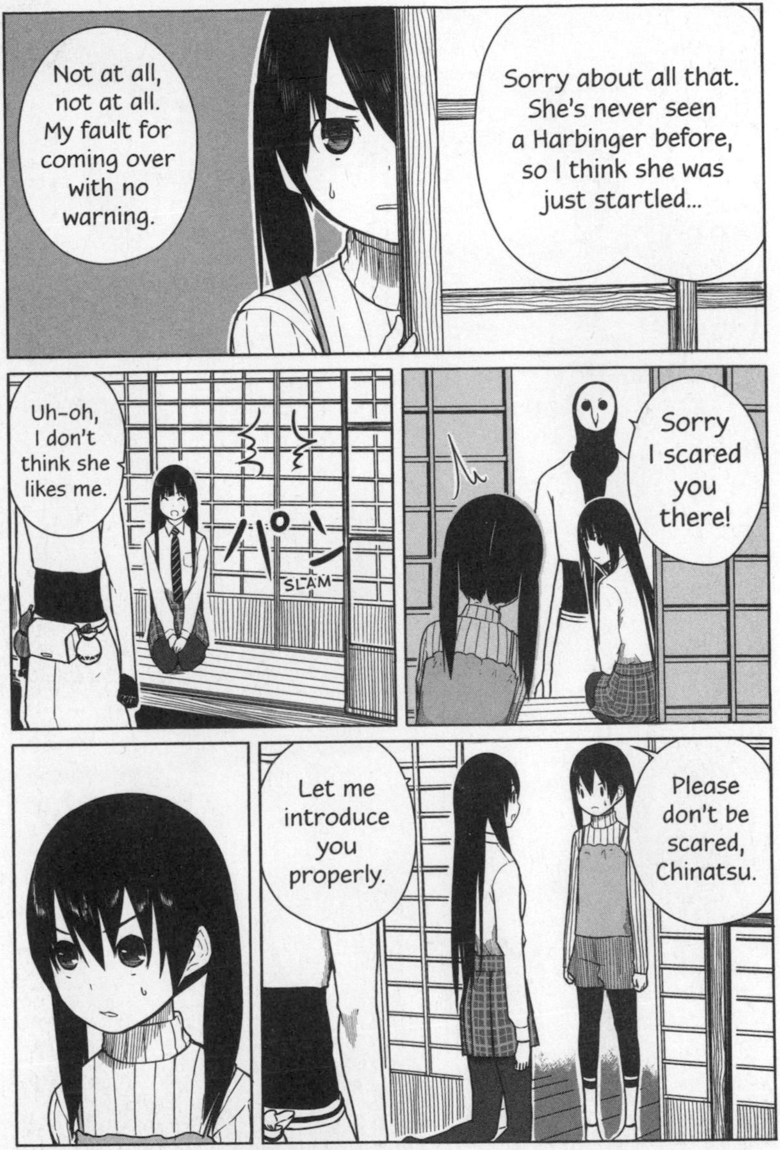
Sorry about all that. She's never seen a Harbinger before, so I think she was just startled...
Not at all, not at all. My fault for coming over with no warning.
Sorry I scared you there!
パン
SLAM
Uh-oh, I don't think she likes me.
Please don't be scared, Chinatsu.
Let me introduce you properly.

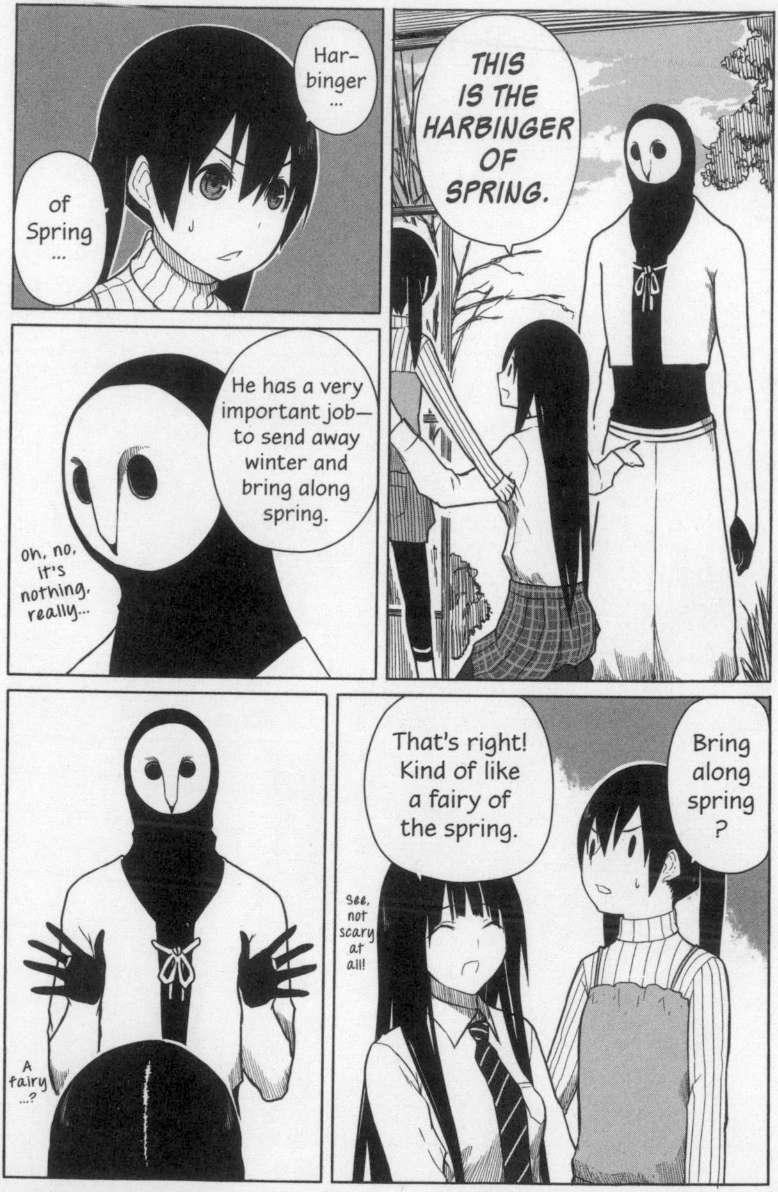
THIS IS THE HARBINGER OF SPRING.
Har-binger ...
of Spring ...
He has a very important job—to send away winter and bring along spring.
oh, no, it's nothing, really...
Bring along spring ?
That's right! Kind of like a fairy of the spring.
See, not scary at all!
A fairy ...?

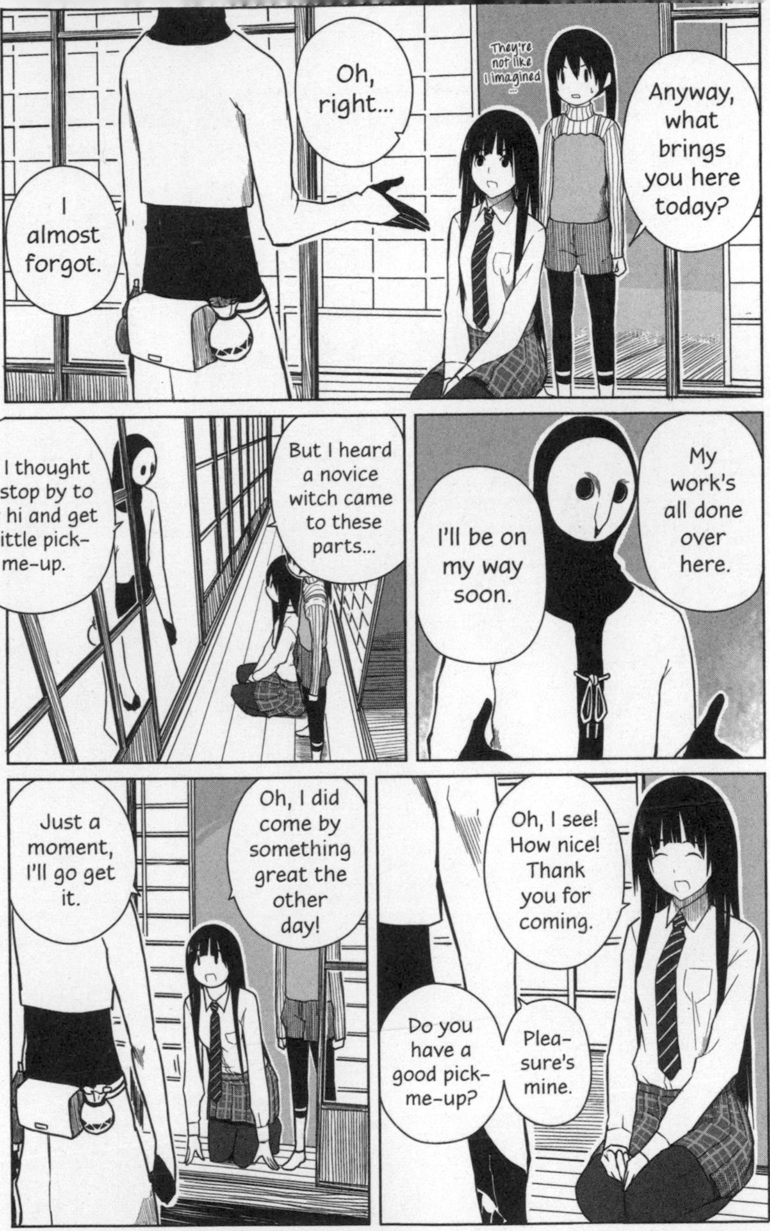
Anyway, what brings you here today?
They're not like I imagined...
Oh, right...
I almost forgot.
My work's all done over here.
I'll be on my way soon.
But I heard a novice witch came to these parts...
so I thought I'd stop by to say hi and get a little pick-me-up.
Oh, I see! How nice! Thank you for coming.
Pleasure's mine.
Do you have a good pick-me-up?
Oh, I did come by something great the other day!
Just a moment, I'll go get it.

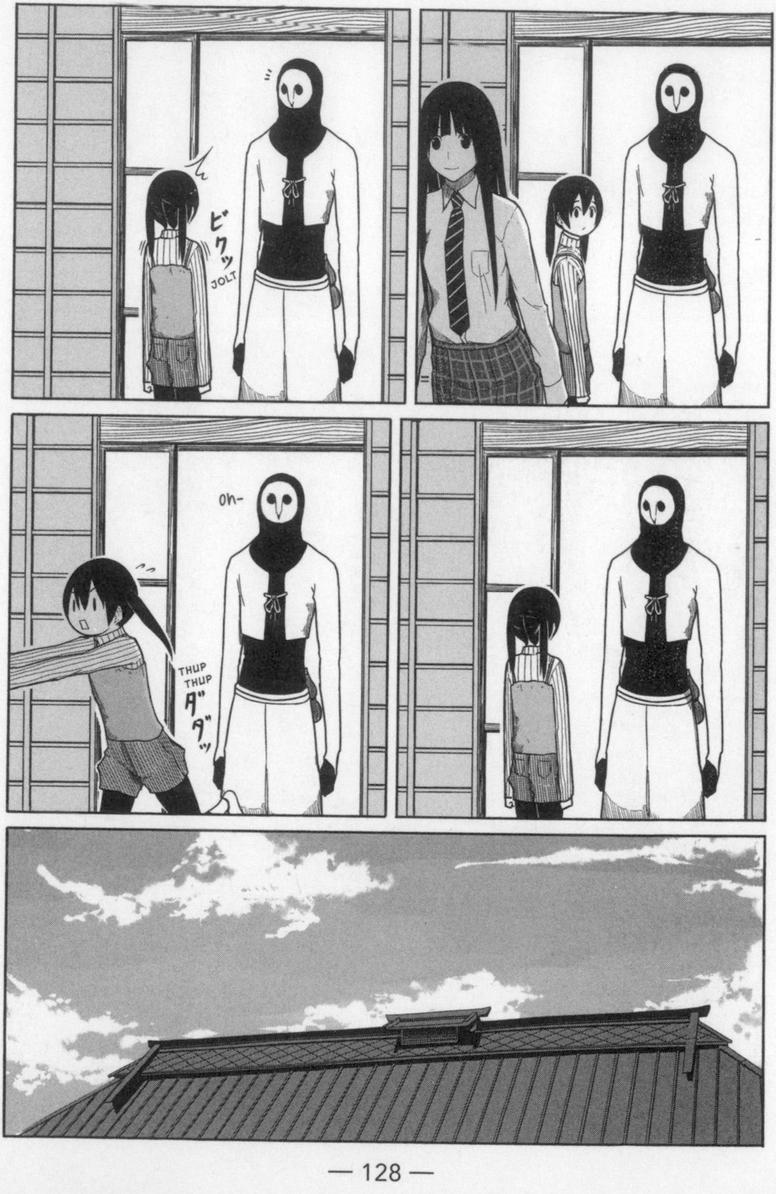
ビクッ
JOLT
oh-
THUP THUP
ダダッ

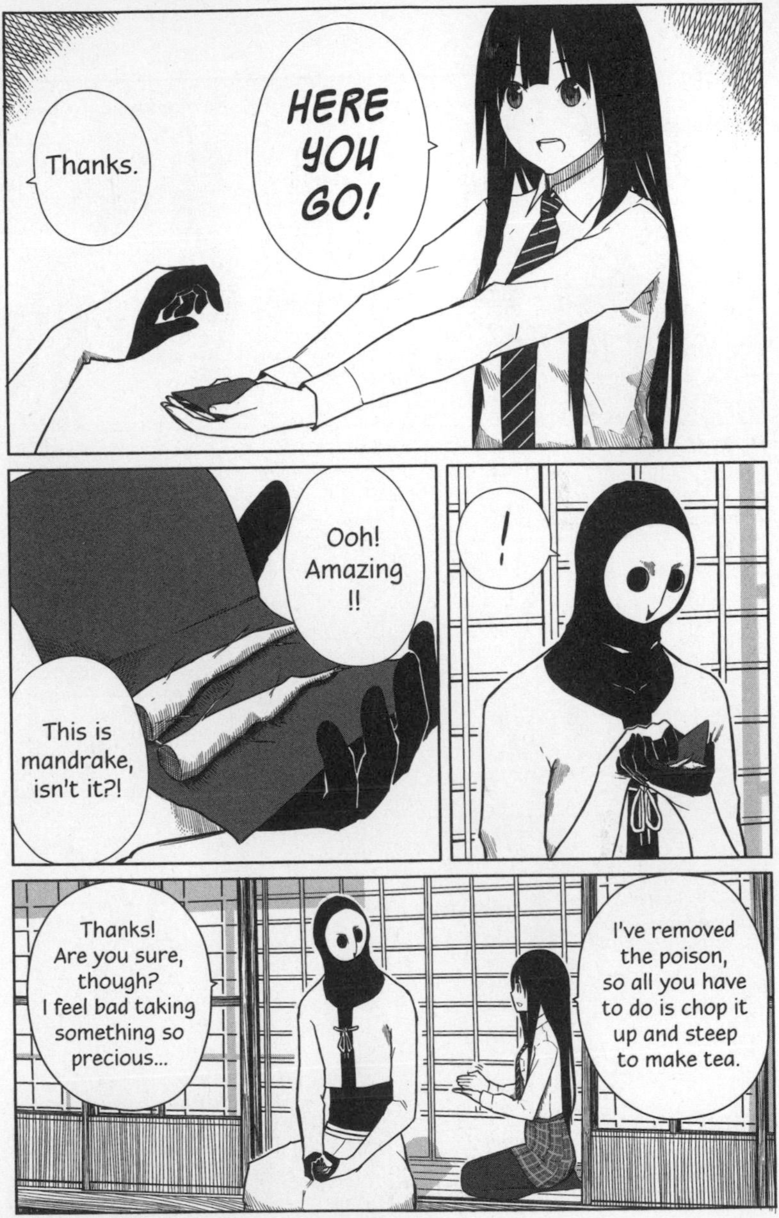
HERE YOU GO!
Thanks.
!
Ooh! Amazing !!
This is mandrake, isn't it?!
I've removed the poison, so all you have to do is chop it up and steep to make tea.
Thanks! Are you sure, though? I feel bad taking something so precious...

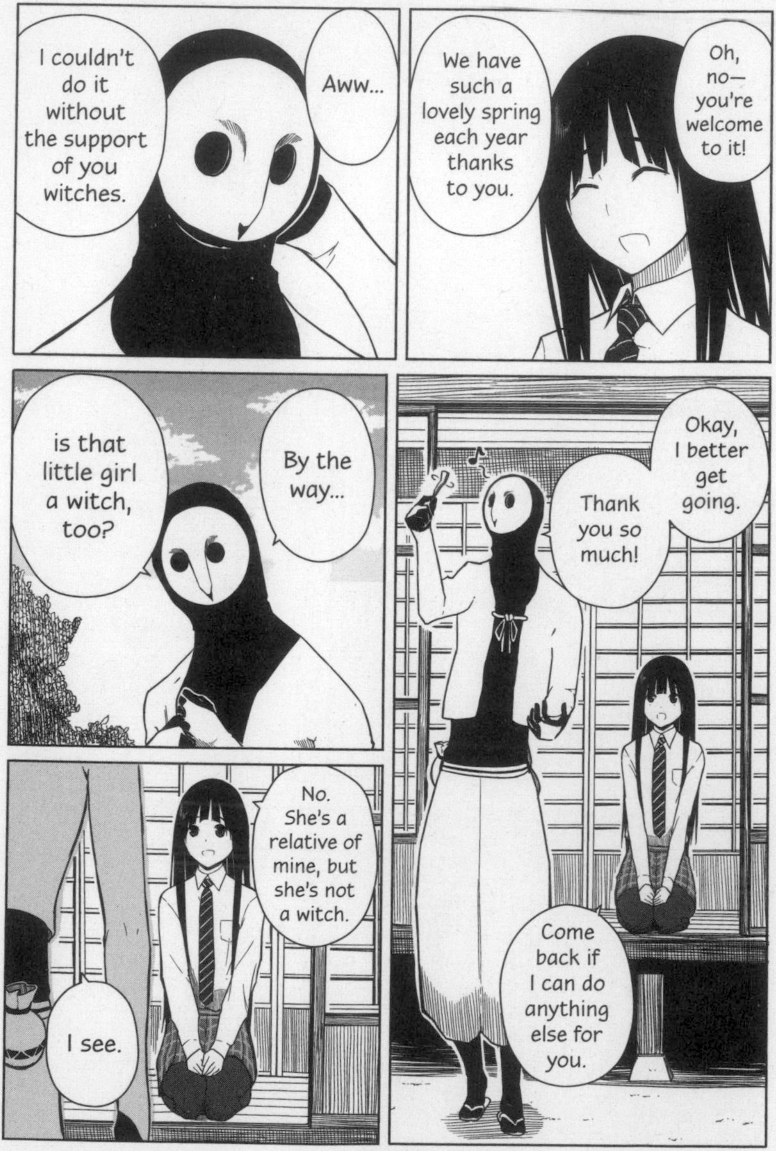
Oh, no— you're welcome to it!
We have such a lovely spring each year thanks to you.
Aww...
I couldn't do it without the support of you witches.
Okay, I better get going.
Thank you so much!
Come back if I can do anything else for you.
By the way...
is that little girl a witch, too?
No. She's a relative of mine, but she's not a witch.
I see.

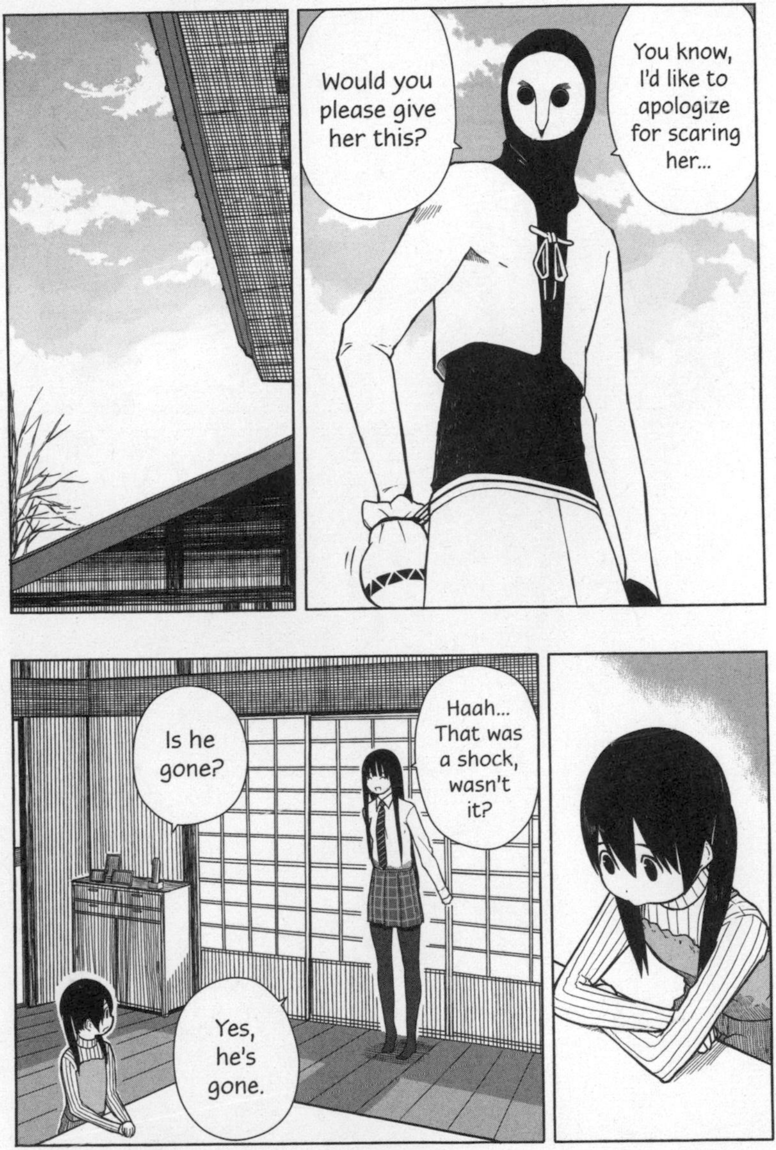
You know, I'd like to apologize for scaring her...
Would you please give her this?
Haah... That was a shock, wasn't it?
Is he gone?
Yes, he's gone.

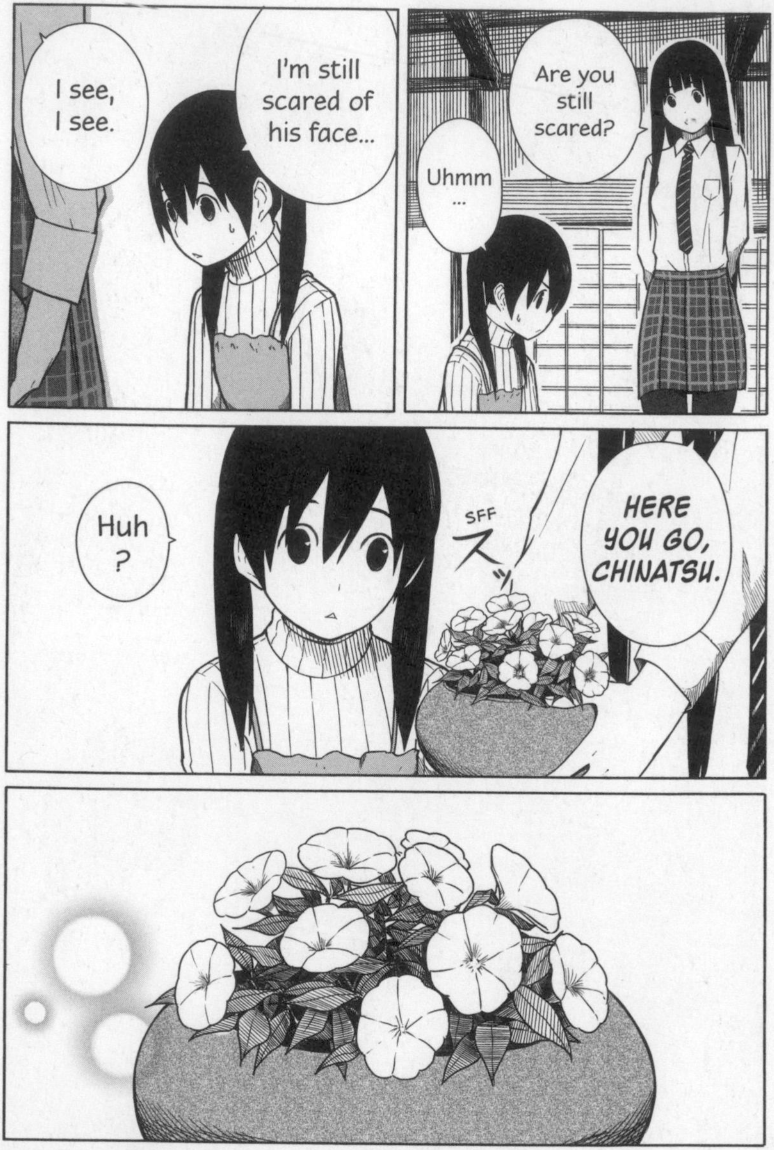
Are you still scared?
Uhmm ...
I'm still scared of his face...
I see, I see.
HERE YOU GO, CHINATSU.
SFF
スッ
Huh ?

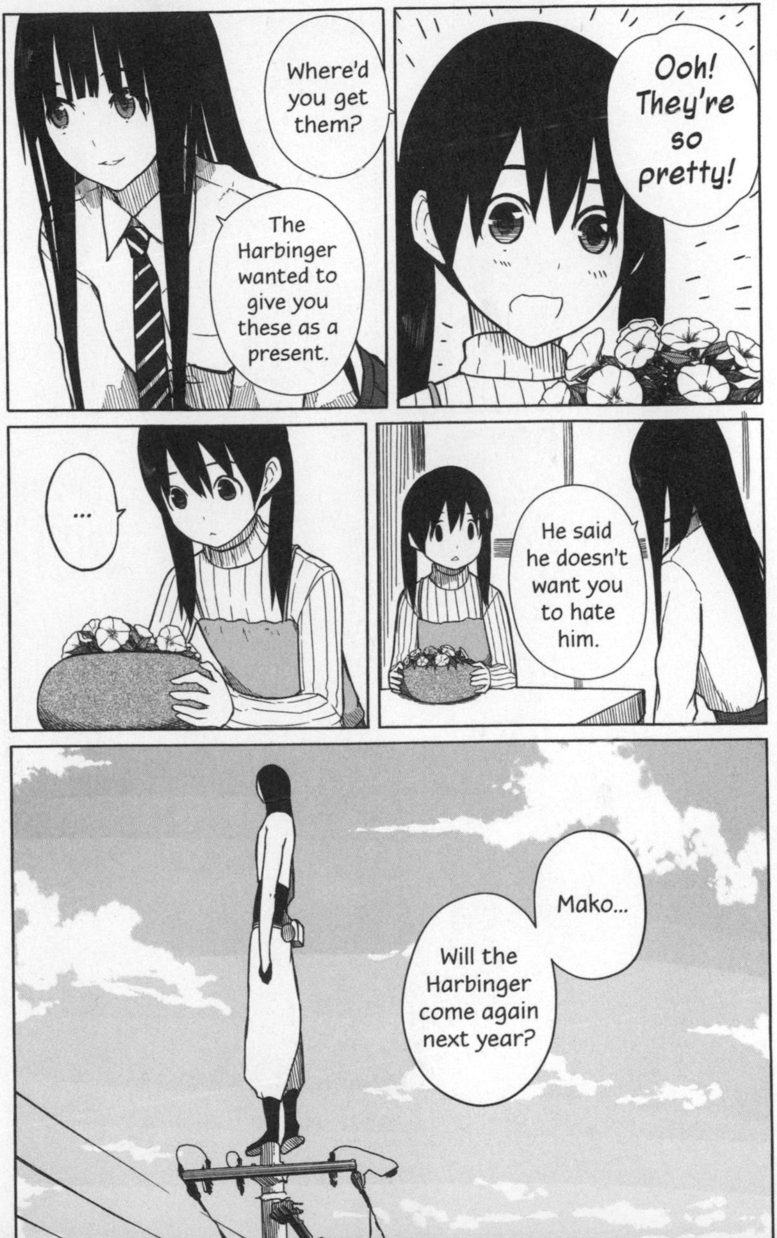
Ooh! They're so pretty!
Where'd you get them?
The Harbinger wanted to give you these as a present.
He said he doesn't want you to hate him.
...
Mako...
Will the Harbinger come again next year?

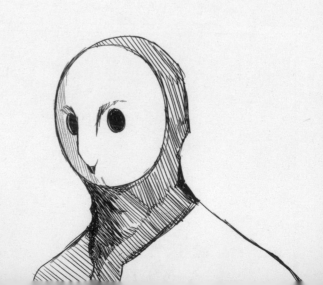

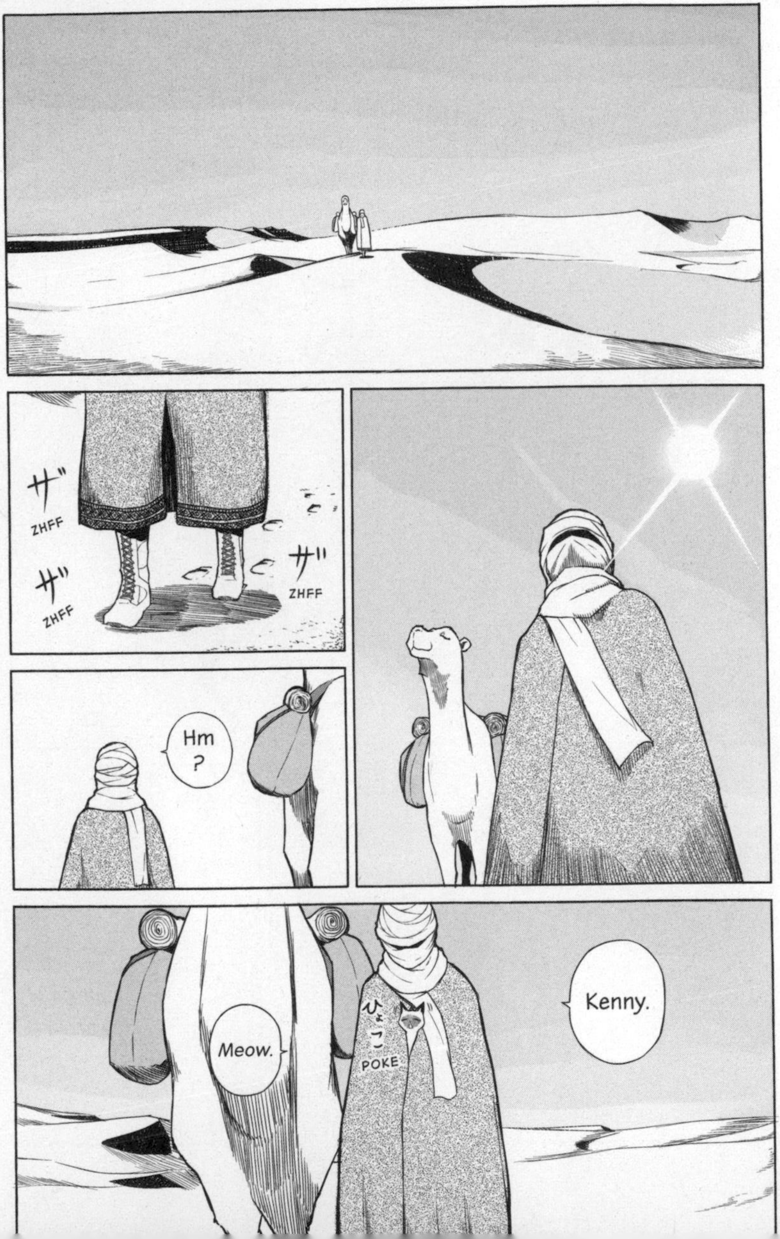
ザ
ZHFF
ザ
ZHFF
ザ
ZHFF
Hm?
Kenny.
ひょこ
POKE
Meow.

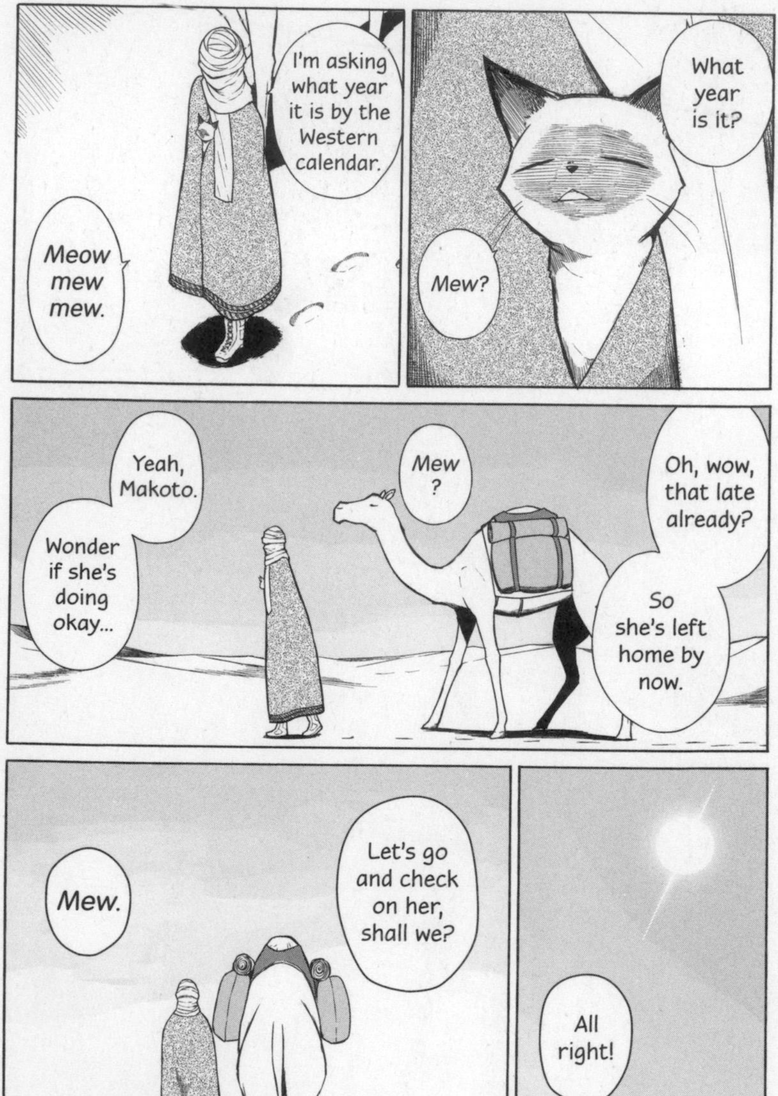
What year is it?
Mew?
I'm asking what year it is by the Western calendar.
Meow mew mew.
Oh, wow, that late already?
So she's left home by now.
Mew ?
Yeah, Makoto.
Wonder if she's doing okay...
All right!
Let's go and check on her, shall we?
Mew.

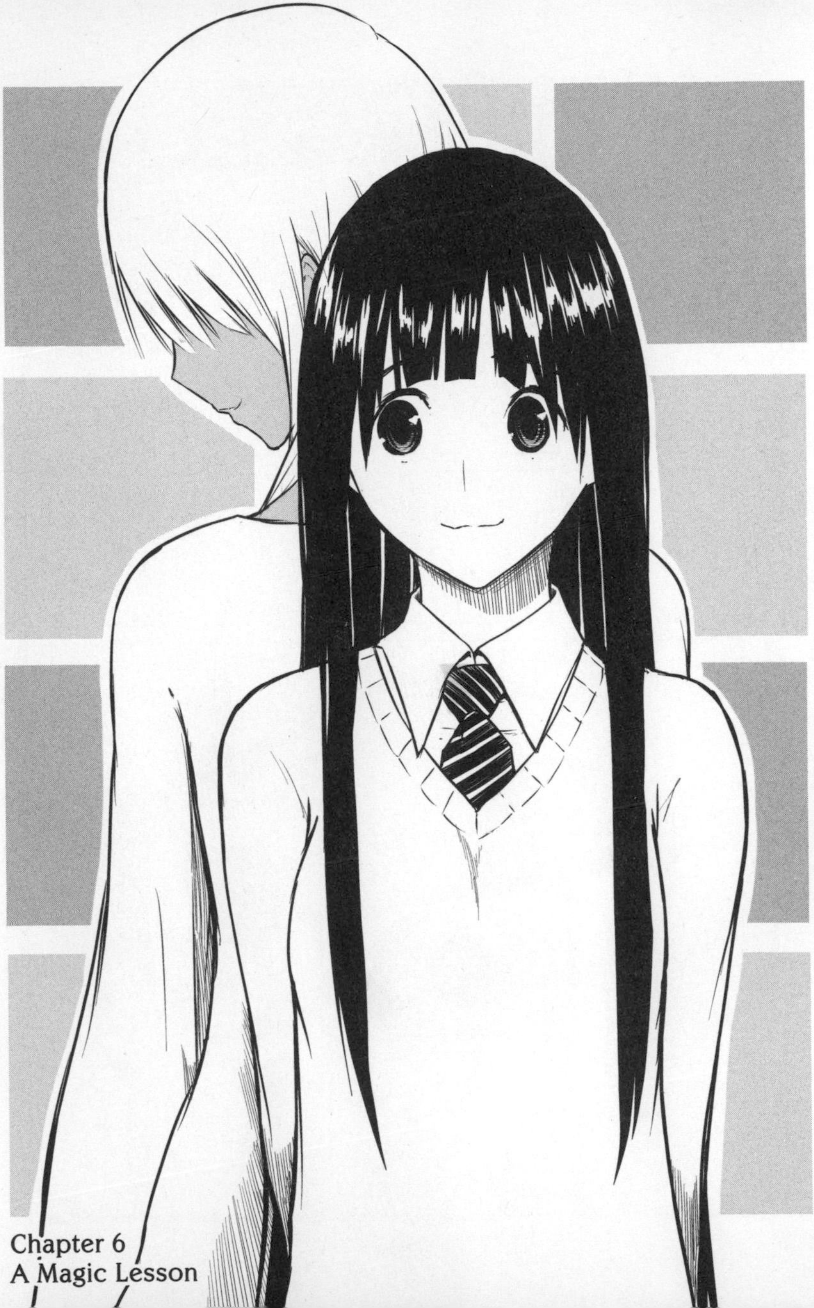

Chapter 6
A Magic Lesson

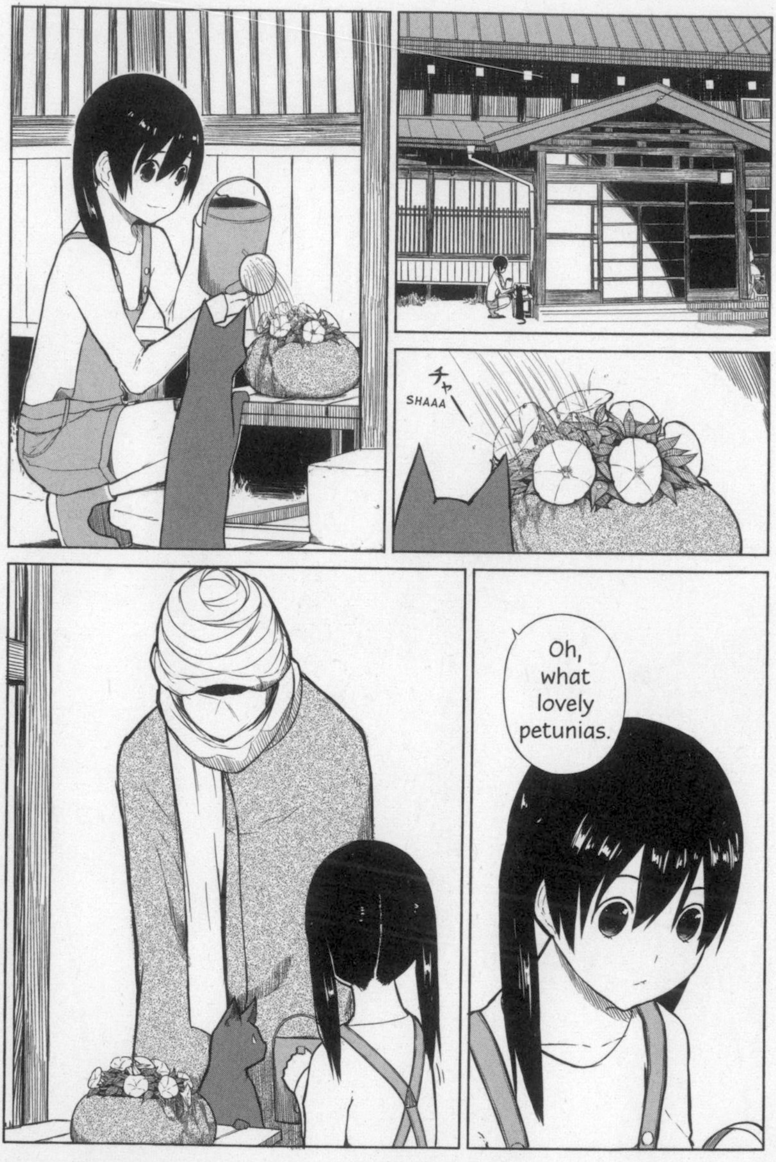
チャー
SHAAA
Oh, what lovely petunias.

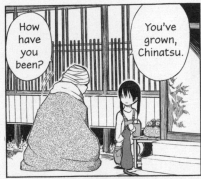

You've grown, Chinatsu.
How have you been?
Uhm, okay...
That's good to hear.
What about your mother?
My mom's home...
Is Makoto home?
No... Not yet.
All right. Then I'll just wait inside
until Makoto comes back.
This brings me back...
SLIIDE ガララ
Hello, Nana!
Yes ?
It's been a while !
Who are you?!
Another weird person...

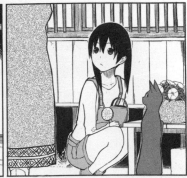

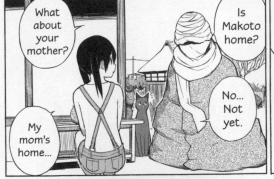

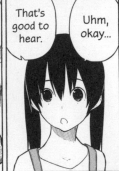

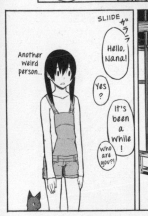

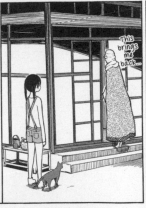

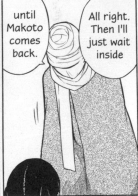

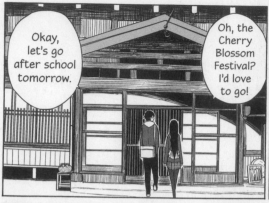

Oh, the Cherry Blossom Festival? I'd love to go!
Okay, let's go after school tomorrow.
Really? We can go on a weekday?
Wouldn't it be better on a weekend?
Nah, the Golden Week holidays are at the same time, so it'll be totally mobbed with tourists. It's no fun that way.
Oh, I see ...
テ TROT
テ
テ TROT
I haven't been to one since grade school...
How exciting!
Meow.
Oh, hello, Kenny.
It's been a long time.

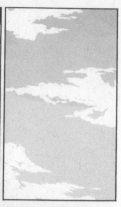

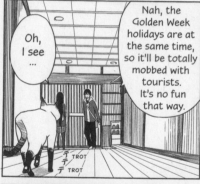

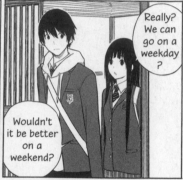

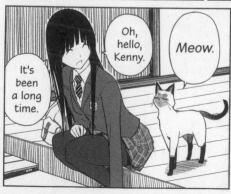

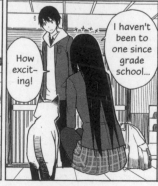

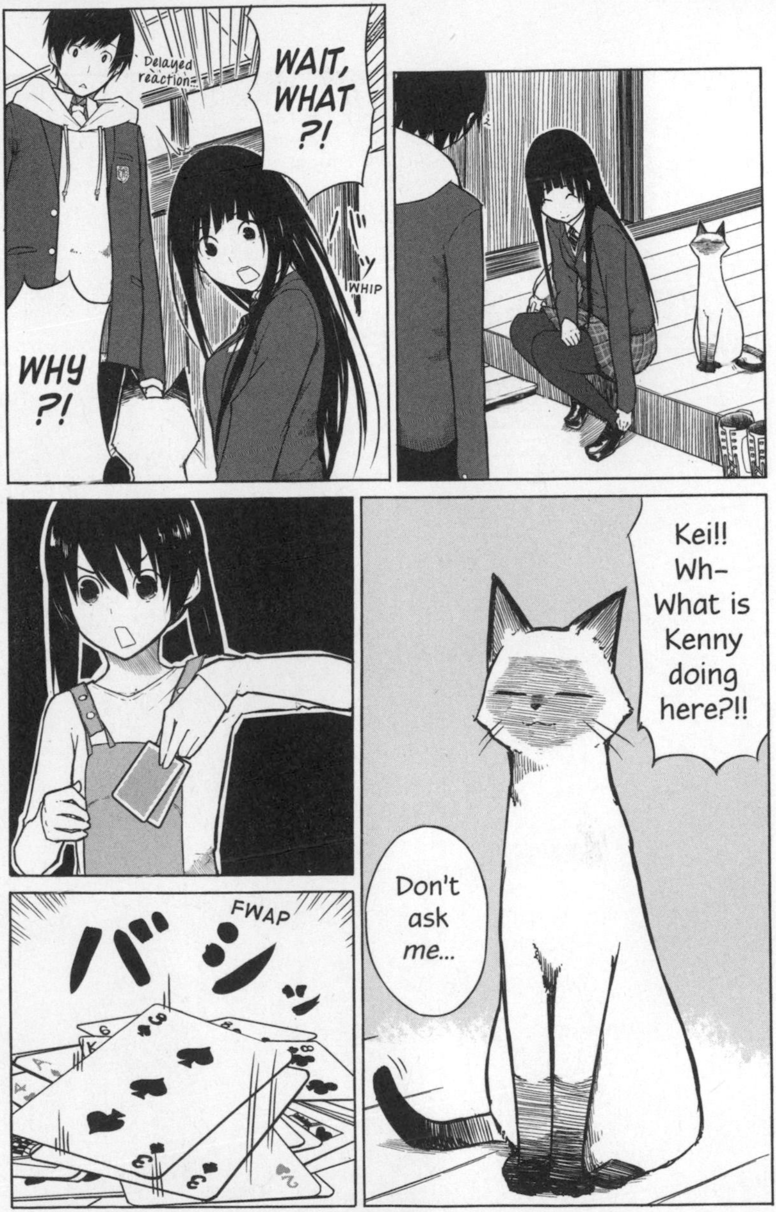
WAIT, WHAT ?!
Delayed reaction...
バッ
WHIP
WHY ?!
Kei!! Wh- What is Kenny doing here?!!
Don't ask me...
バシッ
FWAP

I win!!
Gah! You got me!
HUH? WHA?! NO WAY!!
SIS ?!!
Oh!
Hey, Makoto!

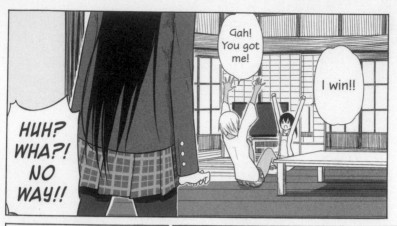

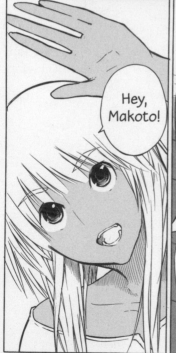

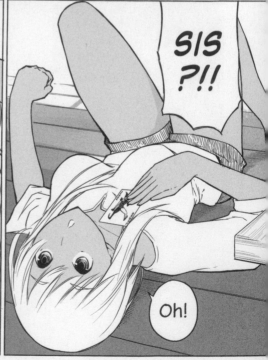

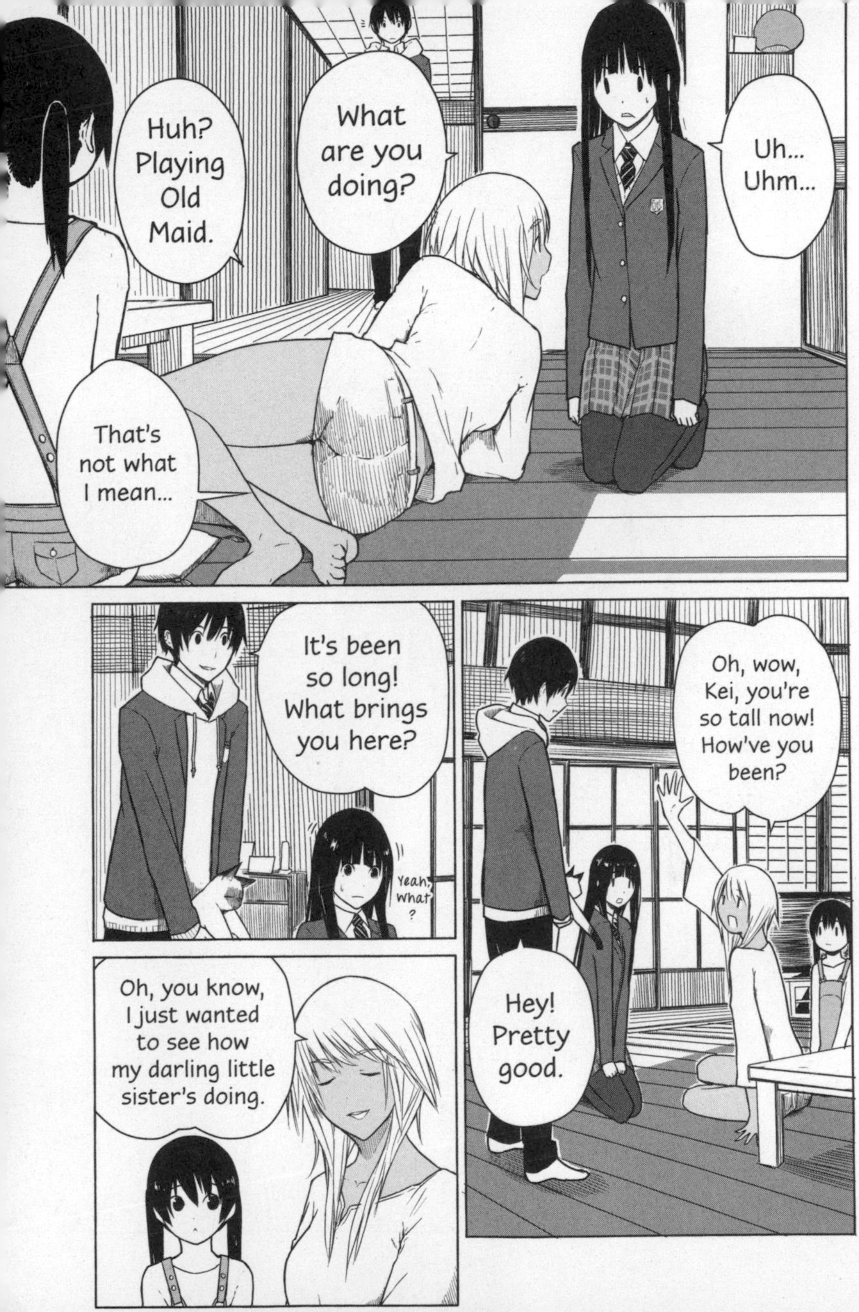
Uh... Uhm...
What are you doing?
Huh? Playing Old Maid.
That's not what I mean...
Oh, wow, Kei, you're so tall now! How've you been?
Hey! Pretty good.
It's been so long! What brings you here?
Yeah, what?
Oh, you know, I just wanted to see how my darling little sister's doing.

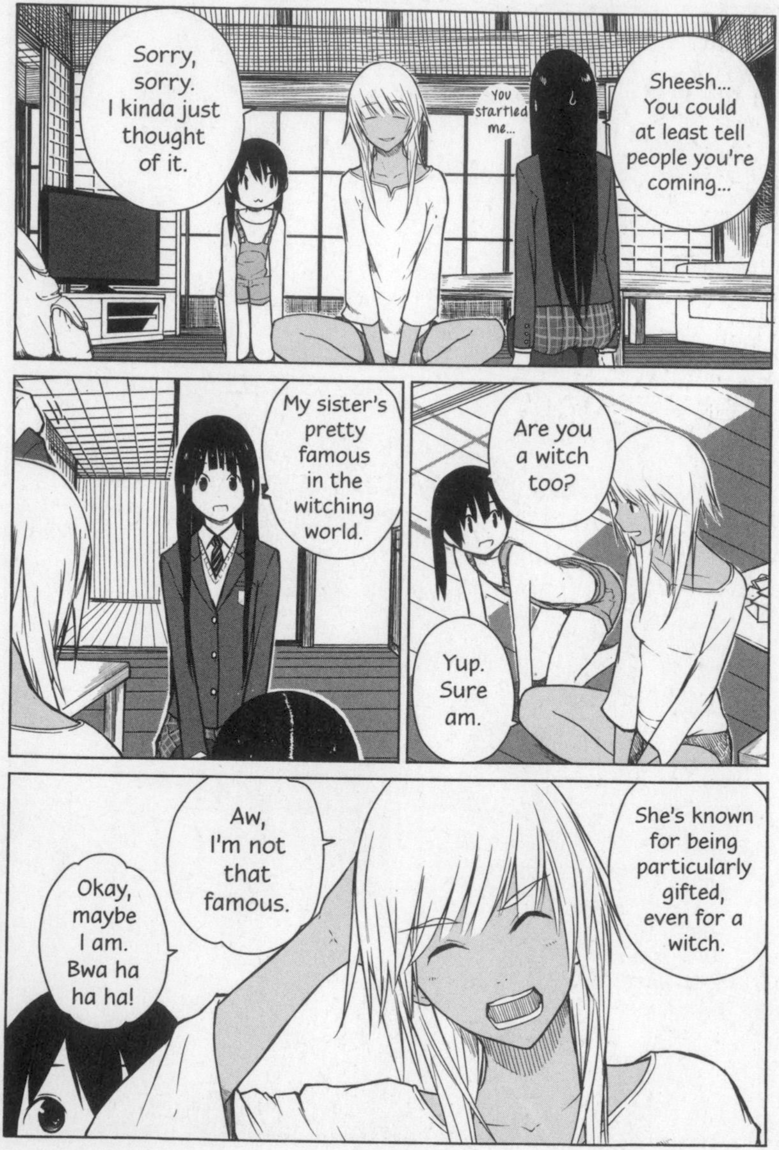
Sheesh... You could at least tell people you're coming...
You startled me...
Sorry, sorry. I kinda just thought of it.
Are you a witch too?
Yup. Sure am.
My sister's pretty famous in the witching world.
She's known for being particularly gifted, even for a witch.
Aw, I'm not that famous.
Okay, maybe I am. Bwa ha ha ha!

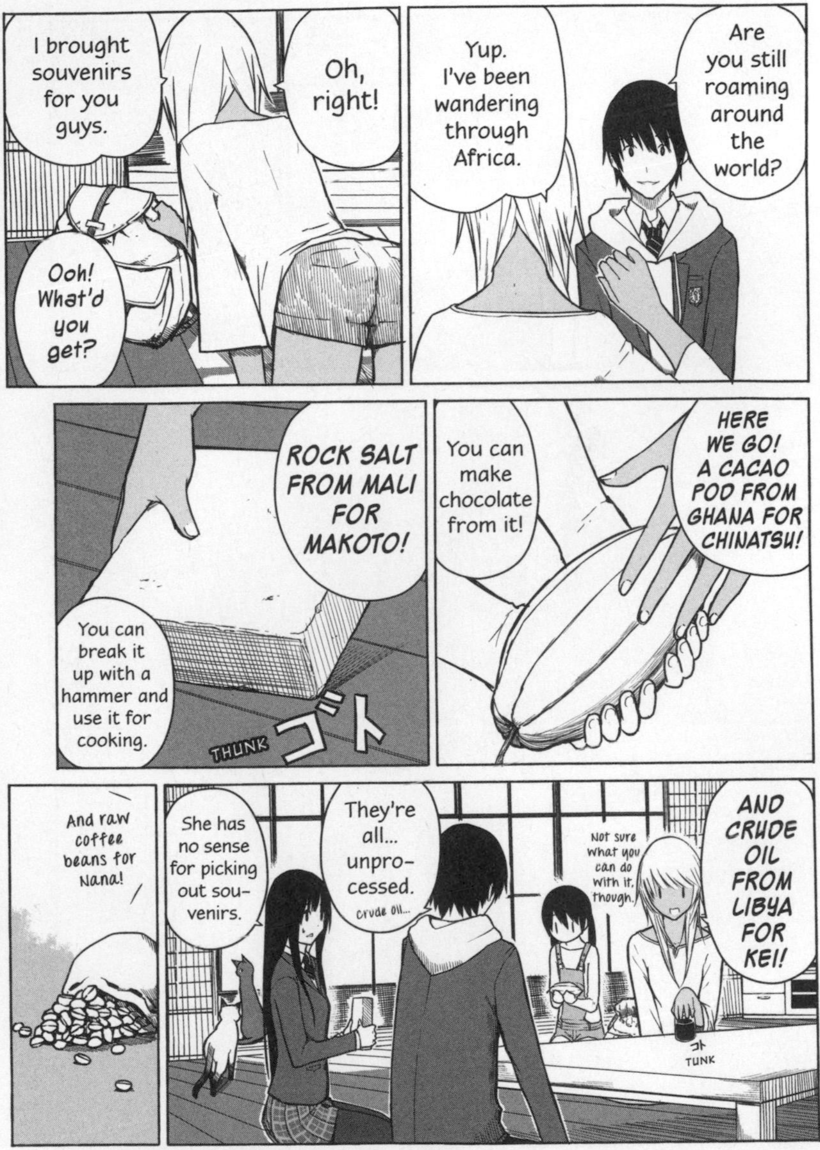

Are you still roaming around the world?
Yup. I've been wandering through Africa.
Oh, right!
I brought souvenirs for you guys.
Ooh! What'd you get?
HERE WE GO! A CACAO POD FROM GHANA FOR CHINATSU!
You can make chocolate from it!
ROCK SALT FROM MALI FOR MAKOTO!
You can break it up with a hammer and use it for cooking.
ゴト
THUNK
AND CRUDE OIL FROM LIBYA FOR KEI!
Not sure what you can do with it, though.
コト
TUNK
They're all... unpro-cessed.
Crude oil...
She has no sense for picking out sou-venirs.
And raw coffee beans for Nana!

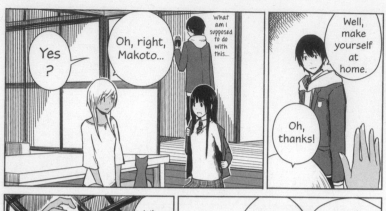

Well, make yourself at home.
Oh, thanks!
What am I supposed to do with this...
Oh, right, Makoto...
Yes ?
You haven't done any serious magic since you left home, have you?
JOLT
ギクッ
AGH !!
Wh... why would you ask...
pbbt
Chito told me.
She said you haven't really done anything besides fly on your broom.
And only once, at that.
Uh... Yes. That's entirely true.
I-I'm sorry ...
Oh, no, don't apologize! Being a witch isn't just about using magic.

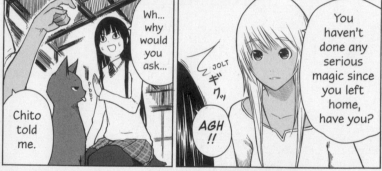

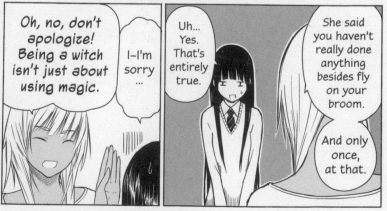

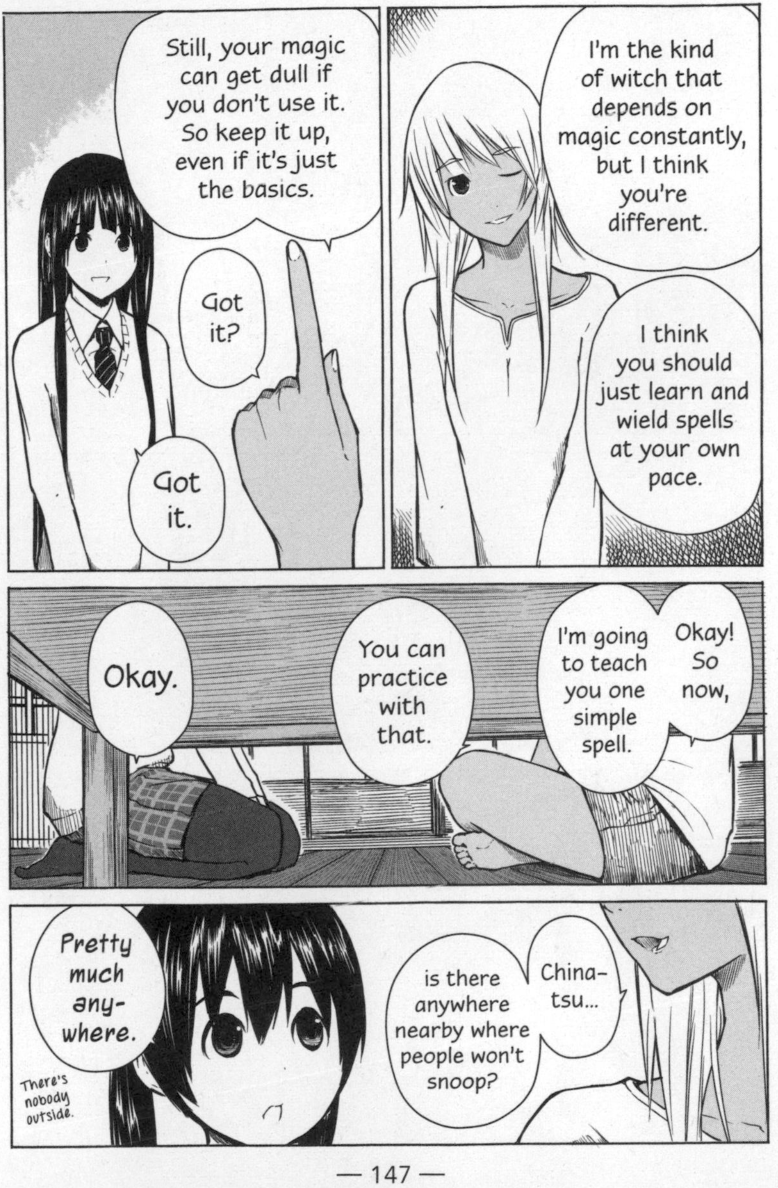
I'm the kind of witch that depends on magic constantly, but I think you're different.
I think you should just learn and wield spells at your own pace.
Still, your magic can get dull if you don't use it. So keep it up, even if it's just the basics.
Got it?
Got it.
Okay! So now,
I'm going to teach you one simple spell.
You can practice with that.
Okay.
China-tsu...
is there anywhere nearby where people won't snoop?
Pretty much any-where.
There's nobody outside.

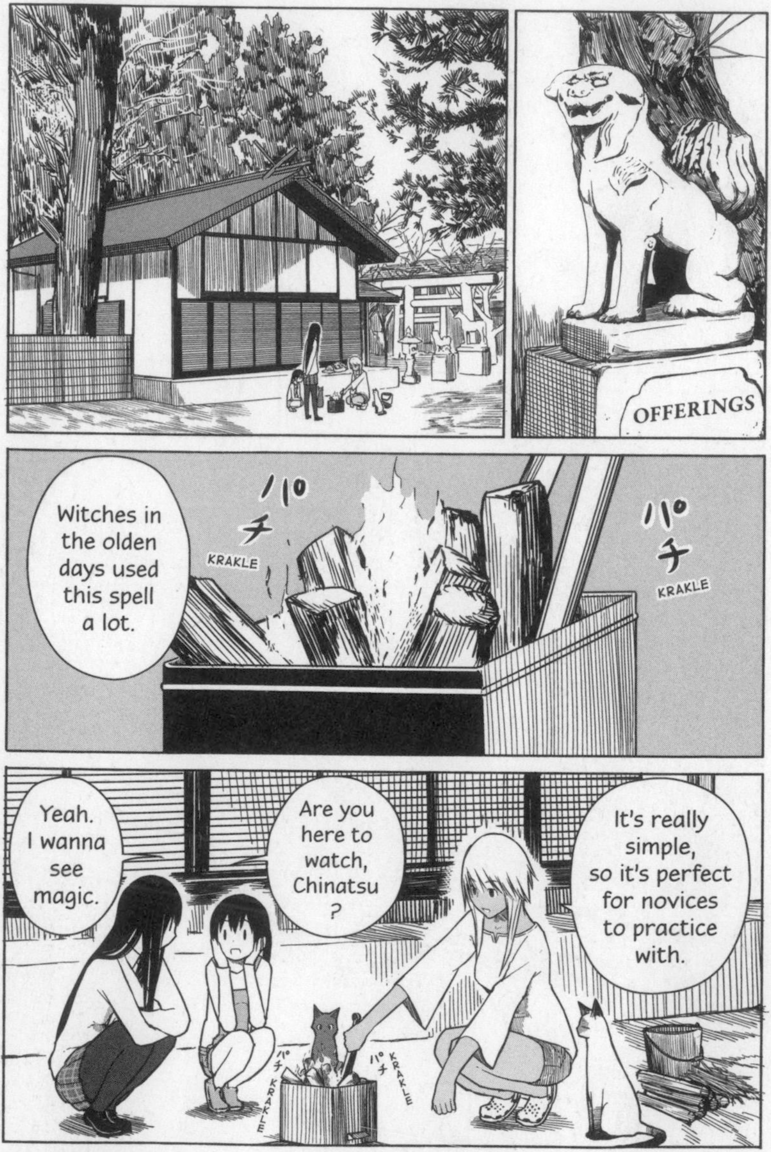
OFFERINGS
パチ
KRAKLE
パチ
KRAKLE
Witches in the olden days used this spell a lot.
It's really simple, so it's perfect for novices to practice with.
Are you here to watch, Chinatsu?
Yeah. I wanna see magic.
パチ
KRAKLE
パチ
KRAKLE

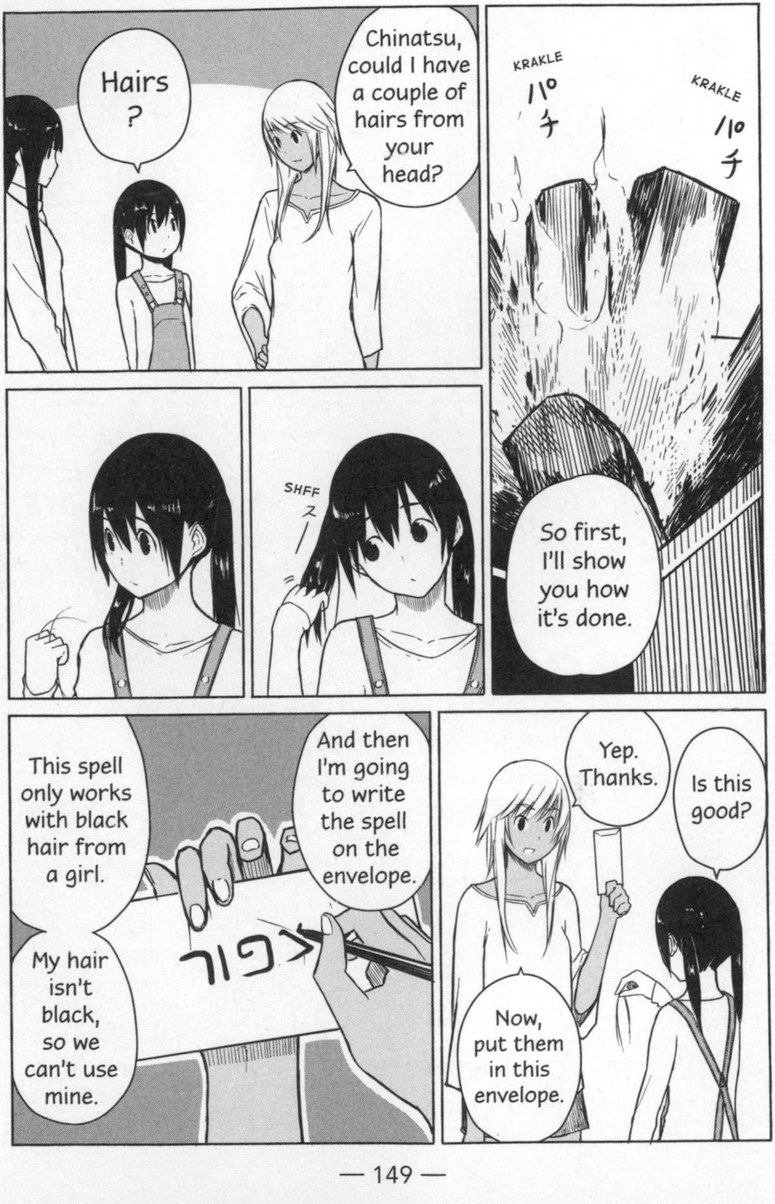
KRAKLE
パチ
KRAKLE
パチ
So first, I'll show you how it's done.
Chinatsu, could I have a couple of hairs from your head?
Hairs ?
SHFF
ス
Is this good?
Yep. Thanks.
Now, put them in this envelope.
And then I'm going to write the spell on the envelope.
This spell only works with black hair from a girl.
My hair isn't black, so we can't use mine.

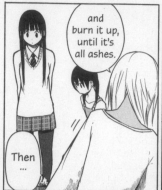

Then we throw it on the fire,
ボウ
VWOOSH
and burn it up, until it's all ashes.
Then ...
DOUSE THE FIRE WITH WATER!
SPLASH
ザパァ
プシュ
HISSSS

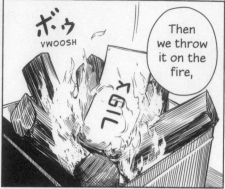

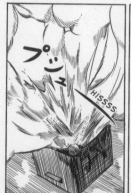

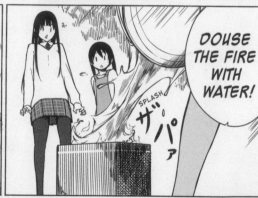

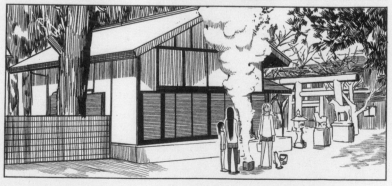

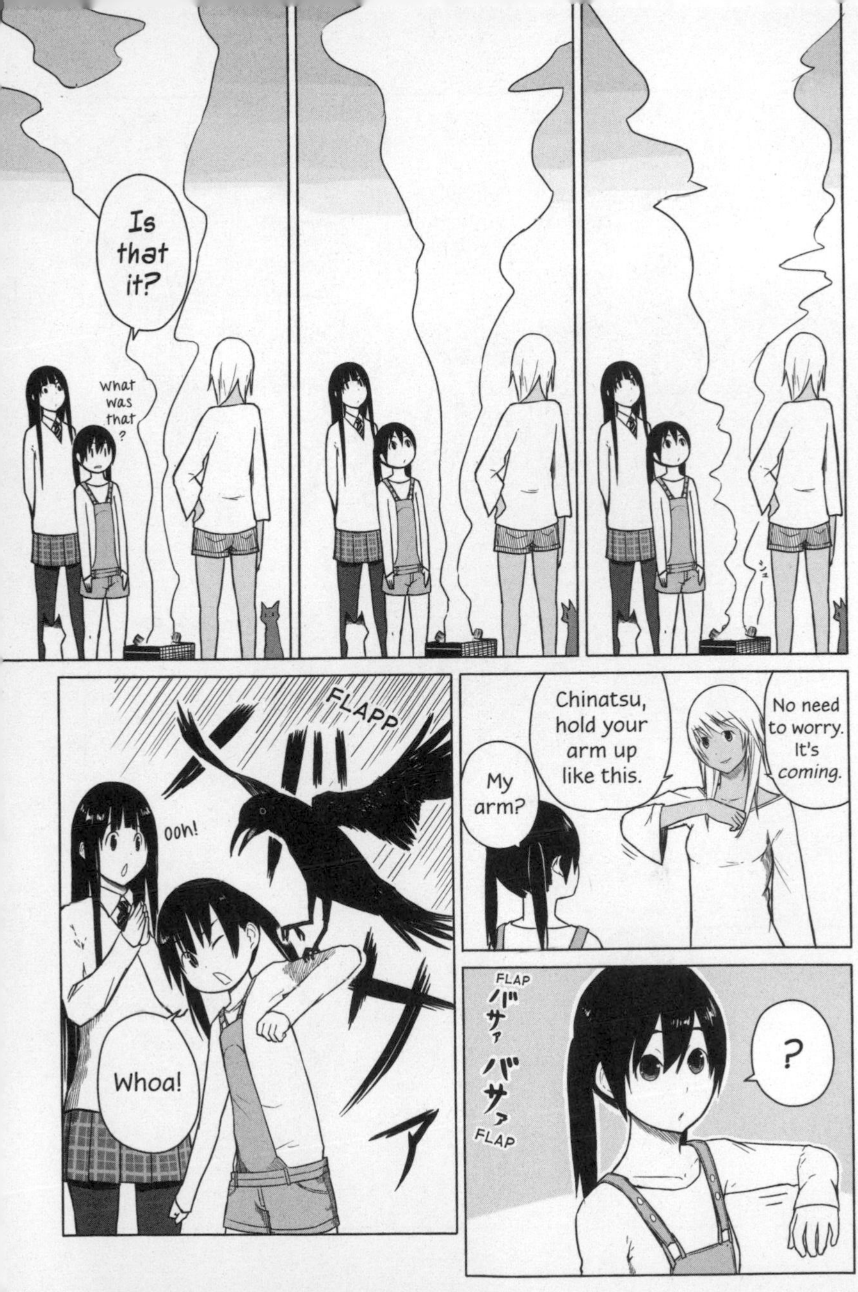
Is that it?
What was that?
No need to worry. It's coming.
Chinatsu, hold your arm up like this.
My arm?
?
FLAP
バサァ
バサァ
FLAP
FLAPP
ooh!
Whoa!

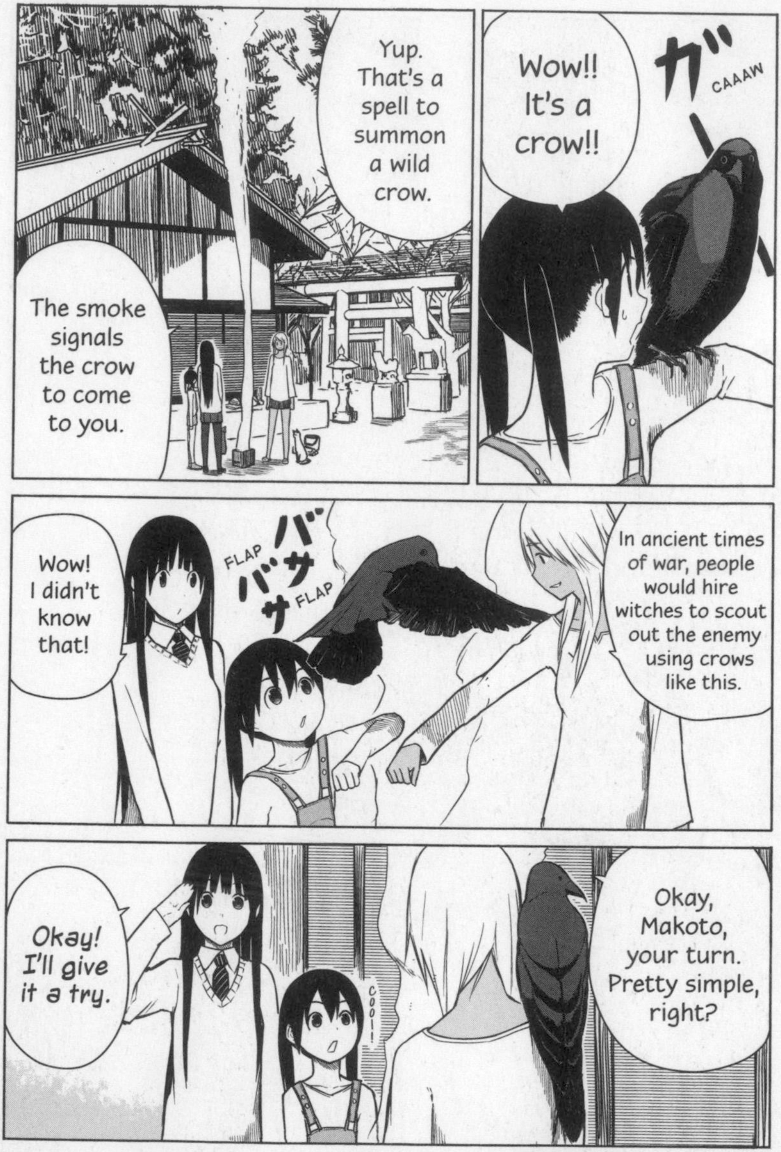

ガー
CAAAW
Wow!! It's a crow!!
Yup. That's a spell to summon a wild crow.
The smoke signals the crow to come to you.
In ancient times of war, people would hire witches to scout out the enemy using crows like this.
バサバサ
FLAP FLAP
Wow! I didn't know that!
Okay, Makoto, your turn. Pretty simple, right?
COOL!
Okay! I'll give it a try.

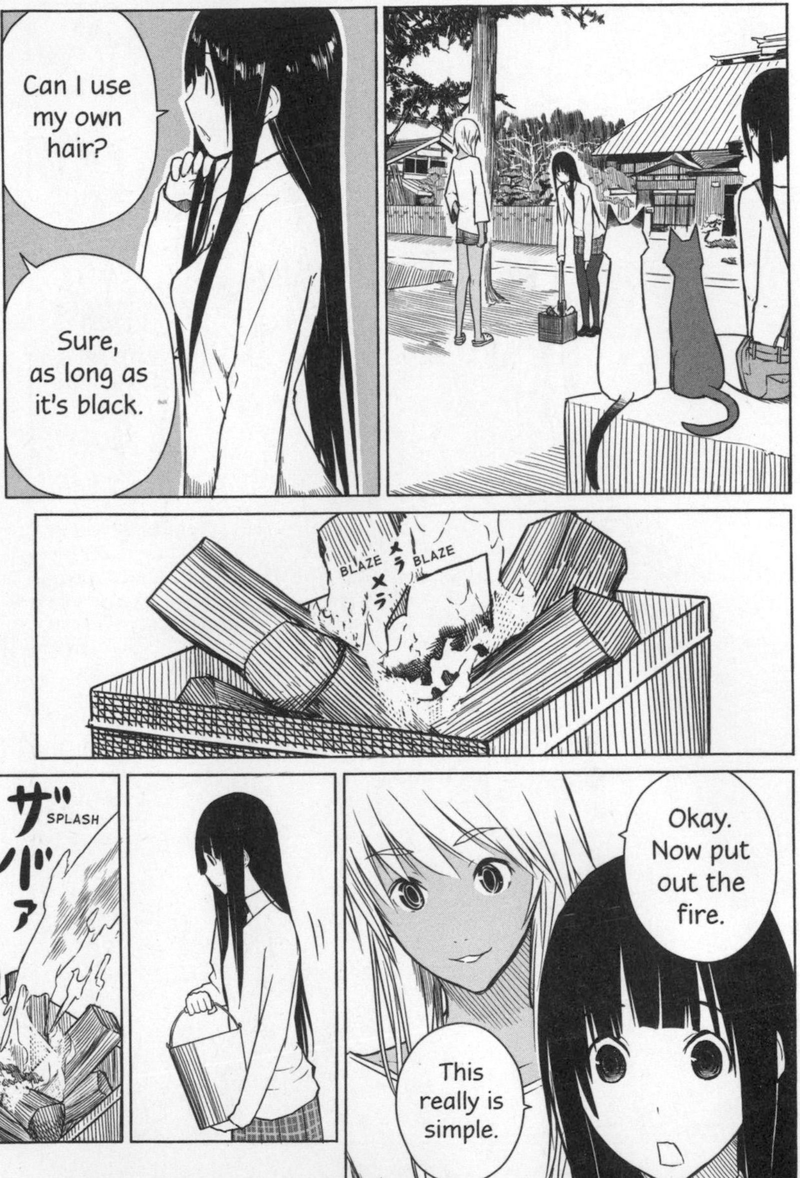
Can I use my own hair?
Sure, as long as it's black.
BLAZE メラ BLAZE メラ
Okay. Now put out the fire.
This really is simple.
ザバァ SPLASH

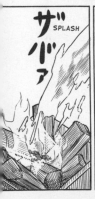

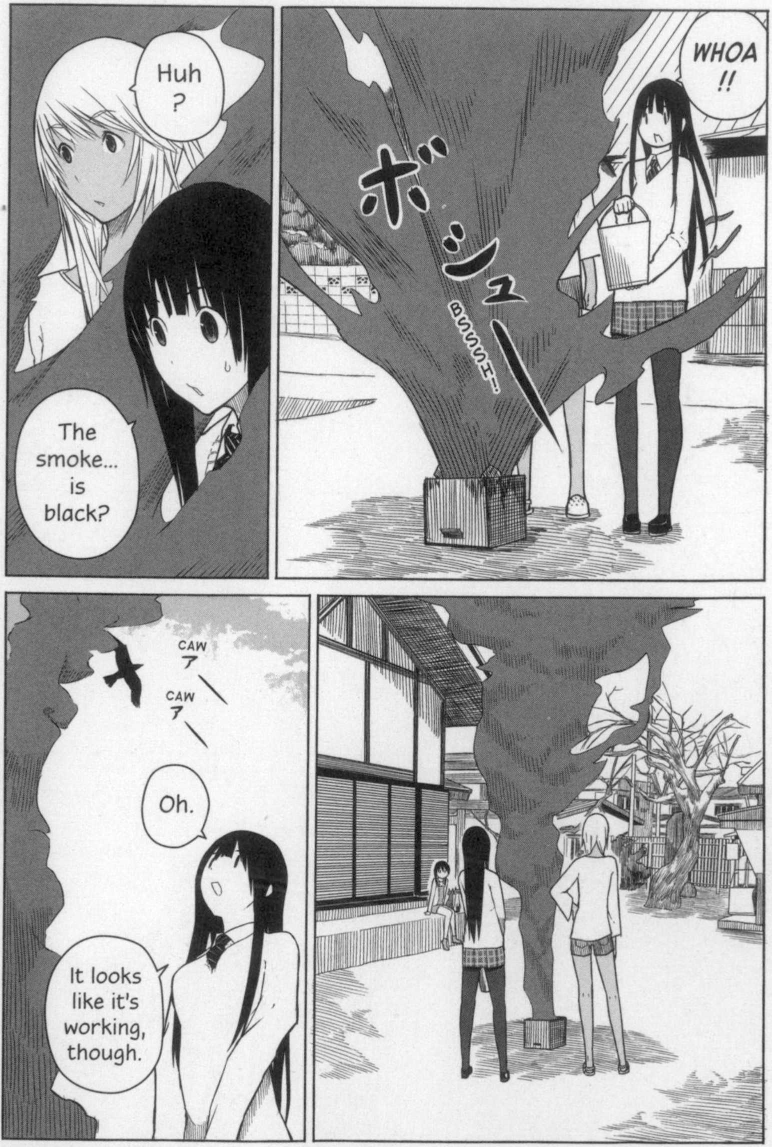
WHOA !!
ボシュー
BSSSH!
Huh ?
The smoke... is black?
CAW
ア
CAW
ア
Oh.
It looks like it's working, though.

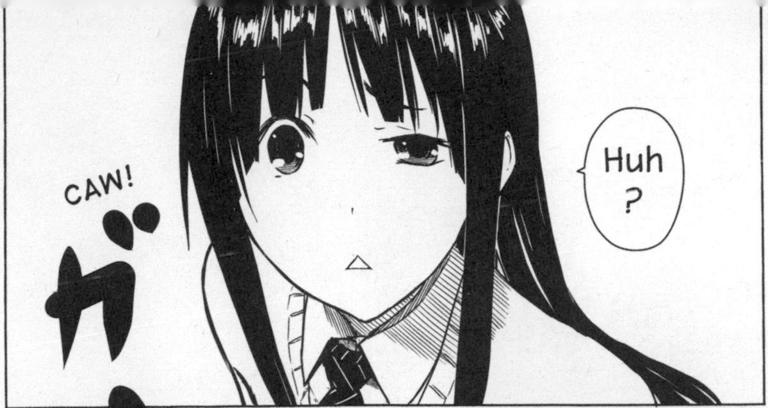
Huh
?
CAW!
ガー

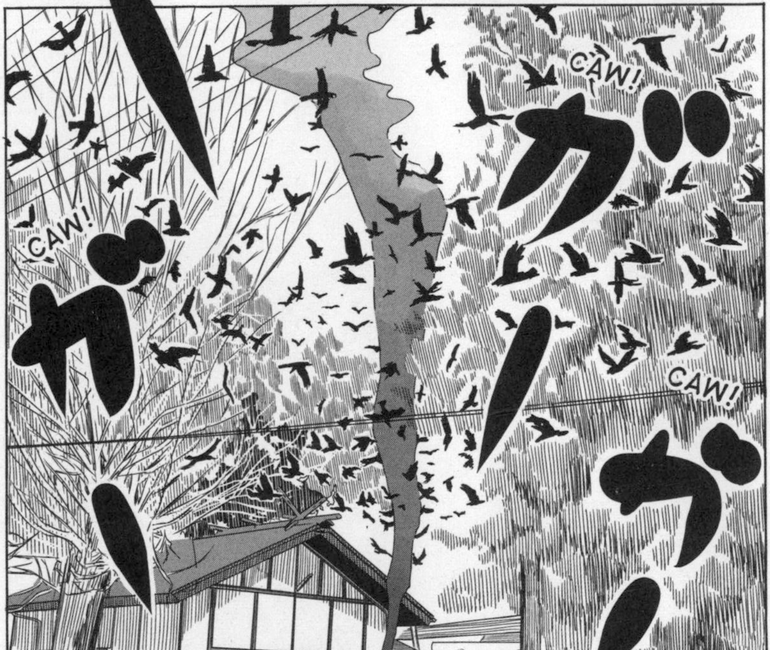
CAW!
ガー
CAW!
ガー
CAW!
ガー

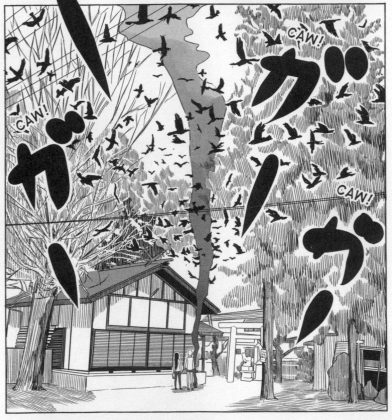

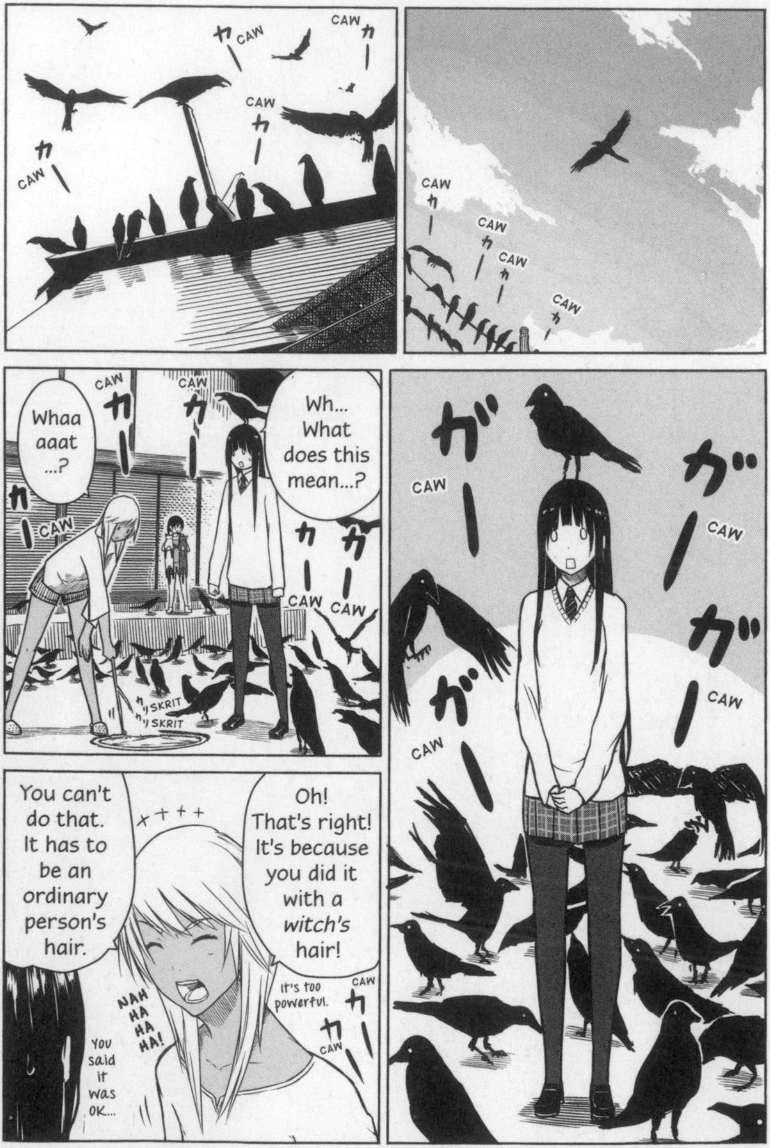
カー CAW
カー CAW
カー CAW
カー CAW
カー CAW
カー CAW
カー CAW
カー CAW
ガー CAW
ガー CAW
ガー CAW
CAW
カー CAW
カー CAW
Wh... What does this mean...?
カー CAW
Whaa aaat ...?
カー CAW
カー CAW
カリ SKRIT
カリ SKRIT
Oh! That's right! It's because you did it with a *witch's* hair!
It's too powerful.
カー CAW
カー CAW
NAH HA HA HA!
You can't do that. It has to be an ordinary person's hair.
You said it was OK...

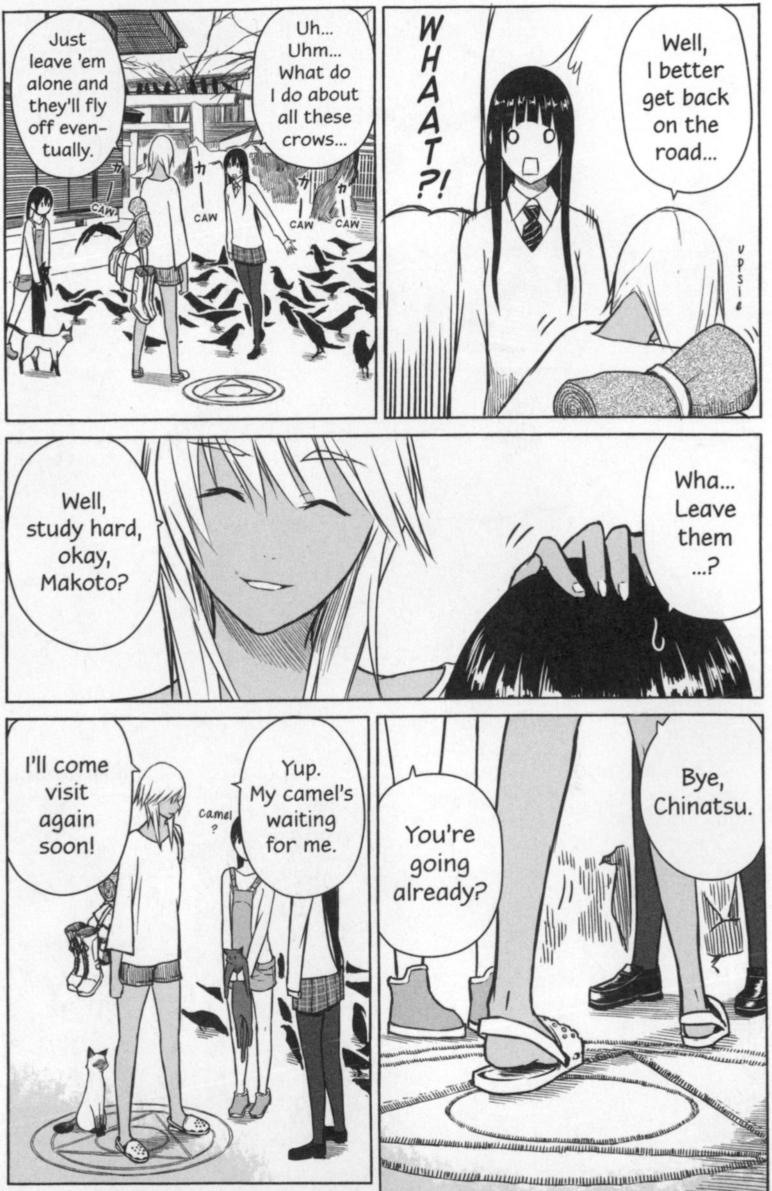
Well, I better get back on the road...
WHAAT?!
upsie
Uh... Uhm... What do I do about all these crows...
CAW
CAW
CAW
Just leave 'em alone and they'll fly off eventually.
CAW
Wha... Leave them ...?
Well, study hard, okay, Makoto?
Bye, Chinatsu.
You're going already?
Yup. My camel's waiting for me.
Camel?
I'll come visit again soon!

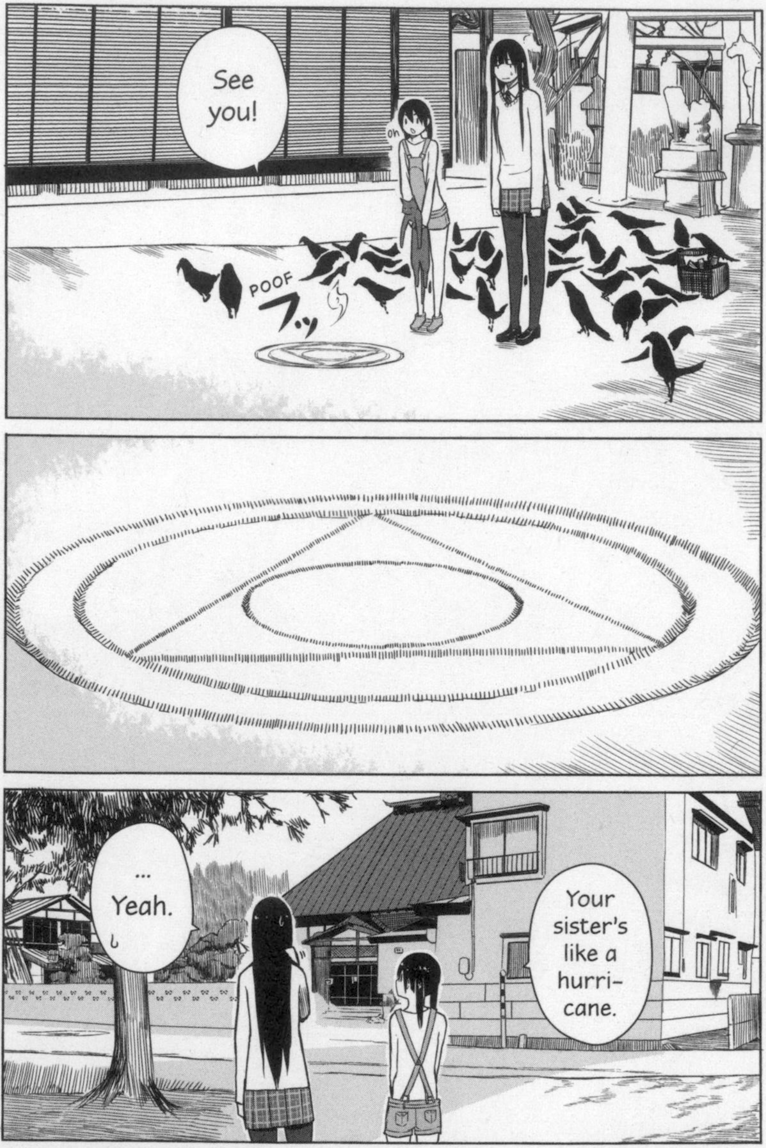
See you!
oh
POOF
フッ
Your sister's like a hurri- cane.
... Yeah.

Fly Again in Volume 2

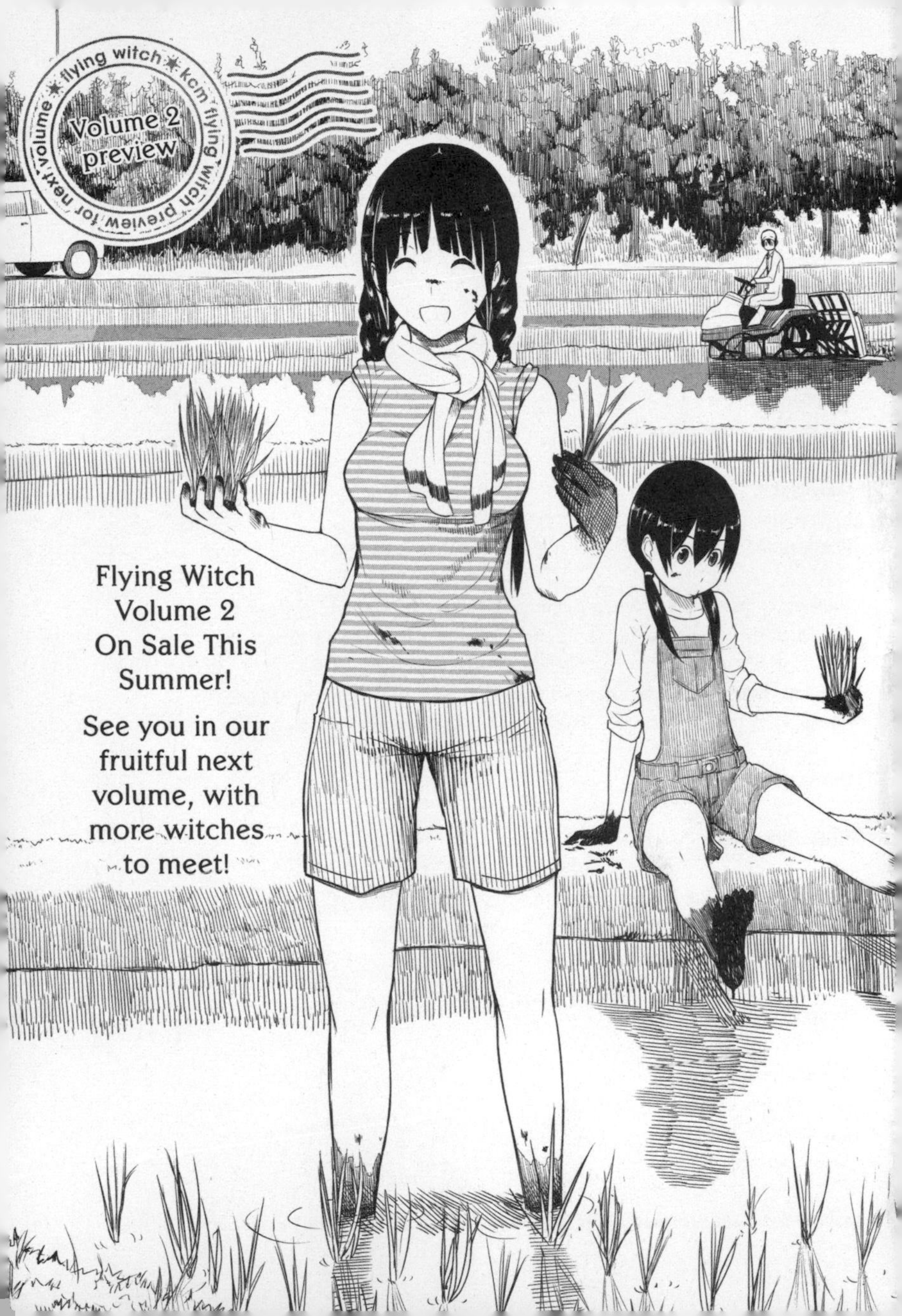
flying witch kcm flying witch preview for next volume
Volume 2 preview
Flying Witch Volume 2 On Sale This Summer!
See you in our fruitful next volume, with more witches to meet!

Flying Witch 1

Translation - Melissa Tanaka
Production - Grace Lu
Tomoe Tsutsumi

First published in Japan in 2013 by Kodansha, Ltd., Tokyo
Publication for this English edition arranged through Kodansha, Ltd., Tokyo

Translation provided by Vertical Comics, 2017
Published by Vertical Comics, an imprint of Vertical, Inc., New York

Originally published in Japanese as *Flying Witch 1* by Kodansha, Ltd., 2013
Flying Witch first serialized in *Bessatsu Shonen Magazine*, Kodansha, Ltd., 2013-

ISBN: 978-1-945054-09-9

Manufactured in the United States of America

First Edition

Second Printing

Vertical, Inc.
451 Park Avenue South, 7th Floor
New York, NY 10016
www.vertical-comics.com

Vertical books are distributed through Penguin-Random House Publisher Services.